CFROI of Customer Relationship Management

Managementschriften

Fachhochschule Ludwigshafen am Rhein
Hochschule für Wirtschaft

Herausgegeben von

Beate Kremin-Buch, Fritz Unger
Hartmut Walz

Band 5

Martin Selchert

CFROI of Customer Relationship Management

Empirical Evidence from mySAP CRM Users

2. Auflage

Verlag Wissenschaft & Praxis

Bibliografische Information der Deutschen Bibliothek

Die Deutsche Bibliothek verzeichnet diese Publikation in der Deutschen Nationalbibliografie; detaillierte bibliografische Daten sind im Internet über http://dnb.ddb.de abrufbar.

ISBN 3-89673-248-X

© Verlag Wissenschaft & Praxis
Dr. Brauner GmbH 2005
D-75447 Sternenfels, Nußbaumweg 6
Tel. 07045/930093 Fax 07045/930094

Alle Rechte vorbehalten

Das Werk einschließlich aller seiner Teile ist urheberrechtlich geschützt. Jede Verwertung außerhalb der engen Grenzen des Urheberrechtsgesetzes ist ohne Zustimmung des Verlages unzulässig und strafbar. Das gilt insbesondere für Vervielfältigungen, Übersetzungen, Mikroverfilmungen und die Einspeicherung und Verarbeitung in elektronischen Systemen.

Printed in Germany

CFROI of Customer Relationship Management Empirical Evidence from mySAP CRM Users

Foreword by *Prof. Dr. Hartmut Walz, University of Applied Science Ludwigshafen, Editor in Chief*   8

Introduction and Acknowledgments   10

1. **Management Summary: High Value Creation Potential Through Using Customer Relationship Management**   12

2. **Research Design: Understanding Value Creation by CRM**   18
   2.1. The Urgent Challenge of CRM Value Assessment   18
     2.1.1. The Urgent Need to Assess Value of CRM   18
     2.1.2. The Empirical Findings: Sparse and Contradictory   21
     2.1.3. The Challenge in CRM Value Assessment   22
     2.1.4. The Aim of the CFROI of CRM Study   24
   2.2. The Research Design: Meeting the Challenge   26
     2.2.1. Key Concepts for Measuring CRM Value   26
     2.2.2. The Structure of the CRM Value Metric   35
     2.2.3. The Individual Business Cases: More than a Survey   43
     2.2.4. The Trustee Model: Ensuring Openness and Honesty   45
     2.2.5. The Study Process: Ensuring Interactivity   46
     2.2.6. The Participants: Focus on mySAP CRM Users in D-A-CH   48

3. **Results: Higher Productivity, Lower Cost, Higher Revenue**   53
   3.1. Project Targets: Met by CRM   53
   3.2. Financial Targets: CFROI, NPV, and Break-Even Period   57
     3.2.1. Financial Targets Including Experience Based Expectations   57
     3.2.2. Financial Targets Excluding Experience Based Expectations   66
   3.3. Productivity Targets: Potential for Cost Reduction   68

Table of Contents

    3.3.1. Improved Customer Information: The Basis for Higher Productivity   68

    3.3.2. Marketing: Valuable Analytic Insights, Improved Campaigns, and Consequential Lead Management   75

    3.3.3. Sales: Operative Process Improvement   80

    3.3.4. Interaction Center: New Opportunities in Telesales and Help Desk Functions   91

    3.3.5. Internet Sales: Automated Order Management   96

    3.3.6. Service: Improvement Potential Not Yet Developed   100

    3.3.7. Other Productivity Effects and Potential Cost Savings   101

3.4. Revenue Targets: More Customers and More Revenue per Customer   103

    3.4.1. Increase in Revenue: Basic Logic-Tree and Aggregated Results   104

    3.4.2. New Customer Acquisition: Leads   110

    3.4.3. "New" Old Customers: Customer Satisfaction and Customer Retention   116

    3.4.4. Increase in Goods Sold: Larger Quantities and Cross Sales   121

    3.4.5. Higher Prices: Absolute and Relative Price Increases   128

3.5. Speed Targets: Time-to-Market, Time-to-Volume, and Time-to-Delivery   130

4. Key Factors of Success: Sector, Situational Fit, and Proficient Project Management   135

4.1. Financial Results by Sector   135

4.2. Systematic Framework for Key Factors of Success   141

4.3. External Situational Fit: Technology, Customers, and Competition   144

    4.3.1. Influence of Production Technology: Service Characteristics and Complexity of Goods and Services on Offer   144

    4.3.2. Customer Influence: Insignificance of Numbers   148

    4.3.3. Competitive Pressure: The More the Better for CRM   149

4.4. Internal Situational Factors of Success: The 7-S of CRM   152

	4.4.1. Organizational Structure: Dynamics Breed High CFROI of CRM	152
	4.4.2. Systems: No Impact of IT Proficiency Before the Project	153
	4.4.3. Staff: Specific Skills and Internationalization Matter	155
	4.5. Good Project Management: A Necessary but Not Sufficient Condition for Success in CRM	157
	4.5.1. Management Support and Involvement	157
	4.5.2. Employee Buy-In	160
	4.5.3. Quality of CRM Targets	165
	4.5.4. Proficiency of Project Execution	166
	4.6. Analysis of Value Drivers by Sector	170
5.	**Closing Remarks: Strengths, Limitations, and Best Use of Results**	177
	5.1. Strengths of the Study: Neutral, Quantitative, and Systematically In-Depth	177
	5.2. Limitations of the Study: Small Sample, and Limited Geographic Scope	179
	5.3. Best Use of the Results: Guidance for the Company-specific CRM Business Case	180
6.	**Appendix**	183
	6.1. References	183
	6.2. Table of Figures	189
	6.3. Glossary of Terms and Abbreviations	192
	6.4. Questionnaire "Value Creation by mySAP CRM"	196

Foreword

*Prof. Dr. Hartmut Walz,
University of Applied Science Ludwigshafen,
Editor in Chief*

CFROI of CRM: A Challenge Well Met

Evaluating the profitability and economic value of CRM investments is an important challenge nowadays. It involves a number of issues that are both interesting from an academic and challenging from a management perspective.

- The overall economic environment calls for investment decisions to be made on a more rational basis
- Speed competition and shrinking profit- and risk margins in most branches make it increasingly important to make investment decisions which are both timely and based on proper analysis
- The ratio of spending on software and services to tangible goods is increasing
- CRM technology is well developed but has not been employed extensively, although a major effort is underway
- It is extremely difficult to measure the profitability of software-related investments in general, especially in CRM as many "hard to quantify" effects play a major role

Prof. Dr. Martin Selchert's study "CFROI of Customer Relationship Management" successfully addresses the complexity of evaluating CRM investments and demonstrates that their evaluation is nevertheless possible.

The convincing results were achieved through:
- Thorough business cases
- Careful avoidance of double counts that all too easily distort results
- Soft and hard factors taken into consideration
- Relevant measures to judge CRM investments

Foreword

This book is ideally suited to all those who have to make CRM-related investment decisions. It also provides a valuable contribution to those responsible for CRM evaluation.

Prof. Dr. Martin Selchert,
University of Applied Science Ludwigshafen

Introduction and Acknowledgements

Customer Relationship Management (CRM) is a familiar term by now – although it is used as a label for many diverse concepts. Numerous books cover the topic as well as articles in leading marketing and management journals. Still: The urgent question of CRM's impact on the bottom line has not yet been answered. This study set out to produce some factual, quantitative evidence, focused on mySAP CRM users in Germany, Austria, and Switzerland. Cash-flow return on investment (CFROI), the net present value (NPV), and the break-even period result from individually crafted, comparable business cases for all participants. These financial decision criteria are founded on a solid analysis of operational improvements through using CRM. The main results are also provided by sector; many of the potential "factors of success" are tested.

"CFROI of Customer Relationship Management" thus provides the best-founded answer to the question of CRM's bottom line impact for a larger number of mySAP CRM users as of now. This answer should be of interest to the current users of CRM to locate additional pockets of value. Decision makers on CRM may find the results useful to give a broad orientation of the range of possible outcomes. Furthermore, the methodology may serve as the blueprint for a business plan. The research design and especially the success-factor analysis contribute to the embryonic state of research in this area.

To provide a quick access to the different levels of interest, the following structure has been chosen:

- For readers under time-constraints, an extensive management summary captures the main results with practical management relevance. One level deeper, each main chapter ends with a gray-shaded bullet-point summary.
- Italics at the beginning of the main chapters give an overview over the flow of thought and thus are to help navigate in the text

- Finally, the main body of text is heavily supported by a visual display of results. Potentially unfamiliar terminology from statistics, e-business, and investment theory is explained in the glossary of terms (appendix). Deeper level statistics are relegated to the footnotes

This research effort has been supported by many. First of all, I want to thank the participants in the study for their time, effort, and trust. I also want to thank SAP for their extremely fair cooperation. To sponsor an open-ended research without insisting to get access to the raw data is noteworthy. My gratitude is especially owed to Dr. Martin Klein, the SAP project manager responsible, for his personal courage to take on the responsibility for an effort that may well have ended in an unpleasant surprise, for many fruitful discussions, and for his relentless effort in organizing whatever was needed. Thank you also to all at SAP who contributed to the study.

I am grateful for the support and guidance from my cherished colleague and editor in chief, Prof. Dr. Hartmut Walz. Several solutions concerning the CRM Value Metric were inspired by my father, Prof. Dr. Friedrich-Wilhelm Selchert: Thank you very much! Furthermore I want to thank my colleague Prof. Dr. Josef Puhani for his very helpful hints on the study's statistics, Veronica O'Looney for her thorough review of the English in this book, and Dr. Brauner for his professional handling of the publication process.

A research effort like the one at hand cannot be realized without compromise on family life. Thus last but not least, I want to thank my wife Karin for her support in any way possible.

Despite quantitative results and thorough methodology, a word of caution is warranted: These findings may guide but definitely not replace a solid CRM business case. As it is deemed impossible to provide a "one-size-fits-all" solution, the author is happy to engage in a bilateral discussion to apply the findings to the reader's specific situation: Please do not hesitate to contact me:

Prof. Martin Selchert

Home Office	Address:
Tel.: +49 6236 46-2480	Theodor-Storm-Str. 5a
Fax: +49 6236 46-2481	D-67117 Limburgerhof
e-mail: martin.selchert@fh-ludwigshafen.de	Germany

1 Management Summary: High Value Creation Potential Through Using CRM

The goal of the *"CFROI of Customer Relationship Management"* study is to systematically quantify the value created through using mySAP CRM, based on the experience of 35 users in Germany, Austria, and Switzerland (D-A-CH). CRM is more than just software. It requires a customer-centric business philosophy, strategy, shared values, organizational structures, and processes to be effective. The CRM application merely supports the overall efforts. Nonetheless, the urgent question for decision makers on CRM is: What are the benefits of investing in CRM technology and all its related changes? These benefits must be examined not only on a qualitative but also on a quantitative basis, not just the potential benefit but the also the results of experience. Operational impact as well as the financial angle must be taken into consideration, such as the cash flow return on investment (CFROI), net present value (NPV), and break-even period.

The *method of this study* to tackle this question is centered on a systematic CRM Value Metric, which served as a blueprint for participant-specific business cases. This method strikes the optimal balance between comparability of results and individualization of assessment. Questionnaire-based telephone-interviews with a prior preparation by respondents provided input that proved highly reliable through a number of plausibility checks. In the discussion, operational productivity gains were evaluated, then aggregated to potential cost savings and revenue increase to finally compute the financial indicators. The systematic approach avoids double counts and ensures that gains can be attributed directly to the use of mySAP CRM. Although sponsored by SAP, a trustee model ensures neutrality and non-biased results, as all raw data remains exclusively with the author whose position as a full-time professor of a publicly financed institution grants full independence.

On first enquiring about *the participants' own initial CRM target achievement*, it was discovered that most participants deployed mySAP CRM with the objective of standardizing their customer information base on the technical side and, on the operational side, optimizing customer interaction and internal CRM processes. On average, participants fulfilled over 75% of their initial project objectives after 14 months of using the system. They were, however, aware of less than 1% of the economic potential of mySAP CRM that had materialized within their own companies. Few participating companies compiled a business case or defined quantitative success metrics before investing in CRM. That's why surveys that simply ask for ROI cannot produce valid results.

Investment in mySAP CRM is financially highly attractive. Using the most conservative financial indicators[1], the median results are as follows:

- A cash flow return on investment (CFROI) of 53% over 3 years, which over 5 years assumes a value of almost 90%
- A net present value (NPV) of EUR 5.8 million, in other words, the mySAP CRM project enhances the value of the company by this amount
- A break-even period of almost 23 months

The investment in CRM has increased the value of more than 90% of the participating companies in the study. Although these results are specific to the sample, for the entirety of mySAP CRM users in D-A-CH it can be concluded with 99.9% certainty that the mean average NPV exceeds EUR 3.4 m, the CFROI exceeds 13.4%, and the break-even period is below 3 years. Evidence therefore contradicts those who claimed that CRM would not show a ROI. These results are based on experiences that had already been made when the interviews were conducted, as well as on experience-based future expectations. If the same profitability figures are assessed with only the operational improvements as of the interview date, only 1/3 of the 3-year CFROI, but 50% of the NPV calculated over 5 years, are dependent on future expectations, which are naturally less secure.

On the most basic level, ***CRM has improved customer information.*** So the quality and quantity of customer information have risen by an average 30%-40% margin. These figures, for example, apply to reductions in the time needed to collect customer information as well as to an increased relevance of the information obtained. These two results naturally explain the fact that employees used customer information 30% more often. Thus market insight is expected to be much deeper than before.

Spurred by the improvement in customer information, significant ***productivity gains were realized in many different functional areas***, which are first analyzed with respect to potential cost savings:

---

[1] The CFROI is calculated with zero interest, the NPV does not contain a terminal value; furthermore it is calculated at the individual participant's weighted average cost of capital; the same applies to the break-even period. The financial measures are defined in the glossary of terms (appendix) and outlined in detail in chapter 3.2.1.

Management Summary

- The time required for ***marketing*** analyses and campaigns has been reduced by a mean average of 15% while maintaining the same profitability level. In the steady state, this figure is expected to rise to 20%-25%. Lead management has improved by 10% on the marketing side.
- In ***sales***, all processes were investigated along the sales cycle, starting from sales planning, through sales lead- and opportunity management, to customer interaction, internal coordination, order management, and reporting. Productivity increases in these sales processes amount to an average of 10%-15% for the external sales force and sales support staff as of now. Order management and reporting are fastest to reap the CRM benefits; reporting, improvements in internal coordination, customer interaction, and order management constitute the highest potential benefit in financial terms. Based on the currently visible effects, potential savings will reach 15%-25% in the steady state, depending on the process in question.
- Productivity gains in the ***Interaction Center*** are represented by a more than 40% reduction in the time for outbound calls in 5 companies at the time of the interview, expected to grow to almost 50% in the steady state. However, results for the help desk and documentation processes were rather mixed: They ranged from a 50% decrease in productivity in one case to up to a 70% increase in another.
- Efficiency gains in ***Internet sales*** are mostly due to an optimized order management. Nine of 35 participants deployed this CRM functionality. The mean average reduction of time for order-taking between online and offline orders was seen at an average of 70%. Related to the entire order management process, Internet sales users achieved a time reduction of almost 25% compared to 10% for those companies that did not deploy Internet sales.
- Few participants in the sample used ***service support***; and when they did, it was mainly the help desk and service order fulfillment that were improved.
- ***Other productivity effects*** witnessed by users were improved cooperation with business partners by collaborative CRM, opportunities for outsourcing of CRM functions, reductions in the annual inventory of receivables by 17%, and a reduction of stock at the magnitude of 15%. With regard to the overall financial impact of CRM, however, these effects were rather small on average.

Productivity gains can be used to reduce cost. However, they can alternatively be "reinvested" to ***potentially increase revenue.*** This "reinvestment" is not just a matter of, for example, employing more sales representatives. It may be far more valuable that the existing CRM staff has more time to spend on more preparation

Management Summary

before seeing the customer. Overall, a roughly 6% average increase in revenue has been achieved by mySAP CRM users in the sample at the time of interview. This figure is expected to double to 12% in the steady state. 90% of all participants see an increase in revenue by mySAP CRM.

- *New customers* only provided 5.5% of the entire increase in revenue, which gives evidence for the widely-held belief that CRM primarily serves to better retain existing customers. New customers originated from 10%-15% more leads in marketing and sales, and a slightly improved lead conversion rate. 70% of all respondents had experienced a positive impact in terms of additional leads at the same level of quality than before. Top scoring participants went up to 180% improvement, although that particular case started from a very poor base. The increase in the number of leads resulted from more focus in marketing and sales on the right customers as well as from a more than 20% reduction in interchannel coordination issues.

- *Customer satisfaction* has risen on average by 15%, expected to exceed 20% in the steady state. More than 70% had experienced that effect immediately and the steady state average is based on an impressive 85% of all participants. The key drivers are an improvement in the quality of customer interaction, for example, a 19% increase in the delivery-to-promise ratio. Higher customer satisfaction led to a 10% rise in customer retention at the time of interview, which in turn added 20.5% of all extra revenue generated by CRM.

- The *increase in the quantity of goods sold* added the lion share of the surplus in revenue: 64%. Thereof 18% were due to higher cross sales, that is, the sale of products or services to customers that had not bought those products before. The better the customer information, the easier the cross sales pin-pointing those areas that the customer is most likely to be interested in. While the Interaction Center and the Internet sales mainly collected rechanneled revenue, almost all extra revenue came through the sales force. The remaining 46% of extra revenue flow from extra sales of the established goods and services was powered by a more systematic and intensified coverage of the customers.

- The last 10% of the increase in revenue result from *relative price increases*. While competitors had to lower prices by 10% to 30% in the situation of economic crisis, users of CRM experienced far less price pressure as customers also appreciated the improvement in the quality of service based on CRM. About 1/3 of respondents confirmed such an effect at the order of 7% of the original prices on average. While that seems negligible, CRM users with relative price increases enjoyed a median CFROI of 112% compared to 48% by those without price effects. Of this outstanding value-added, 75% stem from the price effect alone. The enormous leverage of price increases is simple to explain: Higher prices do not come at higher cost; therefore they impact the bottom-line directly.

More than 25% of the participants have reported *significant savings in process time elapsed* as a result of mySAP CRM: Time-to-market, time-to-volume, sales cycle time, and time-to-delivery have each been reduced by 10% to 25%. In the best-case scenario, the time required to promote new products has been reduced from one quarter to one week as a result of mySAP CRM – a reduction of over 90%. Processes are not only faster, but are also more reliable. In one case, the portion of new products in the top 30 performers has almost doubled from 7 to 13, while in 7 cases delivery reliability has also increased by an average of 20%.

To identify the *factors influencing the success of CRM*, the following aspects have been investigated:

- One of the main *external influencing factors* for this sample has been production technology, and more specifically service characteristics of the market offer. They drive up the return on CRM, as well as the complexity of the market offer spurred by the number of products and the need for customization. The stronger relationship to a few very important customers has yielded higher CFROI on average than the support for the management of a large customer basis. Another finding was that the higher the intensity of competitive pressure, the higher the ranking of the sector group according to its CFROI of CRM.

- *Internal influencing factors* evidenced in the study included the dynamics of organizational structure and demographics of staff. The more the organizations of participating companies had been affected by mergers and acquisitions, by spin-outs, major structural redesigns, and so on, the higher was the return on CRM – as inefficiencies after such events were overcome faster. Furthermore, IT fluent staff with a high readiness to change adopts a new system more easily. The existence of CRM applications prior to the mySAP CRM implementation or the level of process management sophistication had no statistically significant effect on the investment's return or the NPV. Also the degree of internationalization seems to have an impact on CRM benefit.

- Finally, the *CRM project management skills* have been assessed. As expected, management support is a strong influencing factor on success. However it should be considered as a necessary but not sufficient factor: None of the CRM users with poor management support had a high return on

CRM while some participants with excellent management scored poorly. Employee buy-in is important, and can be influenced by dedicated change management efforts. Also, statistically significant evidence was produced in support of the widely-held belief that IT-driven CRM initiatives only yield a return that is less attractive compared to projects where CRM is driven by the CRM functions like sales or marketing. Interestingly, a number of other potential factors have not been supported in the study: the number of CRM modules live, for example, had no impact on CFROI or NPV at all. Neither the quality of the implementation partner, nor the completeness of functionalities when going live, nor the number of users that went live proved to be relevant.

These factors impact the sectors differently and explain the differences in performance. *Sector groups* were formed to protect anonymity. The 3-year CFROI turned out to be highest in IT services with more than 380%, followed by consumer goods/building materials (83%), chemicals (75%), engineering (48.5%), pharmaceuticals/medical supplies (41%), and finally a group of diverse mainly public services (25.5%). Participants in each sector group are still relatively heterogeneous with regard to CFROI and NPV.

In essence, the study provides a quantitative answer to the question of return on CRM investment with a *high quality of results*. Its design ensures neutral and unbiased results, the CRM Value Metric leads to systematic and consistent findings. As explained above, the CFROI is based mainly on experiences and only partially on expectations, which speaks for its reliability. However due to the size and structure of the sample, the results still leave a broad range of probable outcomes for mySAP CRM users. SAP promised not to generate a biased selection when listing potential candidates for the study; the relevance of the results also depends on belief in that promise. While analyses show considerable sensitivity regarding certain input data, even on a 50% reduction of the most powerful input, only one business case turns from positive to negative NPV.

Overall, the results provide initial guidance to all decision makers that currently need to decide on CRM. But the success shown herein does not guarantee success for future CRM deployments. Therefore, the *decision maker should engage in drafting a business plan tailored to the specific situation of the company*.

2 Research Design and Key Concepts: Understanding Value Creation by CRM

2.1 The Urgent Challenge of CRM Value Assessment

2.1.1 The Urgent Need to Assess Value of CRM

Customer relationship management (CRM) – like almost every popular concept – has not one but many meanings. The term originates from the late 1990s when the Relationship Marketing and Customer Retention Management started to be supported by specialized software modules, "Sales Force Automation" (SFA), "Computer Aided Selling" (CAS), and finally CRM[2]. Empirical research from 1999 shows that senior executives in the US, the UK, and Europe at the time had a largely divergent understanding of CRM[3]. Answers to the question of what "CRM" means, contained words like "customer needs", "partnership", "increasing profits", "loyalty", "value", and "satisfaction". The diversity of meanings has not vanished since. As the **CRM definition** underlying this research should represent the most accepted meaning in practice, it is taken from CRMguru.com, that claims to be the world's leading internet community of CRM practitioners: *"Customer relationship management (CRM) is a business strategy to select and manage the most valuable customer relationships. CRM requires a customer-centric business philosophy and culture to support effective marketing, sales, and service processes. CRM applications can enable effective customer relationship management, provided that an enterprise has the right leadership, strategy, and culture."*[4]

It should already be stressed here that although a CRM application is merely an enabler of CRM, it is the most significant part of CRM from an investment point of view. And indeed, investments in CRM have surged in the wake of e-Business; growth rates were at the 90% level[5]. Now, after the hype has vanished, analysts still see CRM spending grow against the overall trend of

---

[2] For this evolutionary perspective of CRM from Sales Force Automation: Schwetz (2001) p. 19-23, also Stojek (2000) p. 37 ff.; Adolf et. al. (1997) p.187 still define CRM as "continuous relationship marketing"; for the roots of CRM in customer satisfaction research Homburg/Sieben (2000) p.6-8; for an exact "year of CRM birth" in 1998 Stengl/Sommer/Ematinger (2001) p.32
[3] Shaw (2001) p. 26, 27
[4] Thompson (2002) p.1
[5] Schneider (2003) quoting Gartner analyst Tom Topolinski

Research Design – The Concept

stagnation and reduction in IT investments. So the Aberdeen group reports CRM spending to grow by 14% in 2003 reaching the worldwide level of USD 15.4 billion[6]. While the numbers vary among analysts[7] and the new-license revenue is even reported to shrink[8], CRM clearly is one of the top IT priorities for a couple of years. In 2001, CRM spending has already consumed 18% of the overall applications budgets for corporates[9].

So already the sheer amount of corporate resources dedicated to CRM classifies these investments as "strategic". Furthermore, the aforementioned CRM definition clearly states that decisions on CRM will affect the whole of the company, not just the IT department. This observation stresses the strategic character of decisions on CRM. Another aspect of strategic decisions, the long-term commitment, also applies in the case of CRM, as the research results will show later. The classification of CRM decisions as "strategic" is also frequently found in practice and literature[10] but every so often this carries the implicit notion that no calculations are needed at all to justify the investment. This is wrong, and the burst of the e-Business bubble has painfully emphasized the fact "that a company that for good strategic reasons continuously invests in projects with an ROI which is lower than the cost of capital is on its way to going out of business"[11]. Strategic decisions need to be based on an especially sophisticated analysis of their impact on the company's value[12]. Gardner even goes as far as to claim that "the objective of information technology systems development in business is to increase the wealth of shareholders ..."[13]. Thus CFOs rightly demand an answer to the question: What is the return on CRM investment? This question gains further urgency by the fact that the economic slowdown is forcing many companies to take drastic savings measures, which also extend to investments in CRM. Given this situation, the question of the value added by CRM takes on particular significance.

---

[6] Morphy (2003), citing from an Aberdeen group survey; figures include hardware, software, and consulting services
[7] According to Rohde (2002), analysts from Garnter saw the total market at USD 25.3 bn in 2002 already, growing to USD 47 bn in 2006; Stokburger/Pufahl (2002) cite the same research firm with USD 15.9 bn worldwide spending for CRM in 2005; Fielding (2003) quotes analysts from Meta Research who report growth in CRM services by 20% in 2003
[8] Schneider (2003) cites Gartner, with their finding of a 25% drop in CRM new-license sales for 2002 which is reasoned primarily with price-discounts in an increasingly competitive market
[9] AMR Research (2003)
[10] The interdependency of corporate strategy and CRM is thoroughly outlined, for example, by Wehrmeister (2001) p. 103 ff.
[11] Kaplan (1986) p.79
[12] Horváth (1988) p.2,3.
[13] Gardner (2000) p.3

19

However, measuring CRM value is not only needed to convince management, namely the CFO, about the financial advantages of future investments in CRM or to justify past investments but it eventually improves the value of CRM itself. This conclusion is drawn by analysts of AMR Research based on survey results: "Developing a metrics-based business case increases the overall effectiveness of your Customer Relationship Management (CRM) strategy."[14] The underlying rationale is straight forward: better measurement leads to better decisions which in turn result in higher CRM success[15]. Of course, decisions should not rely only on financial calculations but a sophisticated business case may include many of the relevant aspects for the decision. Moreover, CRM applications are increasingly not implemented as a monolithic block of functionality but rather in an interactive approach, following a "test, learn, test" philosophy[16]. Therefore, a sequence of decisions is to be made, and the valuation of CRM is mandatory to rationally prioritize the CRM modules. The measurement of CRM success is also crucial to compare the original plans and the actual results, thereby enabling management to learn from the past and make better future decisions. Finally, even when the implementation project has started, a business case helps management to focus on the most important value drivers.

So a business case is the tool to measure and enhance the value added through CRM. While the financial calculus of a business case is ubiquitous and in that sense relatively easy, the link between the implementation of the CRM system and financial impact measurements is challenging and highly dependent on the specific situation of the company deploying CRM. The quality of the business case results depends largely on the quality of the underlying assumptions. In order to ensure high quality assumptions, a decision maker may want to resort to a proven value metric that allows for a mutually exclusive and comprehensively exhaustive assessment and aggregation of CRM effects. Furthermore, he may be interested in relevant and reliable benchmark figures. For both the pragmatic metric and the benchmark figures, empirical research is paramount. So it can be concluded that the valuation of CRM is needed, as well as empirical research to enable sound measurements and that both are urgent in times of economic recession and shareholder value orientation.

---

[14] Keltz/Preslan (2003)
[15] For a similar line of reasoning Stengl/Sommer/Ematinger (2001) p.40
[16] Schneider (2003), Adolf et. al. (1997) p. 191 f.

2.1.2 The Empirical Findings: Sparse and Contradictory

The urgent question about the value of CRM led to a controversial discussion over the question: Does CRM live up to the promise? While many opinions are being published, empirical findings are sparse and highly contradictory. After a time, when CRM was not questioned about its value added, some researchers hinted at scores of failed projects, dissatisfied customers, and the inability of users to identify a return on investment. Gartner, for example, reported that 50% of CRM implementations were considered failures from a customer's point of view, others 60%, and AMR Research puts that number up to 84% - depending on how success is defined[17]. CRMguru.com conducted a survey of 2000 CRM users and computed an overall Customer Satisfaction Index (CSI), including elements such as ease of implementation, customer focus, price satisfaction, support, and functionality. "Industry-wide, the CSI was a dismal 63.1 on a scale of 0 to 100"[18]. In sharp contrast, analysts from Forrester found in a survey among 111 large North American companies: "Nearly three-quarters of respondents say that they are satisfied with the business results from their CRM efforts."[19] So in terms of CRM customer satisfaction, research results widely differ.

The same diversity of findings exists with regard to the return on investment (ROI) of CRM. AMR Research reports that only 16% of all CRM projects under research "reach the promised land and measurably influence business performance"[20]. Half a year later, the same research firm finds "ROI still elusive in customer management"[21], with 43% of all respondents in an IT survey claiming "their investments yield real business benefits and ROI". Only half of these respondents, however, deployed "solid measurements of their success", a figure that makes the authors doubt the quality of their own assessment. Nucleus Research asked SAP customers about the "real ROI" of their IT investment – not only in CRM but also in other applications. "Fifty-seven percent of SAP customers interviewed did not believe that they had achieved a positive ROI, after having used their SAP applications for an average of 2.8 years."[22] For CRM-focused Siebel, even 61% of interviewed customers were unable to identify a ROI[23]. By comparison, a CRMguru.com survey of 448 CRM projects in 2002 reports "two out of three projects are successful, and half generate a

---

[17] Gartner (2003); Johnson (2003), providing four stages of project success; other research summarized by Fielding (2003)
[18] Sims (2001) p.1
[19] Temkin/Schmitt/Herbert (2003)
[20] Johnson (2003)
[21] Keltz/Preslan (2003)
[22] Nucleus Research (2003a) p.1
[23] Nucleus Research (2003b) p.1

payback in 18 months or less".[24] Also, the software vendors and IT service provider display impressive success stories on their websites and in their publications[25]. Despite the fact that it would be naive to consider these case studies as a representative sample from the entirety of CRM implementations, discarding these findings in total as "P.R. flak"[26] is unfounded and simplistic. Some case studies report effects that are publicly observable, some have been crafted by reputable third parties[27]. Finally, the reports are available within the company and non-realistic information will quickly undermine the credibility of the CRM responsible. Certainly not all would be willing to give up their internal standing to do the software vendor a favor.

The contradictory evidence may be due to a number of reasons – different time, different place, different measurements. There is no commonly agreed-on frame of reference in CRM terminology or ROI methodology, and the research companies are regularly tightlipped when it comes to the disclosure of their proprietary methodologies. So it is virtually impossible to compare figures from different studies. As a consequence, the basis of the publicly available empirical findings is insufficient, and *the question of value added through CRM is therefore far from being answered*.

2.1.3 The Challenge in CRM Value Assessment

To understand the sparseness of publicly-available results on the value of CRM, it pays to take a closer look at its reasons. Conceptually, CRM investments evade simple evaluation, and practically, companies avoid making their experiences public.

Conceptually, measuring value creation through CRM investments is not easy for several reasons:

- Based on the aforementioned definition, CRM penetrates the entire company. Moreover, many of the elements affected by CRM are interdependent, for example, customer and employee satisfaction. So

---

[24] Thompson (2003)
[25] For user case studies check the web-sites of some of the leading CRM vendors www.siebel.com, www.sap.com, or www.peoplesoft.com; for case studies structured according to indicators of success Primus (2002); as consultants, for example, Stokburger/Pufahl (2002) for example p.203, Caulfield (2001) p.19ff., Rigby/Reichheld/Schefter (2002)
[26] Sims (2001)
[27] For example the ROI study on The Tyrolit Group by Pirnar/Plazonja/Scalea (2002) of Hill/Holiday reviewed by the Peppers & Rogers Group

complexity is high, which hinders us in identifying and quantifying of all aspects. Therefore it is not transparent, which effects were caused by the implementation of the CRM system. This challenge is known as the *"causality problem"*.

- Along with the "hard factors" of value creation – like cross-/up-sales – there are many "soft factors" such as customer satisfaction, which are more difficult to measure and whose influence on the bottom line is far from being understood. So the second challenge is how to quantify the effects caused by CRM, as *quantification* is needed in order to measure value.
- This leads to the question: ***How do we correctly measure value creation*** through CRM? Besides the financial success indicators of, for example, ROI, NPV, or Break Even, a multitude of alternatives or complementary aspects are discussed.
- Using universally applicable functional relationships between parameters could potentially reduce the workload associated with crafting a business case. This raises the question to which extent *company and situation-specific assessments* are needed.
- Finally – as will be shown in more detail later – it takes more than two years for the CRM application to unfold its entire potential. This raises the question on *when to measure what* and how to capture the value added at a point of time when the full potential has not yet been experienced.

Not only is return on CRM investments difficult to quantify but *companies are also reluctant to make their results public* – again for good practical reasons:

- In practice, many companies invest in CRM without crafting a business case. In addition, they also do not see a need to measure key value drivers like customer churn, leads, conversion rates, sales cycle time, and so on; so a *fact-based comparison of the situation before and after is difficult to achieve*.
- Transparency is sometimes not even achievable for the company because it is *not always in the interest of individuals or departments* to give insight into the potential to increase efficiency and effectiveness. This information regularly carries the implicit reproach of management failure as well as fear about the loss of jobs. This underlying cause for many measurement failures falls into the category of "chicken-and-egg" problems: As it is unclear what the CRM consequences are, employees are afraid to provide information, which in turn reinforces unclarity.

- As CRM is a far-reaching concept, a detailed and comprehensive publication of results creates tremendous transparency about a company's operations and strategy, which is typically ***not in the individual company's best interest***.
- Whenever the CRM project yields ***very positive results***, several additional reasons may stifle the publication:
    - The competition must not find out because this may well be considered as a strategic advantage
    - The shareholders must not find out because they may raise the targets for management
    - The software provider must not find out to avoid claims on the basis of "value-based pricing"
- If the CRM project's ***ROI is marginal or negative***, of course, nobody should find out about it

So in fact, conceptual and practical challenges abound. To sum up Chapter 2 up to this point:
- Decisions on CRM are strategic in nature. Therefore, a sophisticated business case showing the expected financial impact is needed. Furthermore, a valuation of CRM helps to make sure that the value is eventually delivered as expected.
- The quality of the business case depends on the quality of the assumptions and a pragmatic, empirically proven assessment of CRM effects. Both result from empirical research.
- Empirical findings on the value of CRM are scarce and controversial. This holds true for measurements of customer satisfaction as well as ROI.
- Numerous conceptual and practical challenges have been identified as root cause for the lack of coherent empirical evidence.

2.1.4 The Aim of the CFROI of CRM Study

In the situation as described above, the study's objective is
- To develop a pragmatic, transparent, and systematic success metric to overcome the conceptual challenges and
- To measure the actual financial return on CRM investment from a focused group of users with user-specific business cases in an

independent and interactive research process to meet the practical challenges

The success metric has to be *pragmatic*, that is, applicable for practical cases in which the ideal situation of fully available information almost never exists. This means to tread the sometimes fine line between what is theoretically correct and what is doable in practice. The causality problem, for example, cannot be solved in the strict theoretical sense. Nobody will ever know for sure what would have happened if a CRM system had not been installed. So in this sense it is impossible to be sure about the effects that were caused by the implementation of a CRM system. Nonetheless, this is irrelevant because for most practical purposes, a probabilistic assessment of effects is better than not to measure at all[28]. The challenge is to develop techniques that will increase the quality of the assessments.

While many research firms hide their proprietary metrics, the CRM Value Metric developed in this study will be outlined in some detail in the next chapter. Unless the methodology is *transparent*, the value of the results is limited. Furthermore, the metric itself is an end product, which may prove to be valuable for decision makers in assessing the value added through CRM. Finally, the methodology is aimed to tackle the conceptual issues *systematically* one by one. The target is to capture the full spectrum of the pragmatically assessable value added – which may only be 80:20 with regard to the theoretically correct figure. Whenever assumptions for the sake of simplification are needed, they lean towards the more conservative assessment.

The practical challenges that inhibit companies to make their experiences public are being met by the design of the research process. The fact that every company's CRM application is different, and that many companies do not have ready-to-report figures on the shelf when it comes to the value of CRM, has been accounted for by the use of questionnaire-based telephone interviews. They allow us to combine a systematic assessment with sufficient flexiblity to adapt to the *specific situation of the company* and to interactively estimate the scope of effects. Openness and honesty in these interviews require *independence and confidentiality*, which were both achieved by the trustee model. Finally, reliability is warranted by the highly *interactive* feedback process.

---

[28] Huber (1999) p.112 ff.

2.2 The Research Design: Meeting the Challenge

Chapter 2.2. explains the methodology underlying this research; reading is recommended to warrant an adequate understanding of the results. First the fundamental choices for a CRM value measurement concept that build the basis for the CRM Value Metric are outlined. The CRM Value Metric's structure is explained in Chapter 2.2.2, which then in turn serves as blueprint for the user-specific business cases. While these chapters tackle the conceptual challenges of measuring CRM value, the following ones focus on the approaches to overcome the practical challenges: the questionnaire's structure, the trustee model, and the interactive feedback process. Finally, the structure of participants is detailed.

2.2.1 Key Concepts for Measuring CRM Value

Measuring CRM value is challenging – as Chapter 2.1 outlines. To overcome the conceptual challenges, several fundamental choices have to be made, resulting in a CRM measurement concept. These choices also differentiate the landscape of approaches to the topic of measuring CRM value. First, a logic-tree is displayed that structures the numerous choices. Then, each "node" of the tree is explained in more detail.

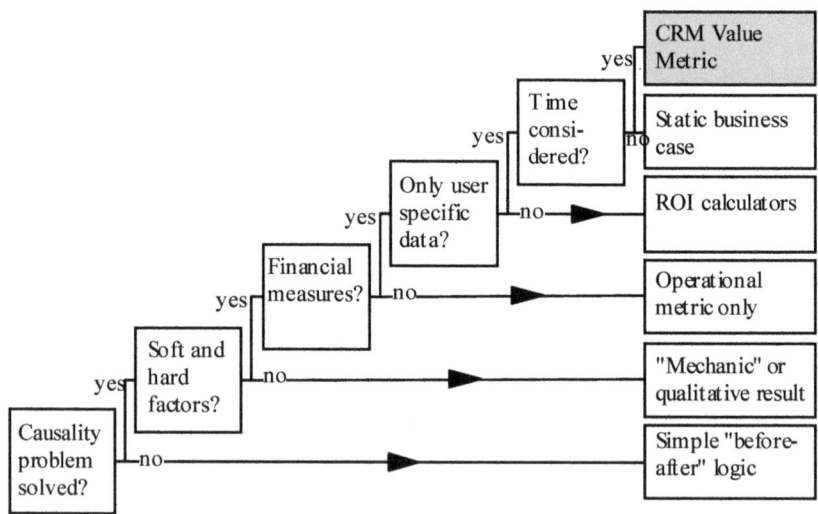

Figure 1: Fundamental choices about the CRM value measurement concept

We start from the most basic question in the framework, the *causality problem*: Are only those effects that were caused by CRM taken into consideration? Some researchers simply assume causality in a "before" and "after" comparison of success indicators. Accenture conducted research based on this implicit assumption of causality to find out how much enhanced customer relationship capabilities can add to the return-on-sales (RoS) of a company[29]. While the assumed relationship between higher performance and a comprehensive list of 24 customer capabilities is plausible, the "before-and-after" comparison is invalid for the question of the return on CRM investments. A change in the operating profit or even the market value of a company has multiple causes, many of which are likely to have a much stronger effect on the overall performance than the CRM-system. Furthermore, the implementation of CRM takes time. The longer the time between the start and the full effectiveness of the CRM system, the less likely are changes in company value rightly attributed to it. Therefore, research like the "Retail Impact Analysis" of MicroStrategy[30] is an unsound "logic shortcut". As this method just evades the problem but does not solve it, causality remains elusive.

While some research neglects the causality problem, other authors capitulate at this step already. So Schwetz claims that it is "impossible to find a causal relationship between the use of computers in sales, marketing, and service and an expected increase in revenue"[31]. And he is right in a strict theoretical sense, as "objectivity" is impossible to achieve. Nonetheless as has been pointed out in Chapter 2.4.1: For practical reasons, an assessment of what would probably have happened is sufficient. So the key to a pragmatic solution of the causality problem is to increase the likelihood of individual, subjectively probabilistic assessments. Judging the effect of a CRM-system on revenue is beyond the cognitive limits of almost everybody. The CRM Value Metric deploys two techniques to ease the assessment and thereby increase its quality: causal chains and a project focus in defining the CRM scope.

The CRM Value Metric is based on *full cause-and-effect chains*, built step-by-step from the initial impulse by the CRM system to the highly aggregated

---

[29] Dull/Stephens/Wolfe (2000)
[30] For example MicroStrategy (2002) states in its "Retail Impact Analysis" that users of the MicroStrategy Business Intelligence Platform have a higher ROA, and simply claims the difference to be due to its software
[31] Schwetz (2001) p.221

financial indicators of success[32]. This way the relationship between the CRM system and the increase in revenue is broken down into several smaller steps. The employee working with the system then only has to report the CRM effects that he or she has observed instead of speculating about unfamiliar aspects. And despite splitting up the larger relationship into a mosaic of single observations, the systematic nature of the causal chains ensures that all effects are taken into account and that they add-up without double counts.

The second technique to increase the quality of the assessment is *a sharp project focus on scoping the CRM efforts and effects* that have to be taken into consideration. The CRM definition from Chapter 2.1 shows the complexity of interdependent effects that span all across the entire company. Moreover, to be theoretically correct, one would have to separate the effects caused by the CRM system from those that were caused by other CRM measures as, for example, the cleaning-up of customer data, the change management which directly impacts employees' values, and so on. However, this fine-grained differentiation between several causes and effects simply surpasses the ability of most CRM employees. It leads to spurious exactness. Therefore, in the CRM Value Metric, the CRM implementation project in total has been assessed by the respondents as a crystalizer of the CRM change efforts. So all measures required for the CRM application have been taken into consideration, that is, the required or induced changes in CRM processes, the improved employee skills based on the CRM training, the customer data clean-up effort, and so on. Subprojects that just took place at the same time as the CRM implementation were not considered. If, for example, the product portfolio changed at the same time as CRM was introduced, and the respondent observed a 10% increase in sales, the question was: What would happen, if the CRM system were switched off now? Only the difference would then be attributed to the CRM project. This focused approach has the advantage of a clearly identifiable and observable component on the investment side. And it fits the situation at most of the participating companies in the survey, where implementing the enabling CRM technology has in practice been the visible signal to the company that a new era was to begin. Furthermore, most project budgets were not divided according to single measures. So even if the CRM effects could be assessed in a more differentiated way, they would have to be all added up to compare the benefits with the associated cost. Finally, as the chosen circle of CRM investments and effects is a narrow one, the reported financial results are on the conservative side.

---

[32] This technique is similarly applied by Wehrmeister (2001) p.30-62 who also develops a full-scoped CRM metric; for simpler model, check Hippner/Wilde (2001) p.20

The next question is how to capture the *"soft" and "hard" factors of CRM success*. "Hard" factors, for example, revenue or time, are easily quantifiable, as two people who measure the same object will come to the same results. By comparison, "soft" factors, such as customer satisfaction, cannot be measured unambiguously. Hard and soft mark the end points of a spectrum of factors according to their quantifiability[33]. CRM is all about "relationships", and they are impossible to understand without soft factor categories such as trust, respect, loyalty, satisfaction, and so on. On the other hand, financial measurements depend on measuring, adding-up and evaluating hard factors. In literature and practice, several possible ways can be identified to solve this dilemma:

- Many authors simply ***neglect soft factors*** and start with the hard effects such as expected cost and revenue benefits[34]. This method is also frequently found in practice when the "generic business case template" has the "estimated cost savings" as the lowest level of aggregation for an input. One significant caveat is associated with this technique: The respondent will regularly be incapable of giving a substantiated assessment because the soft effects, the critical link between the application and the hard benefits, are missing. The figures are all right in a "mechanistic" way but they are not anchored in observations of soft changes, which are needed to do a plausibility check on the assumptions.

- A second group of authors ***neglects the hard effects*** and settles for a qualitative understanding of CRM effects. So many of the popular introductions to the concept of CRM provide picturesque enumerations of potential qualitative advantages, thereby extensively covering the soft factors of CRM success. The reader is, however, not helped in calculating the value of a CRM investment[35].

- A third approach is to bridge the gap between soft and hard factors through ***mathematical functions*** of the kind: If customer satisfaction rises x%, revenue will increase y%. The main practical problem of this theoretically correct concept is the fact that the relationship between soft and hard factors is far from being understood in terms of universally applicable functions. One of the best-researched relationships between customer satisfaction and customer retention has yielded a plethora of divergent results and catalytic interdependencies of other parameters as outlined by Giering[36]. Even in the

---

[33] Horváth (1988) p.11 ff.
[34] For example Gardner (2001) p.209 ff. as an example of a simplistic and mechanistic business case for information technology
[35] For example Rapp (2001), Schwetz (2001), Rajola (2003)
[36] Giering (2000)

focused segment of German car dealers, Fischer et. al. do not rely on universal functions to compute a "return on customer satisfaction" but on individual dealer assessments[37].

The CRM Value Metric again takes a pragmatic approach: Soft and hard factors are directly asked for. Then the "soft" factors are used to check the plausibility of the reported hard CRM effects. If, for example, the revenue was said to have risen due to the deployment of mySAP CRM but neither customer satisfaction nor any other "soft" factor had changed, the number was openly questioned in the interview. The prerequisite for this technique is a complete landscape of potential links between soft and hard factors.

Once it is decided to measure hard effects of the CRM deployment, the question of whether to use *financial success measurements* needs to be answered on the next level of the Figure 1 staircase. Before the background of the detailed rationale in Chapter 2.1.1 it comes as no surprise that this question has been answered with a clear "yes" for the CRM Value Metric. The companies' shareholders and decision makers need it as a basis for rational decisions. This choice, however, clearly differentiates this study's approach from many others:

- Some authors are focused on the *measurement of operational CRM effects* and develop elaborate metrics[38]. Large scale surveys conducted such as those by Gartner or CRMguru.com[39] do not measure economic success but an aggregate "satisfaction index" – a legitimate indicator with a different purpose, just not the answer to the question at hand.

- Others *reject financial measures for reasons of misconception*. So, for example, Zingale and Arndt do not see "short term economic profit" as a valid measurement for e-CRM success, as it was all about "long-term customer relationship and profitable growth"[40]. They seem to have ill-understood the concept of financial measurement by settling for what Meltzer rightly calls "rear facing" and non-strategic accounting measures[41]. The CRM Value Metric uses dynamic financial indicators such as cash flow return on investment, net present value, and break-even period. Neither one of these is limited to the short term. Instead, they have the advantage of integrating past and current experience with a future perspective as they are

---

[37] Fischer et. al. (2001) p.1163-1166
[38] Wehrmeister (2001) p. 62
[39] Gartner (2002), Thompson (2003)
[40] Zingale/Arndt (2002) p.193
[41] Meltzer (2001) p.318

based on a 3 and 5-year future operational cash flow forecast. This future perspective allows us to include expected "strategic" changes in the company's environment that increase or diminish the impact of CRM – for example, increasing competitive pressure. It also allows for the extrapolation of experience with strategic initiatives and competitive advantages[42]. So in some cases, new business opportunities were reported based on the use of mySAP CRM – serving new customers in new ways, which clearly falls under the category of strategic import. Dombrowski/Messinger show another fallacy of thought frequently found in practice: "The economic benefit of the CRM solution at Schott is not so much based on a classic ROI calculation but on all the disadvantages that would have resulted from not using the system"[43]. The only possibility to compute an ROI of CRM is to assess the difference between the situation without the CRM system – the so called "base case" – and the situation with the application in use. Again, not to use financial measurement seems to be the result of its misconception.

- An interesting survey titled "***How You Define CRM Success Depends on Who You Are***" makes an important point: CRM success in the eyes of technology-driven providers of software or IT services is often measured in technical terms while their customers are seeking financial results[44]. The same limitation with regard to the perspective comes into play inside the company deploying CRM. Marketing is primarily interested in, for example, the number of leads generated, the hits on an e-shop, or the time needed to do a marketing campaign. Sales requires higher quality in customer data and a smooth electronic order-taking process, which saves the sales representative some time, and so on[45]. Inside the CRM user company, it is primarily controller or management who prioritizes the financial perspective.

Level four in Figure 1 leads to the next decision that everybody makes implicitly or explicitly before measuring the value of CRM: the use of general assumptions versus company and situation specific information. As an answer to the pressing question of potential customers about the return on CRM investment, the use of

---

[42] So "competitive advantage" is not a "complementary" technique to value CRM investments as Meltzer (2001) p.318 puts it – but rather a prerequisite to adequately arrive at the "traditional" financial measurements
[43] Dombrowski/Messinger (2002) p.246
[44] Johnson (2003)
[45] So Schmidt (2001) p.241 ff. uses the heading of "controlling success of eCRM" to describe primarily techniques which provide statistics of the use of online offers while only hinting at the fact that these statisticts are only the basis for calculating economic success factors.

ROI calculators is widespread among CRM vendors. These tools are typically accessible via the internet, and require the input of very little information by the user, for example the number of sales staff, total revenue, and so on – and then return a prospective ROI. To ensure ease-of-use, these tools largely depend on strong "hard wired" assumptions. Therefore, their results are only rough estimates of ROI – and serious ones do not claim to be any more than that[46]. The CRM Value Metric used in this study does not contain any pre-configured assumptions about values: All values in the business case originate from the respondents.

Finally, it takes a long time for CRM to reach its maximum effectiveness. In the study, it took respondents an average 2,5 years from the project's kick-off to steady state, that is, the point in time when all users have access to the system as planned, when they are able to use the system for their everyday work and when the quality of results from the system is sufficiently high for a continued operation. For most practical purposes, this is too long to not take time into consideration for the calculation of the financial benefit. Consequences from this observation are as follows:

- Decision makers on CRM investments should deploy ***dynamic investment valuation techniques*** like a Discounted Cash Flow (DCF) or Internal Rate of Return (IRR) instead of the static ones like the cost comparison, profit comparison, and so on[47]. This conclusion is important, because despite the convincing rationale for taking time into consideration, still 50% of all participants in a Gartner CRM survey have admitted that they do not consider time in valuing their CRM activities[48].
- Furthermore, "***cash is king***"[49], that is, the cash flow basis is superior to the regular accounting approach in that it provides a "more sophisticated and reliable picture[50]" of the value created. The main conceptual flaw of periodic accounting figures is that they do not reflect the financial consequences adequately with respect to timing. Furthermore, they depend on the different national accounting standards and tax regimes, as well as their use within the

---

[46] For example, check for the disclaimers of the ROI calculators at www.peoplesoft.com, www.siebel.com; the SAP ROI calculator is not "self-serve" but embedded in a consulting process to help the customer to a higher quality of assumptions
[47] Horváth (1988) p.9 draws the same conclusion for valuing IT in general; for an overview of static and dynamic investment valuation techniques also check Selchert (1999) p. 180 ff.; in more detail Walz/Gramlich (1997)
[48] Stokburger/Pufahl (2002) p.34 citing from a Gartner Group CRM survey 2000/2001
[49] Copeland/Koller/Murrin (1995) p.69 ff.
[50] Copeland/Koller/Murrin (1995) p.70

individual company, which are regularly unrelated to the investment decision itself[51]. Empirically, Copeland/Koller/Murrin show that the stock market does not value companies on the basis of periodic accounting results but on cash flow[52]. As the use of the CRM is supposed to increase the value to shareholders, this result is a relevant argument in favor of preferring cash flow over period accounting standards. These findings clearly speak against the frequently used measurement of "ROI after x months" because this is calculated as a periodic result based on accounting figures.

- In the corporate practice, three years is currently the commonly used time frame for an investment in software. However, CRM is more than software. It includes the changes in attitude, behavior, and processes. Therefore, a longer period of time should be considered as the regular ***useful life of a CRM system***. Most practitioners agreed that a five-year period constitutes the upper limit. The less an individual CRM implementation resembles a technical application implementation, the longer the expected useful life should be and vice versa.

- To assess the full value potential of CRM at any given point of time, the users should be asked for ***experience-based expectations***. So based on their own initial experience with the system and the learning curve at the time of interview, users predict which future level of perfection is attainable in their specific situation (as outlined in Chapter 4), how long this will take, and what benefit will result in this envisioned steady state. Participants in the study were regularly not able to provide such an experience-based expectation in a reliable way when the CRM system was productive less than 6 months.

So on the one hand, the CRM Value Metric is a highly sophisticated approach for the large number of companies that were to be investigated. On the other hand, it is not the high end of business case modeling as it falls short in three aspects: the financial evaluation of risk, management flexibility, and business dynamics.

Risk is defined as the deviation of results from the plan. CRM investments have shown some significant risk for several reasons. As mentioned above, CRM takes years to reach the steady state. The longer the timeframe, the less predictable is the outcome. Furthermore, the definition of CRM in Chapter 2.1

---

[51] Selchert (1999) p.201
[52] Copeland/Koller/Murrin (1995) p.77 ff.

stresses that CRM success depends on many factors, some difficult to manage such as corporate culture and customer orientation. From the spectrum of possibilities to assess risk in information technology investments[53], sensitivity analysis and break-even analysis have been deployed in this study. Neither one, however, values the risk in financial terms. Copeland/Antikarov show a pragmatic way to do so, using Monte Carlo simulation[54]. A state-of-the-art business case on CRM should also value *real options*, that is, management flexibility to adapt to future developments. Especially in the case of high uncertainty and high management flexibility – which is exactly the situation of a CRM decision – real options may add significant value to the investment[55].

Finally, ***interdependent self-reinforcing effects*** have not been taken into consideration. So if, for example, CRM improves customer satisfaction, this may lead to a more pleasant work environment, which in turn raises motivation of employees, finally resulting in an even higher customer satisfaction. Feedback loops like this can be modeled in quantitative business dynamics models. A widely recognized study of Reichheld/Sasser analyzed those interdependent effects systematically in the context of customer loyalty to conclude that in some industries, a 5-percentage-point increase in the retention rate leads to a 35%-95% increase in the customer net present value[56].

So despite that fact that each one of the three additional refinements of the CRM Value Metric may be decisive for an individual company's business case, none of them was used in the study for practical reasons. Identifying, modeling, and computing the value of risk, real options, and business dynamics would have required too deep of an analysis of the specific situation of each company. The balance between breadth and depth would have been compromised. As a second caveat, these models are characterized by high mathematical complexity and they require numerous assumptions. Both aspects negatively impact intelligibility and belief of the results. Finally, as option values and dynamic feedback effects are missing, the reported figures will in most cases be too low relative to the "true" value of the CRM investment. This mistake is on the conservative side and it was deemed tolerable in an exploratory research.

---

[53] For an overview check Gardner (2000) p.236-250
[54] Copeland/Antikarov (2001) p.244 ff.
[55] Copeland/Antikarov (2001) p.13 f.; also pleading for the use of real options to value CRM investments Meltzer (2001) p.317 ff.
[56] Reichheld/Sasser (1990) p.106 ff. ; the method and results have been reconfirmed for the Internet Economy by Reichheld/Schefter (2000)

Research Design – The Concept

2.2.2 The Structure of the CRM Value Metric

The CRM Value Metric builds on the foundations of the fundamental choices outlined in Chapter 2.2.1. In this chapter, the goal is to give an overview of the metric's structure; details will then be provided in the context of the results in Chapter 3. Schematically, the CRM Value Metric looks as follows:

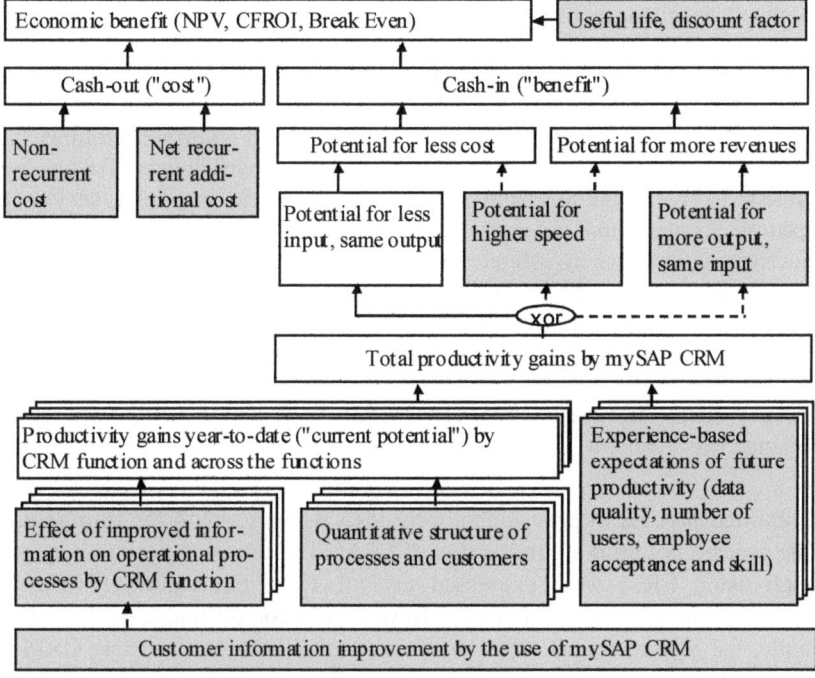

Figure 2: Overview: CRM Value Metric

Although the framework is complex, it is visible immediately that the ***CRM Value Metric systematically builds bottom-up in full cause-and-effect chains*** from better customer information through operational process optimization to improvements of cash flow and the highly aggregated financial economic benefits. All of the shaded areas are input to the metric, separately assessed through the questionnaire, which is available in the appendix. The non-shaded areas are therefore calculated. Calculations are characterized by a full-line arrow, whereas dotted-line arrows indicate a plausibility check only.

35

In order to understand the metric, one needs to start at the bottom. The immediate impact of CRM is an *improvement in customer information. This is the basic driver of productivity enhancements for all of the CRM functions.* The CRM system directly impacts the information on customers as well as the information for customers. But an improvement in information is not sufficient to create an economic benefit for the user. To be effective, these improvements must result in changes of the CRM processes and functions. No commonly accepted model of CRM functions exists. Marketing, sales, and service are almost universally distinguished. The Interaction Center and Internet sales, however, are considered alternatively as one or two functions, as separate functions or as a part of sales or services[57]. In line with empirical findings[58] and SAP's classification[59], which was well known to the participants, the two were separated. So five CRM functions were identified: Marketing, sales, service, the Interaction Center, and Internet sales. For each of these CRM functions, productivity gains were investigated in detail for the most promising operational processes. These processes are outlined in the questionnaire as well as in Chapter 3. For each participant, only those CRM functions were taken into consideration that had gone live before the interview. In many cases, respondents reported updates or additional modules that were to go live soon. These extensions of the existing system, however, were consistently excluded because no relevant experience was available.

The reported process improvements were then weighted with the time required for the process before the introduction of CRM. The resulting productivity gains through using CRM were expressed in Full Time Equivalents (FTE). This measurement needs a word of caution to warrant a correct understanding: If, for example, the preparation of a customer visit took 1 hour before using CRM and afterwards half an hour was enough to reach the same level of preparation, the productivity, that is, the ratio of output over input, has improved. In economic theory, this is referred to as a "general optimization"[60]. It is called "general" because the *productivity gains are neutral as to how they will be cashed in for the company*. Expressing the magnitude of this improvement as FTE suggests a

---

[57] For example Dyché (2002) chapters 2-5 integrates the Interaction Center into service while Internet sales are considered to be a separate CRM function.
[58] Stokburger/Pufahl (2002) report that only 20% of respondents to a Gartner survey from 2000/2001 had added Internet sales capabilities to their Interaction Centers at all
[59] Hauke/Schuh (2003) p.7 outline the 8 "key capabilities necessary for successful CRM operation." Of these, "sales", "field sales", and "integrated sales planning" have been integrated in "sales", "customer service" and "field service and dispatch" are combined to "service".
[60] Selchert (1999) p.4

possible reduction in human resources. But the sales representative's half hour gained could as well be "reinvested" to increase the likelihood to win a deal.

The process of assessing productivity gains per process and then multiplying by the amount of work hours originally spent on this process was carried out with all CRM functions deployed by the participating company. In addition to the analysis by function, *cross-functional productivity improvements were investigated*. A number of positive CRM effects are due to the interaction between CRM functions. For example, marketing generates additional qualified leads based on improved customer information. If this process did not exist before the introduction of mySAP CRM, marketing would have increased its cost due to the introduction of CRM. The associated benefit, however, does not materialize in marketing but in sales. If the user did not deploy CRM in sales, a functional analysis would not have come up with the correct result with regard to the net benefit of CRM. Another example is the time-to-delivery. Only a smooth interaction between marketing, sales, and service will lead to a reduction – not the maximization of efficiency in one CRM function: The weakest link in the value chain determines the speed. So in order to capture these cross-functional effects, they were explicitly addressed in the questionnaire and in the interviews.

CRM is always just in a state of development, so the *time-based nature of CRM results has to be explicitly obeyed*[61]. For this reason, two temporal observation points were distinguished for every single item in the questionnaire: The first measurement concerns the "actual potential" realized at the time of the study, that is, changes in operational processes realized since the production startup of mySAP CRM. The second measurement concerns "experience-based expectations", which describe the state a particular company expects to achieve, based on the experiences made so far. To stress the point: Expectations are not wishful thinking, they do not represent the original and maybe outdated business plan, and they are not rooted in a theoretically possible result, but they reflect the very situation of the user, that is, its given real situation, processes, structures, skills, data quality, culture, and staff. Three components mainly drive the *experience-based expectation*: additional users, enhanced skills in using the software, and improved data quality. The first one especially turned out to be a major driver of productivity as many companies planned to roll out their current installation to other parts of the company – be it other product divisions or other countries. These factors have been reviewed with the participant by CRM

---

[61] For a detailed rationale check Chapter 2.2.1

function. So, for example, a company that went live with the Mobile Sales module 1.5 years ago may have had little or no additional future potential from the sales function – but possibly significant future potential from the mySAP CRM-powered e-shop, which had been live for only 5 months. In case the respondent did not have an experience-based expectation on the granular level of single processes, two closing questions were asked after each CRM-function specific chapter to capture a general perspective on the future development. The respondent first had to imagine the steady state of the entire CRM function. Then the current level relative to this steady state was to be estimated as a percentage. As a last step, the respondent had to assess how long it would take to reach the steady state – given the speed of development so far.

The current and future productivity improvements were mapped over time to get the full picture of *total gains in productivity*. These total productivity gains were to be used in either one of three ways – cost reduction, increase in revenue, or increase in speed. Assuming that all the resources saved through increased productivity were taken out of the company, then the cost would be reduced. In economic theory, this is known as the "minimum principle": same output with less input[62]. If the same amount of time were being spent on a better preparation of customer interaction, an increase in revenue would likely occur. This would be compliant with the "maximum principle": more output with the same level of input[63]. Finally, the speed can also be increased by productivity gains: If the same number of sales representatives worked at a higher productivity and saw, for example, 12 instead of 10 leads a day, the time-to-volume would shrink, as less absolute time is needed to see all potential customers. It is crucial to note that *productivity gains can only be capitalized in one of the three ways!* When the business case is drafted after reaching steady state, there can and will be of course a mixture of cost savings and revenue increase[64]. If however dynamic second order effects are neglected, any mixture can only be a linear interpolation between the extremes at best. When the business case is created before reaching steady state and especially before the CRM project, the challenge is to avoid double counts. The (prospective) user will typically not be able to neatly split up the increase in productivity into cost savings potential and potential for extra revenue. So to simply add up cost and revenue assessments is mathematically correct and frequently found in practice[65] but nonetheless seldomly valid. By comparison, two values were determined in this study to prevent double counts:

---

[62] Selchert (1999) p.4; Dangelmaier/Uebel/Helmke (2002) p.6 call this an improved "efficiency"
[63] Selchert (1999) p.4; Dangelmaier/Uebel/Helmke (2002) p.6 refer to this as "effectiveness"
[64] For example reported by Stokburger/Pufahl (2002) p.203
[65] This simplistic logic is for example applied by Henn (2001) p.44

The first calculation used costs to identify the value of the identified productivity potential; the second determined the value resulting from the freed-up time and improved information flowing into activities for increasing revenue. Besides being the more conservative and sound kind of analysis, this method is also supported by empirical research which indicates that companies fare better when they either maximize revenue or minimize cost but do not follow both paths at the same time[66]. To select one of the two extreme values, a rational choice was assumed: The more valuable of either the revenue driven result or the cost driven result was taken as the basis for the calculation of the financial indicators such as the net present value or the cash flow return on investment[67]. This choice is marked in Figure 2 by the circled "xor".

Higher speed is not a financial category per se, but it ultimately results in either lower cost or higher revenue. So in our example, either sales staff would be reduced after seeing all customers or the higher speed resulted in an improved competitive position, which in turn leads to higher revenue. In this sense, the higher flexibility of CRM users is only an intermediate result.

Potential for cost reduction follows the straightforward notion of taking out the input (resources) saved and valuing them with their respective prices, that is, FTE were multiplied with full labor cost and materials by market prices. It should be noted that the result of this calculation is labeled as a "potential". To which extent it will be captured for the company depends on several factors:

- If the productivity gains have not been properly identified jointly with the users step-by-step as described above but if they were rather estimated "top-down", management will have a hard time locating the potential cost savings.
- If management simply does not do its unpopular duty to "collect" the productivity gains by reducing the input of, for example, work hours, with unchanged goals, no cost reduction will result for the company.
- National labor laws or strong unions may altogether prevent realizing gains in productivity via cost reductions.

Besides the potential reduction of labor cost, other cost positions were favorably affected through using CRM. So, for example, marketing campaigns can be

---

[66] Rust et. al. (2002) p. 13 ff.
[67] The result based on additional revenue is not the more "valuable" only because it is higher than the one from cost reductions. Additional cost caused by the additional revenue has to be deducted to calculate the additional value.

lowered by a more targeted selection of customers as well as a higher quality of addresses, resulting in less returned mail. A deeper understanding of customer buying patterns may lead to reduced inventory, an effect that materializes even outside the "classic" CRM functions. Also the improvement in speed may have a positive impact on cost as mentioned above.

Revenue can also be increased by improved productivity through CRM. In our sales example, cited above, this may be the case by having the sales person invest in a better preparation for the customer visit. Alternatively, the time gained through CRM could be spent in seeing more customers with the same level of preparation as before. A more detailed framework for the generation of extra revenue will be introduced in Chapter 3.4.

While the calculation of the potential cost savings is straightforward, the assessment of the potential extra revenue is not. ***Two possible methods are to be distinguished***: a mathematical transformation of productivity gains to additional revenue or a separate question asking the respondent how much more revenue he could make given the changes by the CRM system. The mathematical transformation is only theoretically possible. In practice, the reinvestment of freed-up additional time cannot be assumed to yield the same return as the time spent before. While a decreasing rate of return would be expected, Stokburger/Pufahl even experienced an increasing rate of return where CRM doubled productivity and increased the average revenue per customer by the factor 2.6^{68}. So no universally applicable functional relationship between the two parameters is known. Therefore, the revenue potential was assessed separately to account for any decreasing rate of return. To do so, the drivers of additional revenue potential were structured by logic trees to capture all possible effects but only those that are due to the CRM system[69]. The gains in productivity were used as plausibility check. So if, for example, a respondent reported an increase in the number of leads by 30% but did not see any improvements in productivity then the reported increase would have been questioned. So any revenue increase reported in this study is double-checked: once against the explicitly assessed changes in the drivers of revenue and once against process enhancements that resulted in the total productivity increase. This method has the advantage of values being reproduced and clearly attributed to CRM, rather than to economic or other changes. In addition, double counts are avoided.

---

[68] Stokburger/Pufahl (2002) p.203
[69] For an overview of the logic trees check Chapter 3.4

Additional revenue constitutes "*cash-in*". At the same time, more goods sold also result in "cash-out" for raw materials and production. So as a next step, value added has to be calculated as revenue multiplied by the participant's individual EBITDA-margin, that is, the earnings before interest, tax, depreciation, and amortization in relation to revenue. This measurement is adequate to the cash-flow perspective as argued in Chapter 2.2.1. As the EBITDA-margin is pre-tax, this measurement also avoids incomparability of CRM results due to different national tax regimes. There is one notable exception to this rule: If revenue rises through price increase, no extra cost will be incurred. Therefore, the EBITDA-margin should not be applied to this kind of revenue increase as it already has a direct impact on the bottom-line. Cash-in may also originate from cost reductions but as explained before: Only the more valuable of the two should be chosen.

The *additional cost caused by the decision in favor of CRM consists of recurrent and non-recurrent cash-outs*. The following positions have been taken into consideration:

- All cash-out from pilot and test installations' hardware and license fees
- Licenses for the mySAP CRM application as well as for other software needed in the CRM project plus all hardware which was deployed as prerequisite for the CRM implementation. If the participating company bought the license, the expense has been classified as non-recurrent, whereas a leased application or hardware resulted in a recurrent expense.
- The entire cost of the implementation project, including change projects, external support as well as internal staff
- All cost of initial and ongoing training, that is, external and internal trainer as well as trainees' time-out
- Reductions in the users' personal productivity due to on-the-job learning, problems with the system, data quality issues, and so on
- Cost for the maintenance and operation of the CRM system, including updates, hotline support, and so on.

If legacy systems have been switched off due to the mySAP CRM implementation, potential cost reductions have to be deducted from the sum of the aforementioned extra-cost. The deduction of cash-out from cash-in results in the gross operational cash flow from mySAP CRM. This gross operational cash flow has been calculated in detail for a five-year period. A terminal value was added for the time after.

Research Design – The Concept

Based on this cash flow and the discount rate, several indicators of financial investment success were computed: the cash flow return on investment, the net present value, and the break-even period. Details of the calculation and interpretation of these measurements will be provided in Chapter 3.2.1. The question to be dealt with now is: Are there any alternative financial measurements that meet the requirements developed in the previous chapter? Some authors favor the customer lifetime value (CLV) concept or the related customer equity as the correct measurement of value added by CRM[70]. The customer lifetime value and customer equity are defined as the present value of all returns from a customer over the lifetime of a customer relationship. The decision of implementing a CRM-system or not would then be based on the impact of this system on the CLV. There is not one CLV concept but many variations, some of which are non-compliant with the requirements for this study, for example, some do not adequately take future values into consideration[71], others neglect all company-internal effects of CRM and only focus on the customer interaction[72]. If all decisions were taken as it was described in the context of the CRM Value Metric, the result from the CLV would be expected to be identical to the CRM Value Metric – only that it is expressed as a value added per customer[73]. However, the calculation would almost inevitably be more difficult, as the absolute CLV would first have to be calculated which is widely recognized as very difficult[74]. Thus, it was decided to express the value added by CRM by such commonly used and easily understood indicators as CFROI, NPV, or the break-even period, instead.

The characteristics of the CRM Value Metric exactly mirror the basic decisions described in Chapter 2.2.1:

- Hard and soft factors of CRM value are explicitly assessed and related to one another in full cause-and-effect chains to ensure the utmost consistency and plausibility
- Operational measurements build the basis for the indicators of financial success

---

[70] For customer lifetime value in the context of CRM Homburg/Sieben (2000) p.12 ff.; for the customer equity concept, for example, Blattberg/Getz/Thomas (2001) p. 132 ff.
[71] For example the customer equity formula of Blattberg (2001) p. 133 who does not discount future profits; some scoring models of CLV do not result in financial evalutation, as highlighted by Homburg/Sieben (2000) p. 18 f.
[72] For this criticism Hippner/Wilde (2001) p. 24
[73] The similarity of strengths and weaknesses of these two approaches are also stressed by Stojek/Ulbrich (2001) p.189 f.
[74] For the problems of using the CLV concept in practice Homburg/Sieben (2000) p. 14, Hippner/Wilde (2001) p.24

- No "general applicable functional relationships" were deployed, neither to relate "soft" to "hard" factors of CRM success nor to transform hard productivity gains into the potential for additional revenue
- The time-based nature of CRM results has been taken into consideration by the inquiry of experience-based expectations

The CRM Value Metric is the blueprint for all business cases that were drafted jointly with the CRM users. Therefore, it is important to understand the metric's structure as detailed as described in this chapter. Moreover, the CRM Value Metric may well be used as a methodology for a business case by all decision makers who currently need to assess the value of CRM. Finally, it fulfills the requirements of a balanced scorecard, so it can be used directly for continued controlling and management of the CRM investment[75].

2.2.3 The Individual Business Cases: More than a Survey

The most refined metric does not deliver a reliable value of CRM if the information input is invalid. Therefore, instead of simply asking a user for the financial impact of CRM, each figure in this study is the result of *user-specific business cases on the basis of questionnaire-based interviews*. Experience from the study shows that these business cases were critically important. One of the first questions in the questionnaire was: To which extent did you notice an impact on cost or revenue. *The answers to these questions summed up to less than 1% of the final value identified in the business cases!* So naturally, any survey that simply asks users for ROI like the ones from Nucleus Research or the Gardner CRM Sales Suite Survey[76] falls short in producing valid evidence. Even if respondents had their pre-calculated ROI figures, the methodologies would hardly be comparable. Therefore, in this study, a new business case was created for all participants to ensure full comparability.

The *questionnaire-based telephone interview* was chosen as method to gather the required information for the business cases. The questionnaire was used as a systematic guideline to cover all relevant aspects. The telephone interview allowed for a flexible reaction to the different CRM situations of respondents. This flexibility proved to be very important. It would not have been achieved

---

[75] Proposing the balanced scorecard approach in the context of CRM Hippner/Wilde (2003) p.24-27, Meltzer (2001) p.318; the scarcity of the balanced scorecard approach for CRM in practice is documented by Wilde (2002) p.43, indicating that only 19% of 45 respondents used this instrument

[76] Gartner (2002) question no. 7.10., Nucleus Research (2003 a) and (2003 b)

with any kind of written questionnaire. These two elements, the questionnaire and the telephone-based interviews, are to be further detailed.

The ***questionnaire*** starts out with general information about the participant and the situation of the CRM deployment. The main part of the questionnaire is then split into four sections: Benefits from mySAP CRM, additional cost incurred, the quantitative structure of the CRM processes, and finally selected potential factors of success. The interview regularly progressed in that sequence.

Most items in the questionnaire are combined with predefined ***ranges of change***. There are regularly five answers from 0% (no significant effect) to more than 30% change and three equidistant groups in between. For a few questions, the top end reached up to 60% or even 80%. The range of change was chosen based on prior experiences as well as the scarce quantified results from literature. If the respondent was able to give a precise answer or a more narrow range, that one was used instead of the predefined range. To process figures in the CRM Value Metric, medians of the chosen sub-range were taken. Besides the quantitative assessment, ***narrative evidence*** was asked for, especially if answers were inconsistent or surprisingly high or low. Then respondents were asked to give an example or to explain how this number came about. This proved to be valuable to avoid misunderstanding and to get an even more complete picture of the situation.

Each section of the questionnaire starts with an open question about observed effects. The purpose of this item was to record all known effects and to adequately reflect the participant's awareness of effects. Asking for more specific aspects then complemented this open question. As most respondents were well prepared for the interview and the time for the interviews was to be kept to the minimum, the general up-front question was skipped in 9 out of 10 cases to directly proceed with the specific questions. Closing this section, it was always asked if there were any other activities impacted. This was regularly not the case.

Interview time per respondent was roughly 1.5 hours, of course, not sufficient to go through the entire questionnaire. Therefore, the relevant sections have been jointly identified at the start, depending on the CRM functions supported by mySAP CRM. The nature of the interview was in most cases more a discussion than a one-way flow of information: Questions were explained, examples given, answers challenged. So sometimes effects were reported that did not result from the CRM project but from other decisions and thus they needed to be filtered out.

Whenever respondents left the ground of experience and resorted to "strategic plans" which had not yet been proven as realistic, these speculative effects were not considered. The possible mistake – to not accept those figures when they materialize – was considered to be less critical than the opposite. Sometimes, participants had monitored and fully measured the effect of CRM. If not, fact-based estimates of the effect in question were used as long as the respondent had made some relevant observations. If no factual evidence of the CRM impact was available, no effect was marked – even though the respondent expressed his or her certainty of a positive impact. Speculative assumptions are not included in the study.

2.2.4 The Trustee Model: Ensuring Openness and Honesty

The trustee model describes an information flow that ensures anonymity of participants and creates an atmosphere of openness and honesty in the interviews. Several respondents stressed that they were only willing to participate under conditions of guaranteed anonymity. The trustee model, which is frequently used in benchmarking studies, can be characterized as follows: Information is provided in the interview to the trustee only, in this case to the author of the study. He alone verifies the information with the company. No third party is involved. So not even the study's sponsor, SAP, had any access to the raw data. The results are published only in an aggregated and anonymous manner. Therefore, the spheres of public and privately held information are strictly separated. So due to the personalized interaction, the results are reliable and of high quality, and because companies names are not revealed, each participant retains anonymity. This combination of advantages is not feasible with alternative models of surveys. Surveys with anonymous participants achieve the same level of anonymity but fall short in reliability, and publicly known participants will always be tempted to tweak results due to the problems outlined in Chapter 2.1.

And the results of this study prove the trustee model right: Extremely positive cases were reported and some respondents mentioned that they would never make this information public to retain their competitive advantage through CRM. In other cases, respondents were open to address negative experiences and missed targets due to the guaranteed anonymity. The participants may only publish their results with author's written consent. Thus, even involuntary disclosure by being the last remaining non-public case is prevented. While the trustee model has many advantages for the participants, it comes at a risk for the study's sponsor, SAP: The results are known at least to the participating companies, no matter if they are good or bad. Nonetheless, at no point in time has any pressure been exerted by SAP to get access to the raw data or to alter results. The author maintained absolute independence, which is eased by his position as a full-time professor at the Ludwigshafen University of Applied Science, a publicly-financed institution with no financial ties to SAP.

2.2.5 The Study Process: Ensuring Interactivity

The study process can be characterized by 5 phases as follows:

Phase	Development	Test	Contact	Interview	Analyses
Main activitities	Drafting of overall study concept and tools	Test of question-naire and metric	Selection of adresses and first contact	Interviews with participants and business cases	Analyses across all participants at several stages
End products	• CRM metric • Questionnaire	Improved metric and questionnaire	List of participants and interview dates	Individual 20-30 p. report per participant	Interim and final report
Timing	Oct./Nov. 2002	Dec. 2002	Dec. 2002/ Jan. 2003	Jan./Feb. 2003	Mar./Apr. 2003

Figure 3: Phases of research on CFROI of Customer Relationship Management

In the ***development phase***, the overall study design and general possibilities of value creation were drafted, based on literature and the author's experience with measuring the return on software. In a round of interviews with mySAP CRM product managers and other specialists from SAP, the list of possible effects was completed and prioritized. On the basis of this wealth of experience, logic trees were created to ensure a mutually exclusive and collectively exhaustive system of potential effects. From the worldwide knowledge base of SAP, quantitative evidence from user experiences was pooled to generate expectations about possible ranges of outcomes. Required input for the CRM Value Metric determined the structure and main items of the questionnaire.

The questionnaire has been ***tested*** by a number of project managers from SAP to check for clarity of concepts and descriptions, completeness of aspects covered, and the ability to answer the questions with reasonable effort. The improved version was then tested by SAP representatives from Germany, Austria, and

Switzerland to get a broader view of the target region. After each round of tests, the questionnaire and the CRM Value Metric were updated, taking the feedback into consideration. Finally, there was a test drive of the questionnaire and the metric with a user under "real conditions".

The *contact phase* started while testing and perfecting the tools of the study, in parallel. SAP selected 50 mySAP CRM user addresses from Germany, Austria, and Switzerland. Participants were required to use the CRM system productively for at least three months. Furthermore, a broad scope of different industries and classes of revenue was included in the sample in order to find out if the patterns of value creation differed. Participation in the study was free of charge and voluntary. The SAP customers were first contacted by SAP headquarters by e-mail to introduce the project. In a next step, the author sent out the questionnaire[77]. In January, participants declared their willingness or unwillingness to participate[78], and a date for the phone interview was fixed.

Most of the *interviews* were conducted in January and February 2003. Each participant received the questionnaire before the phone call, and most prepared for the interview by collecting data. Some respondents collected user experiences from colleagues ahead of the interview. In the roughly 1.5-hour phone interviews, the questions provided a helpful discussion guideline. The modular structure worked especially well by quickly prioritizing the relevant sections. But a high degree of individualization was needed always. CRM functions differ largely among participants: Some sales forces sell by visiting their customers, some sell by outline agreement, some do not sell at all but consult only; some call centers are customer service only, some are charged to the customer, and some do not have customer contact at all but merely serve as internal coordinator. The value assessment always had to be tailored to the situation while maintaining the same methodology for all. All interviews were conducted by the author himself to ensure the utmost comparability across all participants.

After each interview, an interview report was written. In the report, all missing information and inconsistent data was marked. The report was then cross-checked and completed by the participant. Many respondents double-checked the data with colleagues from other departments. In three cases, separate phone interviews were conducted with more than one respondent from the participating company. Once the interview report had been completed and approved, the business case was built and the CFROI, the NPV, and break-even period were

---

[77] As attached in the appendix – but in German
[78] For further information about the response rate and structure of participants, go to chapter 2.2.6.

Research Design – The Concept

calculated based on the CRM Value Metric. The results from this calculation went into a 20-30 page individual report that linked the observed operational improvements step-by-step to the highly aggregated financial results. With one exception, no changes were allowed once the individual report was out to avoid potential "tweaking" of results to get a desired outcome. Finally, in March 2003, the main part of the *analyses across all participants* was completed. Results from a first sub-sample went into a brochure that was presented at CeBIT 2003. The final results are documented here.

2.2.6 Participants: Focus on mySAP CRM Users in D-A-CH

The research has been *focused on mySAP CRM users in Germany (D), Austria (A), and Switzerland (CH)*. The overall economic situation, differences in national cultures, or different functionality of the software were thus to be excluded as explanations for differences in performance. The sample size of 50 initial contacts represents a balance between depth and breadth of the investigation in time. Given the scarcity of quantified results on CRM investments so far, a smaller scale exploratory research design was considered to be more adequate than a large-scale superficial survey.

The addresses have been provided by SAP. It was promised not to pre-select positive cases. In fact, most of the "mySAP CRM show-case examples" were not part of the study. Furthermore, as the study results will show, 20% of the participants did not have a positive 3-y-CFROI. Finally, the distribution of CRM modules used well fits the empirical result of the German market[79]. These observations, however, along with the promise of SAP are the only evidence that the sample is not biased and values are therefore representative. Another, frequently encountered bias, however, can be excluded: the potential bias from contacts not answering to cover up negative results. Of the 50 companies contacted, only 5 expressed no interest in participating which results in an *extremely high response rate of 90%*. Of the 10% that did not participate, not a single contact reasoned non-participation with negative results. The reasons for not taking part are known through phone contact or reply e-mails – at least the official ones. Two excused themselves because of time-constraints due to software update rollouts under way, two respondents were new to their jobs and did not feel that they were able to provide any information, and in one situation, the respondent had just left the company without a substitute being appointed yet. Nonetheless, the structure of the sample and the selection process result in

---

[79] For a distribution as a result of a survey with n=45 observations compare Wilde (2002) p.43

two limitations that should be borne in mind to adequately interpret the study's findings:
- The small size of the sample relative to the base population of CRM applications supported by SAP does not allow for precise conclusions about all mySAP CRM users in D-A-CH, and even less so for all mySAP CRM users worldwide or even CRM users in general
- The applicability of results to CRM users outside of the sample depends on trust in SAP's promise – backed by some evidence – to not filter out potentially problematic cases from the sample

While only 5 contacts refused outright to participate, another 10 companies were excluded after a short phone discussion for various reasons: They had not yet gone live, did not have sufficient experience with the system to be ready for an assessment, or were not granted permission by top management. ***The study is thus based on the experience of 35 companies***, still a high proportion of 70% of those initially contacted. As two companies refused to provide all information needed to calculate a return on CRM and another failed to collect the information needed in time, the CFROI calculations are based on 32 observations.

As the goal of the research was to assess and quantify ***experience with mySAP CRM***, a minimum experience was required as precondition for participation. The participants had to use the system productively for at least three months from the day of going live. Only two companies were at the minimum; a total of four companies – that is, about 10% - had less than 6 months of experience. Now, after the study, it is apparent that this is still too short of a time after the implementation. Respondents had a hard time to report quantified experiences. Three of the four companies with less than 6 months of experience were below average, not due to negative experience but due to careful assessments caused by limited observations. Nonetheless, all four cases have been taken into consideration in the computation of the study's results. On average, the participants had been using the system productively for 14 months. However, the range is considerable, as can be seen in the following bar chart (which is not to be read as a histogram!)[80]:

---

[80] This figure - as all other bar charts in this report - is not a histogram, as the frequency of each group is not represented by the area of the rectangle but by the height. For practitioners of CRM, this representation of frequency has been easier to understand correctly

Research Design – The Concept

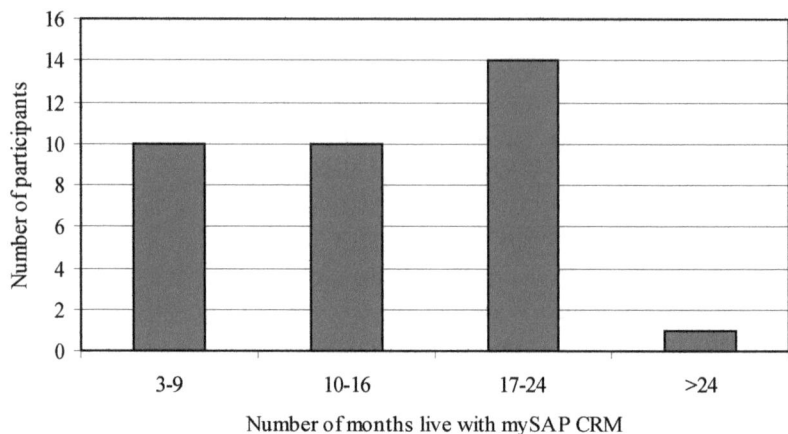

Figure 4: Range of participants' mySAP CRM experience (in months)

Closely linked to the span of experience is the ***mySAP CRM release*** that participants use. More than half of the participants used mySAP CRM 3.0, another third used 2.0c, and the rest deployed version 2.0b. The experience reported, however, is rooted to a larger extent in release 2.0 than in 3.0, as some users only changed to the newer release lately.

Another structural aspect is the ***breadth of the mySAP CRM deployment***. Five key CRM functions are supported by mySAP CRM: Marketing, sales, service, the Interaction Center, and Internet sales. However, almost all participants used fewer than three of these CRM functions. All in all, 35 participants supported 57 CRM functions, that is, on average 1.6 CRM functions per participant. The most frequently function supported by far was sales, followed by marketing, Internet sales, and the Interaction Center. Implementations of the mySAP CRM service module were rare.

In terms of the ***industry sector***, a broad scope was sought to gain insight into potentially different ways of creating value; this goal was clearly achieved. In this report, sectors needed to be grouped in order to protect anonymity. Engineering companies, producers of pharmaceuticals and medical supplies, the chemical companies, and of course IT services are relatively homogeneous, while two sector groups are highly heterogeneous in nature:
- Diverse services include all service businesses other than IT services, for example, financial services, utilities, or transportation companies. Most participants from this group are publicly owned or have a strong public influence.

- Consumer goods entail participants as diverse as consumer electronics, building materials, food, and so on. On first viewing, it may seem awkward to cluster these highly different sectors. However, an analysis in Chapter 4 shows that this group displays astonishingly similar results, thus it seems to be homogeneous in terms of CRM factors of success.

The distribution of participants by sector groups is displayed in Figure 5:

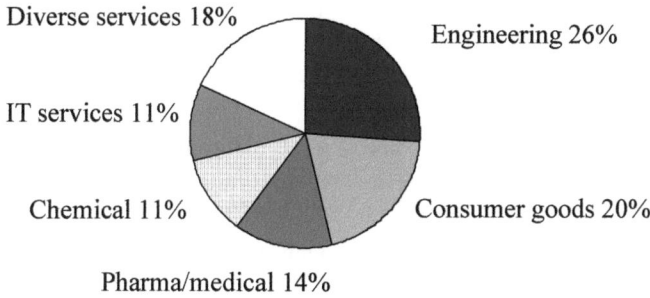

Figure 5: Structure of participants by industry sector groups

Participants were split by **country** as follows: Germany 27, Austria 4, and Switzerland 4. As there were only 4 participants from Austria and Switzerland each, no separate analysis will be displayed by country.

In terms of the **annual sales**, again diversity has been sought and achieved:

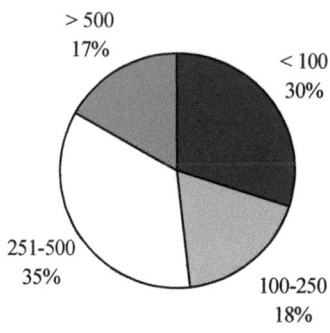

Figure 6: Structure of participants by size (annual sales in EUR millions)

Research Design – The Concept

The purpose of this broad array of company sizes is to check for value effects of size, especially to test the proposition that the larger the company in terms of annual sales the more it pays to deploy CRM.

To summarize the key elements of the research design:
- The CRM Value Metric links soft and hard factors from operational to financial CRM results in full cause-and-effect chains. Thus, a high likelihood exists that all effects considered are truly caused by the CRM project. The metric's systematic structure ensures a mutually exclusive and collectively exhaustive consideration of CRM effects. Due to the time-based nature of CRM results, experience-based expectations were explicitly assessed.
- The CRM Value Metric served as a blueprint for user-specific business cases. Information has been obtained in questionnaire-based telephone interviews, which allowed for a flexible adaptation to the user's situation.
- Honesty and openness of respondents resulted from the trustee model, in which the trustee alias the study's author maintained full independence of the sponsor.
- The interactive study process led to a very high response rate of 90%. All 35 participants are mySAP CRM users in Germany, Austria, and Switzerland. The relatively small effective sample size and the sample procedure limit the applicability of the study's findings to all mySAP CRM users.

3 Results: Higher Productivity, Lower Cost, Higher Revenue

3.1 Project Targets: Met by CRM

The primary goal of this study is to assess the financial results of CRM projects. However, participants had many different objectives for introducing CRM, for example, the technically required replacement of legacy systems or the improvement of customer interaction. Overall, regardless of the specific contents of the CRM goals, 75% of all single CRM targets have been met after 14 months.

In order to analyze the structure of objectives and their relative degree of fulfillment in more detail, five groups were created:

- ***Technical objectives*** mostly aimed at a higher level of customer transparency by technically pooling all internally available customer information and by improving its quality. Goals of this group were explicitly stated in 70% of all participants' projects. So respondents wanted to "integrate customer data", "all CRM staff was supposed to have access to the same files", or a "consistent, centrally directed, worldwide available, and fully integrated information system". The essence of all these goals is the same – to overcome fragmentation of customer knowledge.

- The group of ***internal process optimization targets*** includes all anticipated changes in internal business processes, for example, coordination among sales channels, higher speed and flexibility in setting up a marketing campaign, improved techniques for marketing analyses, better integration of sales and logistics, and so on. The immediate impact of these measures will be experienced in-house while the customer will only be indirectly affected. Frequently, the changes in internal business processes build on an improvement of customer information, for example, when the sales representatives in two countries use the same integrated customer data base and therefore know about each other's activities, they no longer compete against each other for the same key account. Internal process optimization has been the predominant category with 80% of participating companies having one or several CRM project targets from that group of goals.

- **Customer advantages** were also sought with the introduction of CRM. Most participants in this category wanted to improve the quality and the availability of information that was provided to customers. So one participant with a large, worldwide customer base of small and medium enterprises reported customers who ordered from paper catalogues that were more than a year old. The project led to a CRM-powered e-shop, which now provides real-time information about changes in products or prices, as well as an online availability check. Improved service was another concern. In one case, all information accumulated about the customer was made available to service, so that unnecessary questions were avoided. Many respondents wanted to use the time gained from internal process optimization to make sales spend more time supporting customers. Several respondents wanted to achieve increased customer satisfaction and/or a higher conversion rate. As the examples show, most of the time, information and/or internal process improvement will be the relevant lever to create those advantages for the customer. Nonetheless, only about 40% of the participants linked their project goals directly to their customers' benefit.

- **Financial objectives** like the increase in revenue, the decrease in cost, or the reduction in accounts receivable were also defined but only by 15% of all participants. This is amazing, given the current concern with ROI. Nonetheless, this figure is fully consistent with other empirical research conducted by AMR Research who reported that 16% of CRM users were able to answer the question about financial benefits based on measurements[81]. Wilde's results from a survey are somewhat more optimistic, stating that 29% of 45 respondents have calculated a Return on Investment[82]. In part this may be due to the fact that most participants opted for mySAP CRM during the IT boom phase, a period when profitability was a somewhat secondary concern. One participant admits: "Our company was doing too well. We could afford not to think about ROI." Another explanation may be that financial objectives are unpopular. Increases in revenue potential raise the individual revenue targets. Cost savings carry the danger of job losses. So one respondent admitted that they started to compute the savings potential and then stopped to avoid a negative attitude towards the project. Finally, all the problems to calculate a return on CRM that were listed in Chapter 2.1. of course also apply with the participants. Therefore, it takes a significant effort and some know-how to compute those figures in a reliable way. So in most cases, when the CRM decision was

---

[81] Johnson (2003); also check Keltz/Preslan (2003) which argue that out of 43% which claim to have identified an ROI, only about half did measure the CRM impact
[82] Wilde (2002) p. 43;

based on a business case or when quantified results existed, a consultant had been involved.
- In the group of *other objectives*, a heterogeneous mixture of rationales was assembled. Some participants considered CRM as strategic means to enter a new business arena. IT service providers especially, indicated that they needed to use the system themselves be credible when selling CRM projects. Other targets for the introduction of CRM comprised improved employee satisfaction, a "face-lift to the company image in order to make it look more modern", or an urgent key customer's request to introduce an online sales function. Several respondents reasoned CRM with a "strategic decision" made by top management.

If the average degrees of target achievement are plotted in one graphic, the following pattern emerges:

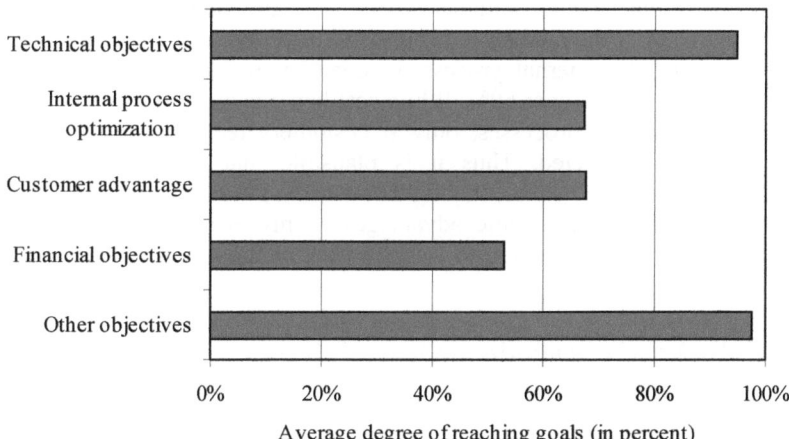

Figure 7: Average degree of reaching mySAP CRM project goals (after 14 months of productive use)

The *sequence of target achievements* is plausible, as it indicates the normal progress in a CRM implementation project – from the technical realization to the financial success. At first, technical objectives were achieved almost to their entirety by participants in the study, which enjoyed a 95% success rate in that respect. That does not mean, however, that all of these mySAP CRM customers were fully satisfied about the implementation project or the software – but it indicates that whatever problem arose, it was solved by the time of the interview.

Results – Project Targets

It is statistically safe to say that reaching the technical targets is a precondition for meeting the overall CRM targets[83]. From the respondents' interviews and questionnaires, the link between the technical and overall target achievement was also evident. Whenever the implementation project ran into problems, it was confirmed that this dramatically reduced acceptance. Vice versa, a speedy implementation with all functionality available working at high quality was considered to be an important factor in overcoming barriers to change.

These barriers of change are high as the next figure indicates: Improvements to operational processes depend on employees changing their habits, a goal which participants have achieved at only 67% on average by the time of the interview. This can be seen as a confirmation of the widely-held belief that the real challenge of CRM is not so much the technical implementation as the change in attitude, behavior, and ultimately, a change in processes. As customer advantage targets frequently build on improvements in customer information or business processes, they should not see a higher degree of target completion and they do not; it is again 67%. If the median of fulfillment rates were considered instead of the mean average, the internal process optimization would lead the customer advantage targets by 65% over 60%. While cost benefits already accrue with the optimization of internal processes, only if customers feel the difference, can revenue targets be affected. Thus it is plausible that the financial target achievements are lagging behind, staying below 55%. Furthermore it needs to be borne in mind that the economic advantages of mySAP CRM about which companies were aware, amounted to less than 1% of the potential identified in the interviews.

The key findings can be summarized as follows:
- 75% of all single CRM project targets were achieved on average within the average 14 months after going live
- While 70% and 80% of participants are driven by technical targets and internal process improvements, only 40% explicitly aim at improvements for their customers, and a mere 15% set explicit financial targets.
- Target achievement rates strictly follow the project sequence, starting at 95% for the technical implementation, progressing via 67% for operational

---

[83] The Bravais-Pearson correlation coefficient (abbreviated by "r") measures the strength of the linear relationship between two variables. Between the degree of target achievement in technical and in overall targets $r = 0.76$. As the correlation coefficient ranges between -1.0 and 1.0, 0.76 is considered as a strong positive relationship. Testing with a two tailed t-statistic, the correlation proves to be significant at the 1%-level.

improvements and customer benefits to 55% for the financial targets. Smooth technical implementation is a necessary but not sufficient precondition for all the other targets.

3.2 Financial Targets: CFROI, NPV, and Break-Even Period

3.2.1 Financial Targets Including Experienced-Based Expectations

As outlined in Chapter 2.3.2, cash flow has been derived from two values: the situation at the time of the interview as well as the "steady state" as an experience-based forecast. In this first chapter, both of these values are considered as valid and relevant to calculate the financial indicators of CRM success. In Chapter 3.2.2, only the status quo at the point of time of the interview will be extended into the future. Three financial indicators have been used to describe the value created by mySAP CRM: net present value (NPV), cash flow return on investment (CFROI), and the break-even period.

The **NPV** is often cited as the decisive criterion for evaluating investments on the basis of a single company. It denotes the current value of an investment. As the concept is crucial to understand the results of this study, a graphical as well as mathematical explanation are given in Figure 8:

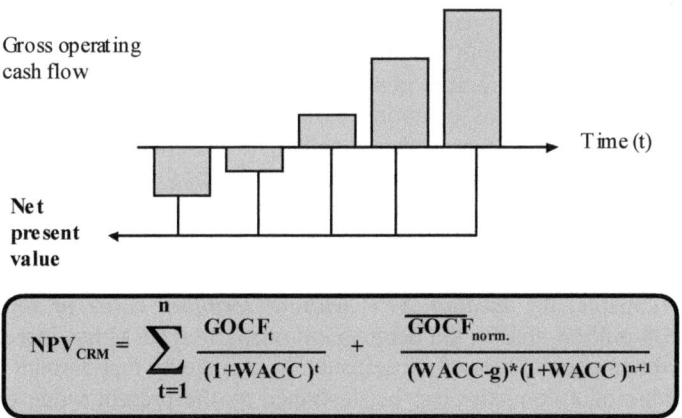

$$NPV_{CRM} = \sum_{t=1}^{n} \frac{GOCF_t}{(1+WACC)^t} + \frac{\overline{GOCF}_{norm}}{(WACC-g)*(1+WACC)^{n+1}}$$

Figure 8: Conceptual framework for NPV of CRM

Results – Financial Targets

The abbreviations used in the formula of Figure 8 have the following meaning:

GOCF = gross operating cash flow
$\overline{GOCF_{norm}}$ = normalized gross operating cash flow
n = the last year of the explicitly modeled forecast period
t = time
g = the expected growth rate of the cash flow in perpetuity
WACC = weighted average cost of capital

If the NPV is positive, the investment is generating more than the minimum yield stipulated by the capital market (hurdle rate) and is increasing the shareholder value. From a financial point of view, the NPV is calculated as the sum of an investment's discounted gross operating cash flow (GOCF) over a predefined period of time, which is also referred to as earnings before interest, tax, depreciation, and amortization (EBITDA). Chapter 2.2.1 provides the rationale for the use of cash flow as the basis for financial measurement of CRM value added while the computation of the relevant cash flow has been outlined in Chapter 2.2.2. The gross operating cash flow has been modeled over a five-year period (n=5). Typically, in the beginning, cash-out is higher than cash-in resulting in a negative value while at the end, a higher cash-in leads to positive values. All values computed were then discounted at the weighted average cost of capital (WACC), the market-determined risk adjusted cost of capital of each participating company. This figure has not been calculated but obtained from the participants – typically the corporate controlling department; it constitutes one item in the questionnaire. Gross operating cash flow and WACC describe the first term in the equation in Figure 8, the so-called NPV without terminal value. It is expressed as the sum of the discounted cash flows of years 1 to 5. Before moving to the second term, the terminal value, the results for the NPV without terminal value will be reported.

Across all participants, the **median NPV without terminal value of mySAP CRM** is EUR 5.8 million, that is, the deployment of mySAP CRM has increased the fundamental company values of participants on average by that amount. The fundamental value of a company can be described as the present value of all expected future earnings. The market value of a company, instead, is determined by many more factors, generally speaking by supply and demand.

The **range of NPVs without terminal value** is considerable, varying from the negative to almost EUR 50 million:

Results – Financial Targets

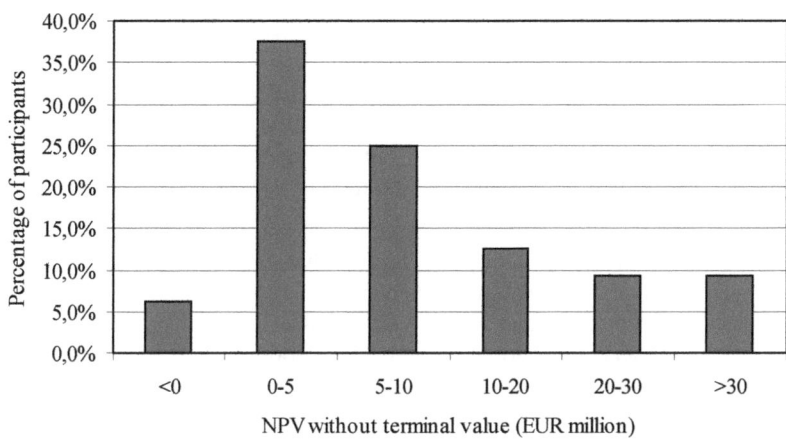

Figure 9: Increase in fundamental company value through mySAP CRM as NPV without terminal value in EUR millions

The NPV in Figure 9 does not yet consider the **terminal value**, that is, the value of the CRM project remaining in the company after 5 years. Again, as outlined for the question of how long the cash flow ought to be modeled, it should be taken into consideration that CRM is more than just software, and changes made to processes, culture, skills, data, and behavior continue to generate value even after the software has been replaced. The more that holds true for a specific CRM project, the more appropriate it is to apply a terminal value. So only in cases where the CRM project is predominantly a technical software installation or where an especially careful calculation is intended, an NPV without terminal value adequately reflects the value added by CRM.

According to the formula shown in Figure 8, the terminal value can be calculated as the perpetual annuity of the normalized cash flow in the first year after the explicit forecast period[84]. This "growing free cash flow perpetuity formula" delivers better results than most other terminal value calculations, and is equally good but a lot less cumbersome than the long explicit forecast[85]. In three ways, careful assumptions were made with regard to this formula:

---

[84] Copeland/Koller/Murrin (1995) p.277
[85] For an overview of different techniques of terminal value calculation Copeland/Koller/Murrin (1995) p.276 ff.

Results – Financial Targets

- The parameter "g" expresses ***the future growth of the cash flow*** from CRM. There is a high likelihood that cash flow will increase in the future, for example, because the company grows and the benefit of CRM will be experienced by even more CRM staff. Nonetheless, as this growth figure would have been entirely speculative, in this study, the growth rate was conservatively assumed to be zero.

- The normalized cash flow (cash flow$_{norm}$) and the assumed growth rate ("g") are interdependent: The higher the growth rate, the lower the normalized cash flow and vice versa[86]. As the future growth rate is assumed to be zero, and as this value is clearly less than the growth rate in the observed period between the productive start of the CRM application and the time of the interview, the ***normalized free cash flow*** should be higher in the future than in the past. However, in the study it was conservatively assumed that the normalized cash flow stays at the same level that had been achieved before lowering the growth rate.

- Finally, the constant normalized cash flow according to the widely used "investment banker formula" should be equal to the last cash flow modeled in detail. That would, however, overestimate the value of the CRM investment as the last cash flow includes all the extra-benefit of CRM but almost no extra-cost any more. In the case of software investment, cash flow will change significantly with a new release. After every new release, processes and skills have to be adapted. Because the extent to which such an adaptation will be required varies, the study conservatively assumes that half of the initial investment in CRM will be lost after five years. This is conservative as the license-fees make up on average below 30% of the overall CRM investment. So the normalized free cash flow has been calculated as the average gross operating cash flow over the first 5 years.

It is important to understand the concept deployed for calculating terminal value, as the difference between the NPV with and without terminal value is very significant: The median NPV with terminal value is almost EUR 15 million compared to EUR 5.8 million without terminal value. So about 2/3 of the entire value added through CRM will materialize after 5 years of productive use. This clearly proves the popular wisdom right which claims that CRM is an investment for the long-term, not necessarily a "quick-fix". Again, not all companies enjoyed such a high increase in value. The value added to companies by mySAP CRM, taking account of the terminal value, is distributed as follows:

---

[86] Copeland/Koller/Murrin (1995) p. 277

Results – Financial Targets

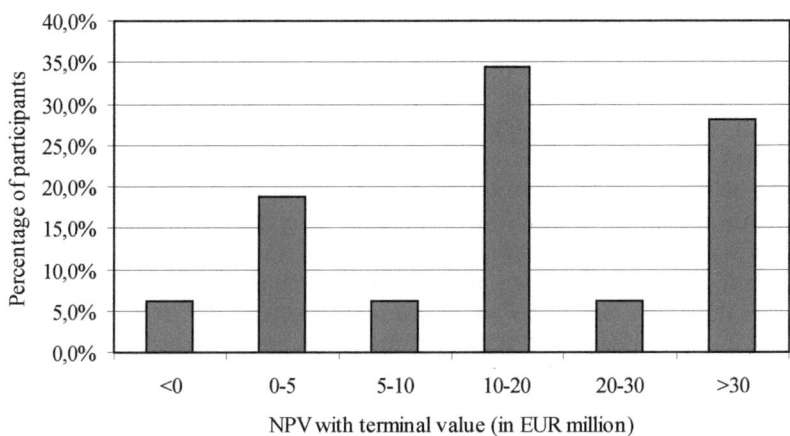

Figure 10: Increase in company value from mySAP CRM as NPV with terminal value in EUR millions

The terminal values reach up to a maximum of more than 165 EUR million. Due to these extremely positive values, again, the mean averages of the NPV are by far higher than the medians. The mean average NPV without terminal value is at EUR 10 million, with a terminal value, it surpasses EUR 27 million.

While these are NPV values for the participants in the survey, it is even more interesting to understand the implications for all mySAP CRM users in D-A-CH. Given the limitations outlined in Chapter 2.2.6, it can be concluded with a probability of 95%, that the mean average (not the median!) NPV without terminal value will be somewhere between EUR 6.7 million and EUR 13.3 million[87]. With a probability of even 99.9% it can be concluded, that the value will be above EUR 3.4 million. This means that using CRM has almost certainly on average increased the fundamental value of companies. So for sure, it makes sense that decision makers take a close look at this value lever. However, these results do not imply that all CRM users will experience such a positive result. Again, it is the "closer look" that counts, that is, the decision maker should engage in drafting a business plan as outlined in Chapter 2.

---

[87] This is referred to as the "confidence interval": With a likelihood of 95%, the "true" mean average NPV without terminal value of the base population of mySAP CRM users will fall into that range. The values are calculated on the basis of a two-tailed Student's t-distribution which is seen as adequate: The NPVs without terminal value in the base population follow an approximated normal distribution. The sample size of slightly above n=30 also allows for a normal distribution to be used. However, the more conservative Student's t-distribution was chosen, instead.

Results – Financial Targets

NPV is a convenient measurement of investment success from an individual company's point of view as it is easy to read: If the NPV is positive, the investment increases shareholder value, if it is negative, it destroys value. Nonetheless, using the NPV to compare profitability of investments, for example, between companies of different sizes, is not so appropriate because the value of an investment with a low profitability in a large company can well be above the NPV of a highly profitable investment of a small company. This is due to NPV being an absolute figure, not a ratio. As comparisons of investments are crucial for this study, the *cash flow return on investment (CFROI)* is introduced as the key measurement. CFROI denotes the return on the invested capital in the CRM project. So a 10% CFROI, for example, means that on average, 10% of the invested capital will be returned every year throughout the calculation period.

CFROI builds on the gross operating cash flow just like the NPV does. In fact the two measurements are closely connected: The CFROI can be interpreted as the discount rate at which the NPV of a given gross operating cash flow turns zero. So it is also referred to as the internal rate of return of the investment's gross operating cash flows. While the NPV was analyzed on a 5-year basis, the CFROI has been calculated for a 3 year and 5 year investment period respectively[88]. *The median CFROI of mySAP CRM users in the study amounts to 53% over 3 years and almost 90% over 5 years.*

These figures are likely to be attractive for most companies that have to decide on an investment in CRM. However, as apparent as for the NPV is the fact that the range of CFROI of CRM for participants is very broad. Peak values reach far beyond 300% and the worst cases have experienced a negative return on investment, which grew ever more negative the longer the company operated in this dismal mode. While the extremely positive and negative values do not affect the median, they cause the mean average CFROI to reach 127%, that is, more than twice the median. So the extremely positive ones outweigh the negative outliers. The CFROI over 5 years has a median of 87% and a mean average of 152%. Figure 11 illustrates the distribution of CFROI of CRM after 3 years among participants.

---

[88] The rationale of the three- and five-year periods is provided in Chapter 2.2.1

Results – Financial Targets

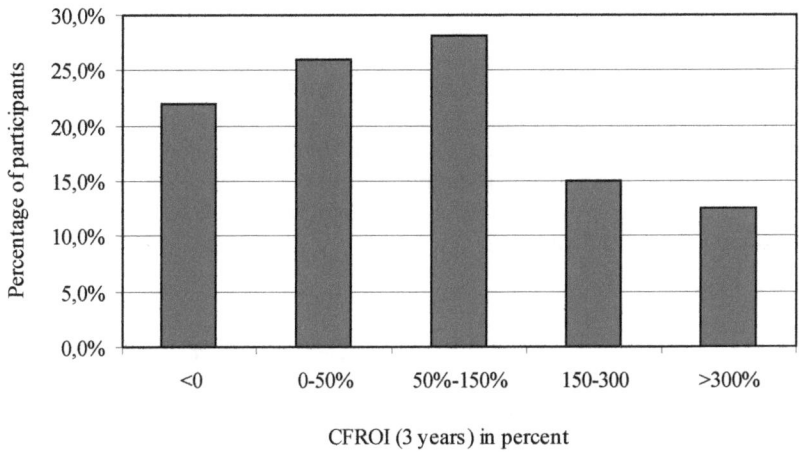

Figure 11: Cash flow return on investment (3 years) from mySAP CRM in percent.

While the results in Figure 11 only show the spread among study's participants, it is interesting to see what that means for the entirety of mySAP CRM users in D-A-CH. Their true mean average 3-y-CFROI is unknown. From the sample it can be concluded, however, that it has a 95% chance to be somewhere between 70% and 183.5%. With 99.9% certainty, the mean average CFROI for the mySAP CRM users in D-A-CH will be above 13.4%. Thus the claim of some analysts mentioned in Chapter 2.1., that CRM does not yield a positive return on investment can definitely be rejected as wrong: Indeed the average of all mySAP CRM users in D-A-CH almost certainly has a positive return on their CRM investment.

NPV and CFROI describe the value added through the CRM investment with the implicit assumption that the future values are as certain as the effects that have been observed in the past. However, the risk that the expected values will not materialize is higher for the far-out future than for the short term. The timing of the payback from the CRM investment can therefore be considered as a measurement of investment risk. This is the basic rationale underlying the ***break-even period***. The break-even period is the period of time (in months) it takes before the positive and negative effects of the CRM investment cancel each other out in the present value. The present values of the positive and the negative payments are thereby calculated as it was outlined above for the NPV: All

Results – Financial Targets

payments that originate in the CRM investment are arranged according to sequence in which they occur and then discounted with each participating company's individual WACC. As only three data points are available over time (the productive start, the time of the interview, and the arrival at steady state), the monthly break-even period was assessed by linear interpolation. According to investment theory, this is incorrect, as monthly data would have been needed to make a break-even assessment on monthly terms. However, the chosen method overestimates the break-even period and is therefore on the conservative side as the following figure illustrates:

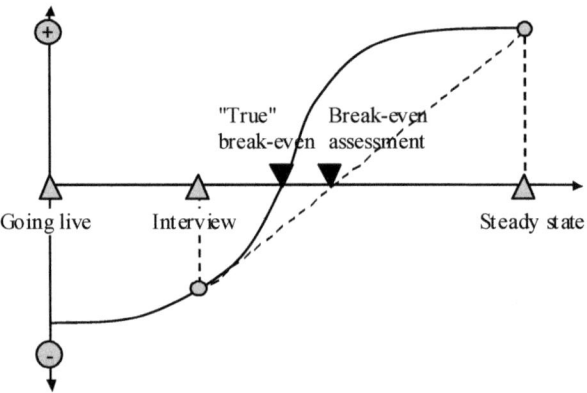

Figure 12: Break-even period interpolation for typical cash-flow structure

The typical cash flow "s-curve" over time has a theoretically correct, "true" break-even period. The time of the interview was on average 14 months after going live while the medium break-even period equals 23 months: Thus the time of the interview is before the discounted cash-flow over time reaches the positive. The interpolation between the cash flow in that point of time and the arrival at steady state is marked by the upwardly-sloped dotted line. It is evident that the calculated break-even period used in this study is longer than the true one; therefore it is on the safe side.

The break-even period is one possible measurement of risk but others exist as well. So the amortization period describes the point of time at which the aggregated project profitability in non-discounted values is equal to zero. The break-even period has been the measurement of choice as it is marginally longer than the amortization period, so, again, the more conservative choice. Sometimes ROI is not expressed as a percentage but in months. An "ROI in x months" describes the point of time when the additional earnings in accounting terms exceed the additional cost for the first time. This measurement is rejected, as it is not based on cash flows[89]. Regularly, the "ROI in x months" – frequently used in software vendor marketing – is significantly lower than the break-even period because in the accounting figures, the up-front investment in CRM does not show in the first months of productive use except for the depreciation incurred.

The median of participants' break-even periods for deploying mySAP CRM is almost 23 months. The mean average of break-even periods across all participants is identical with the median. The following figure illustrates the respective distribution:

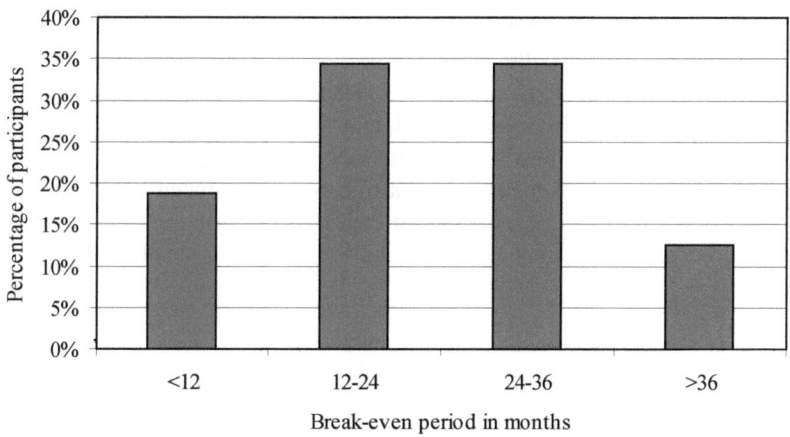

Figure 13: Break-even period for investment in mySAP CRM

The mean average break-even period for all mySAP CRM users in D-A-CH falls in the range between 19 months and 27 months – at 95% probability. This value will almost certainly be well below 3 years for the base population[90].

---

[89] The cash flow has been firmly established as the basis of financial measurement in Chapters 2.2.1 and 2.2.2
[90] The upper boundary of the 99.9% confidence interval for the two-tailed Student's t-distribution which indicates the worst case has a value of g+ = 33.7 months

65

Results – Financial Targets

In conclusion:

- The investment in mySAP CRM has increased the value of more than 90% of the companies that participated in the study, with a median of EUR 5.8 million. The mean average NPV for all mySAP CRM users in D-A-CH will almost certainly be above EUR 3.4 million
- The return on the mySAP CRM investment for participants was at least 53%. With 99.9% probability, the mean average CFROI for the entirety of mySAP CRM users in D-A-CH will be above 13.4%
- The break-even period for the investment in mySAP CRM stayed below a median 23 months for the participants in the study and with 99.9% below 3 years for all mySAP CRM users in D-A-CH.

3.2.2 Financial Targets Excluding Experience Based Expectations

The figures above all partially include experienced-based expectations which could potentially be rejected as speculative, despite the fact that only application modules already in place were considered, and that the experience was reasoned and illustrated with examples in the interview. To take these concerns into account, the same financial measurements that were introduced before, are now computed excluding the experience-based expectations. To stress the point, it is interesting to take a closer look at the distribution of time-to-steady state:

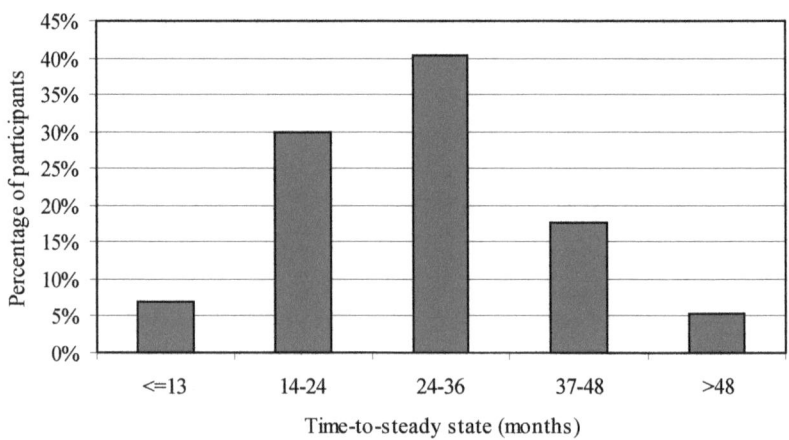

Figure 14: Time-to-steady state for mySAP CRM functional modules (months)

Looking at Figure 14, it is immediately clear that 70% of all 57 mySAP CRM functional modules in the survey reached the steady state after two to three years. By comparison, only 8% accomplished the steady state within those 14 months, which will now be assumed to mark the cut-off point of development. Contrasting these 14 months with the 30 months to reach the "steady state" as a mean average across all mySAP CRM functional modules, it is apparent that this assumption is extremely careful up to the point of being unrealistic.

The 3-year-CFROI without experience-based expectations reaches 36% - relative to 53% with the future developments included. That means that roughly 1/3 of the original 3-y-CFROI is due to future expectations while 2/3 are computed on the basis of observed changes in fundamental productivity. A similar relationship applies to the 5-y-CFROI figures. So it can be concluded that, most of the value is based on "solid" experience, not "speculative" future expectations.

Another thought and analysis further strengthen the validity of the numbers. If hyped future expectations were the reason for the strong CRM performance, one would expect that the absolute difference in percentage-points between the CFROI with and without experience-based expectations would be the highest for those participants that had the lowest absolute performance without future expectations. But that correlation is not statistically significant[91]. So only a marginal 4% of the difference in CFROI, with and without expectations, is explained by the absolute level of performance of participants. Therefore, hyped expectations are an unlikely explanation for the results regarding CFROI of mySAP CRM.

Computing the NPV without experience-based expectations results in a median NPV without the terminal value of EUR 2.1 m, and a mean average of EUR 5.5 m. This figure is down more than 50% on the value with experience-based expectations. The difference between a 30% reduction in the 5-y-CFROI and a 50% reduction for the NPV is due to the fact that the average WACC is lower than the CFROI. Therefore, long-term cash flows are discounted at a lower rate and are worth more in the NPV than in the CFROI. As long-term values in particular are reduced by the subtraction of experience-based expectations, NPV is reduced more than CFROI. Nonetheless, it needs to be noticed that even under

---

[91] The Bravais-Pearson correlation coefficient of $r = (-0.2)$ indicates a very weak linear relation between the variables under research which is statistically insignificant at either the 1%- or the 5% level using a two tailed t-test. Also no non-linear functional relationship between the spread of CFROI with and without expected values vs. the absolute CFROI performance is implied by a visualized scatter chart

these unrealistically cautious assumptions, there is still significant value created by mySAP CRM projects. The median NPV with terminal value but without experience-based expectations is at EUR 5.4 million, the respective mean average at EUR 15.5 million.

Finally, also the break-even period without experience-based expectations has been calculated. It moves up to a median of 26 months, that is, an additional three months relative to the values reported in Chapter 3.2.1. That is an increase of only 13%, so the break-even period proves to be the most robust measurement with regard to future expectations. This is easily explained by the fact that up to 14 months, there is no difference between the values with and without experience-based expectations. So only for the last 7 months, the difference becomes relevant, and even that is only a gradually increasing effect.

To conclude, the results on financial success indicators without expectations:
- More than 50% of the NPV is due to experience-based expectations, and only about 30% of CFROI. The break-even period is increased by only 13%.
- Even under unrealistically conservative assumptions of stopping developments long before the steady state, the financial results of CRM are still attractive
- The attractiveness of mySAP CRM deployment is not due to experience-based expectations

3.3 Productivity Targets: Potential for Cost Reduction

The financial targets are ultimately rooted in improved productivity through the use of CRM. Jumping from the top of the CRM Value Metric to the very bottom, the following chapters provide details about these productivity improvements within each of the 5 functional areas of CRM. As it is one of the main factors, customer information improvements are investigated first. The productivity gains constitute the potential for cost reduction as explained in Chapter 2.2.2.

3.3.1 Improved Customer Information: The Basis for Higher Productivity

IT directly impacts the quality and quantity of information, but only indirectly influences the processes that depend on this information. So, the improvement of customer information has to be investigated first. The main problem with customer information is that employees have several reasons not to share it:

- To have a personal monopoly on customer information makes the employee indispensable, it provides him with power and freedom, because management efforts then lack the informational basis[92].
- The normal inertia and resistance to change and the fear that the software will cost jobs have to be overcome – for CRM as for any other software-supported change process[93]. Nonetheless, this fear of job cuts is especially dominant in the context of CRM because of the so called "channel conflict": Shared customer information enables the company to substitute expensive sales representatives by cheaper electronic channels to the customer, for example, an e-shop or a call-center. Channel conflict – irrelevant if it is real or just subjectively perceived – reduces the readiness to share information.
- Furthermore, especially in sales, the use of technology may lead to alienation from the job as it creates a fundamental mismatch with the sales representative's self-perception[94]. The sales representative typically enjoys higher autonomy than his colleagues from other departments; he is usually not tied as closely into the informal network of a company due his being at the customer site for the main part of his work-time. This freedom is granted as the sales skills are more difficult to box into standard regulations than many other capabilities. Therefore, this freedom is seen as being endangered, if the CRM system is perceived to be taking over crucial skills that the sales person considers to define his value for the company.
- Finally a simple reason may raise the barriers to acceptance: To keep customer information up-to-date requires effort and care.

All of this makes the introduction of a CRM-system to a company a challenging endeavor. However, the real threat to the improvement of customer information is a different phenomenon: Most respondents with whom this topic was discussed stated that the sales representative gets little immediate benefit from the extra effort of using the system as he is at least subjectively convinced he knows his customers anyway. And in the self-perception of many sales representatives, knowing the customer is seen as the key competitive advantage. Therefore, they are not enticed to use the system. But the benefit of the improved information first materializes when (nearly) everybody keeps the customer data at a high level of quality and the entirety of customer information is available to

---

[92] Rapp (2001) p.79-81; Stengl/Sommer/Ematinger (2001) p.44 f., Stojek/Ulbrich (2001) p.199
[93] Dyché (2002) p.263 ff., Helmke/Brinker/Wessoly (2001) p.294-298, Campbell (2003) p.376 f.
[94] Speier/Venkatesh (2002), esp. p. 109 ff.

Results – Productivity Targets

everyone. This requires trust in an up-front investment, which creates a hurdle for acceptance.

Both the participants who successfully deployed CRM as well as those who failed to do so, shed light on a dynamic process in customer information improvement through CRM that is paramount for its success:

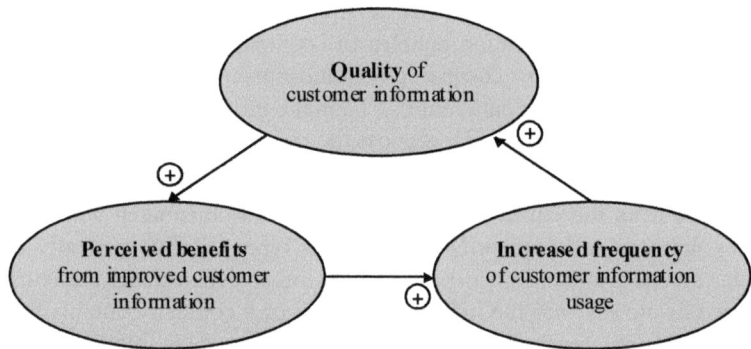

Figure 15: Positive feedback loop of customer information improvement through CRM deployment

First, a massive improvement in the quality of customer information is needed. This initial impulse has often been linked to the CRM implementation project. A successful participant said that "all of a sudden, the 'manual fixes' of lousy customer files were not possible any more – and everyone was aware of those who did not take care of customer information as they were supposed to – and that's the kind of management attention nobody was after ...". One of the least successful participants was hinting at exactly the opposite cycle: Management did not care about the project. So many prospective users refused the up-front investment of time to achieve higher data quality. As the customer data quality did not improve, the few that had started to use the system properly became increasingly frustrated and defected from the system. At the time of the interview, only a handful of users were left; the project was considered as a complete failure. When the first major improvement in customer information is achieved, management and employees perceive an added value from CRM. To make the impact more directly felt by the employees, some companies have resorted to providing material and immaterial incentives[95]. In turn users more

---

[95] Campbell (2003) p.380 f. reporting about Canadian banks

frequently access customer information, enter new information, and thereby continuously increase the quality of information.

Following this cycle, the quality and quantity of customer information was operationalized to assess if a sustainable improvement had taken place:

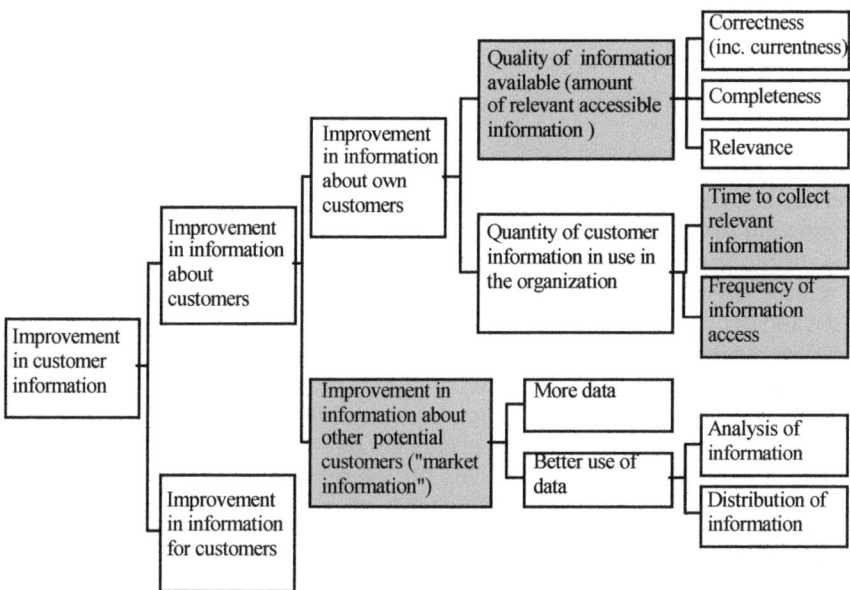

Figure 16: Overview: Customer information improvement through CRM (shaded information contained in questionnaire and discussed in this chapter)

Quality customer information needs to be correct, complete, and relevant. **Correctness** is crucial to avoid employees going back to their own method of filing information, thereby obstructing the pooling effort. In order to be correct, the information must be faultless, and it must have been updated. Therefore, an integral part of correctness is how current the information is. **Completeness** of the customer profile is another characteristic of quality but only in conjunction with relevance. Otherwise, the adverse effect may be experienced, that is, CRM employees get confused with an abundance of irrelevant information and abandon the search altogether. Respondents were asked for the percentage change in relevant information contained in customer profiles before and after the use of mySAP CRM. To check for the plausibility, any one of the three factors of customer information quality needed to be positively impacted as well.

Besides information quality, the second aspect of improved customer information is its *availability* and use within the organization. Better customer profiles are worthless, if they are not accessed by CRM employees. Two indicators have been singled out:

- The required time to collect all relevant information about a customer
- The frequency of information access

The *time to collect information* was considered with respect to its relevance. All interviews used the example of a sales representative who wants to collect the information relevant to prepare for the next customer interaction. This aspect of relevance is crucial for useful results. If respondents had been asked for the time to collect all customer information available, the result would have been irrelevant, as nobody potentially ever needs to do so. Another misleading question would be to ask for the time spent on the collection of customer information. Some respondents admitted that employees started to "play around" with the new analytic tool, spending considerably more time on information processing than before. The time to access the relevant information however had very much shortened, and for now, only this aspect counts. The "playing around" with the CRM system might have led to a deeper level of customer understanding ultimately resulting in higher revenue, but that will be dealt with in Chapter 3.4.

Due to the discreteness of events and automated observation through IT-logs, the *frequency of customer information access* is easily measured. This indicator serves as a proxy for the information in use. And only this information can unfold its potential benefits.

Another aspect of customer information improvement is to not only get a better insight into ones own customer base but into the *entire market*. Several sources of increased market insight are possible. Due to better tool-supported analytical marketing skills (analytical CRM), the available data can be turned into more information for CRM staff. But also, the amount of available market data might increase, such as the information obtained by sales representatives who learn about new products or competitors' pricing moves from the customers. Finally, even if the amount of information for the organization as a whole did not change, CRM might result in a better distribution of the market information available among CRM staff.

The improvement in customer information has been repeatedly cited as the most immediate, most obvious, and most impressive benefit reaped from the introduction of mySAP CRM. These are the figures from the study:

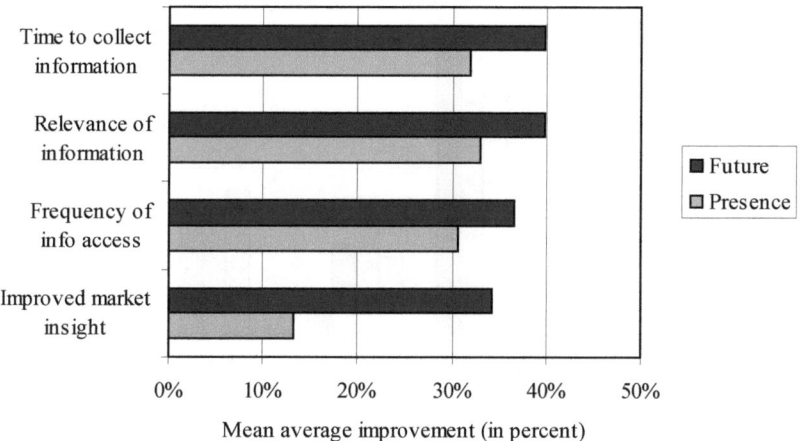

Figure 17: Improvements in customer information through mySAP CRM

The *immediacy of benefits* is apparent at least in the first three categories, that is, the time to collect customer information, the information's relevance, and the frequency of access: For all three categories, the difference between the benefits that already materialized ("presence") and those expected for the steady state ("future") is small. Information improvements also have a *broad base of support*: More than 50% of all participants report a positive effect in the first three categories. Only three participants stated that they had not experienced an effect – the rest did not provide information on that question. Finally, the *results are impressive*, indeed. Improvements of 30-40% set a strong basis for improved CRM processes and the financial results that have already been discussed. As these figures are average values, some participants went far beyond and experienced drastic changes: "Today, people access customer information three times as often as before the system was in place – and the amount of quality information in the average customer profile has more than tripled." There were many very high scores on behalf of the customer information improvement. Therefore, the mean average change surpassed 30%, that is, the high end of the range stated on the questionnaire.

Results – Productivity Targets

Not all participants scored in the 200-300% improvement range as the one respondent cited above. The following figure illustrates the distribution of present values for all four categories of information improvement:

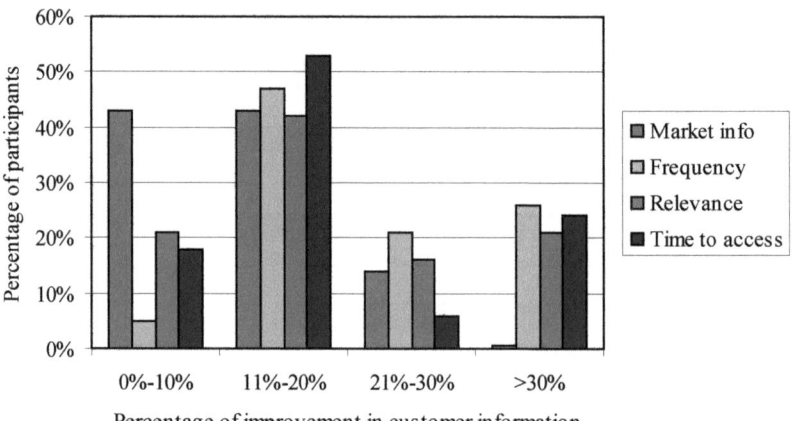

Figure 18: Distribution of improvements in customer information through my SAP CRM (present values)

Almost 25% of participants experienced top scores above 30%. Nonetheless, the distribution's mode is in the range between 11% and 20%. Therefore the median value of time reduction to access relevant customer information is at 20%, the information's relevance has increased at a median of 17.5%, and the frequency of customer information access went up by a median of 15%. It is interesting that the top three categories perform equally strongly – almost to the percentage-point. This result may be interpreted as supporting evidence for the dynamic cycle shown in Figure 15. Each "spin of the cycle" impacts all three categories alike.

Present values with regard to the ***improvement of market information*** are significantly lower than for customer information. Only seven participants experienced a positive effect in this category at the time of interview; not a single one came even close to the level of 30%. Comments of participants shed light on this phenomenon: They all concentrated on analyzing their own customer data. Obtaining additional data and cross-analyzing it to get a full perspective on the relevant market was considered to be the future. And this also finds its way into the data: Expectations for market information improvements are at the same level as all the other categories. Those that did report a positive effect for the present usually operated in narrow markets where their own customer base provided for a representative perspective on the market as a whole.

The reason, most frequently cited to explain the speed, breadth, and strength of this remarkable improvement has been the pooling of formerly fragmented information. "Hidden" information became instantly available to all of the CRM staff. That also corresponds to the fact that the technical goal of pooling information has been reached almost to its entirety, as shown in Chapter 3.1. One respondent compared the sudden improvement in available customer information to the German "Wirtschaftswunder": As soon as it was beneficial, hoarded goods were put up for sale and the supply shortage ended "overnight". Such an impulse is needed to get the information improvement cycle spinning.

3.3.2 Marketing: Valuable Analytic Insights, Improved Campaigns, and Consequential Lead Management

Marketing is a term used for a broad variety of concepts. For the purpose of this study, marketing is defined as a "process of planning and executing the conception, pricing, promotion, and distribution of ideas, goods, services to create exchanges that satisfy individual and organizational goals"[96]. So it is not used to denote decisions, a social task, or an organizational department. This process-orientated definition has the advantage of obtaining comparable results as the processes under investigation existed in most participating companies – but not always in the marketing department. Three distinct marketing (sub-) processes were explicitly assessed: marketing analyses, marketing planning and campaign management, and lead management. These information-driven processes are all rather on the planning side than on the executional side of the classic marketing mix functions, that is, product, price, placement, and promotion. This is plausible, as a CRM system only directly impacts the information side of marketing.

Marketing analyses include the whole spectrum of analyses of market data as well as customer data such as customer lifetime value (CLV), customer profitability, segmentation of markets, customer activity, and so on. The purpose of these analyses is to identify the most promising customers and customer segments and the best way to address them. Activities in this process are data collection, analysis and conclusions, as well as the preparation of results for communication.

---

[96] Kotler (2000) p.8

Marketing planning has been grouped with campaign management, as these two processes were too closely interwoven in the eyes of respondents to warrant a reliable distinction. Within the marketing planning process, targets for sales and revenue are computed and broken down to products and services, to sales areas, and so on. The marketing plans also include the blueprint for market communication and a sequence of planned campaigns. Campaign management then complements the marketing plan with campaign planning, execution, and controlling.

Leads are defined as potential customers which are supposed to be followed up by sales because they show a higher than average likelihood to buy. The process of ***lead management*** in marketing comprises primarily the generation and qualification of leads that are then handed over to sales for further processing.

Besides the three processes, only one additional marketing activity has been mentioned repeatedly by respondents as being supported by CRM: ***event management***, for example, preparation and follow-up of trade shows and fairs. However, this activity is covered in the realm of marketing planning and campaign management in terms of the preparatory part and by lead management with respect to the desired follow-up of the business contacts that were established during the event. Therefore the event management has not been investigated as a separate marketing process.

The deployment of mySAP CRM can save cost in marketing in two ways:
- Directly within the marketing processes, that is, less work hours are needed for marketing activities to achieve the same results
- Indirectly within other CRM functions such as sales or the IC, where effects spill over from an improved marketing output

The critically important aspect is to avoid double counts – not as stressed in Chapter 2.2.2 between revenue- and cost-induced benefits – but as double counts between different CRM functions. So CRM benefits must not be taken into account once within the marketing function and then again, for example, through the information improvement in sales. For the purpose of this study, the respondent was first asked where results of the mySAP CRM were experienced at all. This provided a complete landscape of the value added. Then the productivity improvement has been assessed for each of the CRM functions separately. All direct and indirect effects were taken into consideration. So even if a respondent did not use the marketing module of mySAP CRM, he potentially was able to report a positive impact in the functional area of marketing because, for example, the quality of customer data improved as a side effect of a Mobile Sales project.

The 16 participants who deployed the mySAP CRM *marketing function* reported the following mean average growth in productivity:

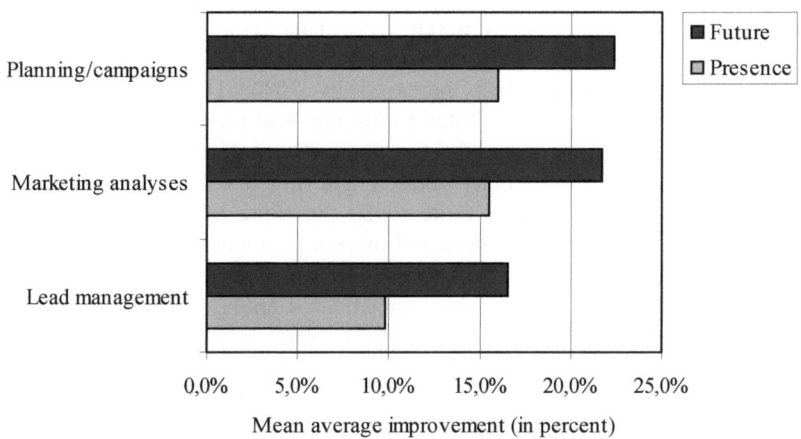

Figure 19: Average productivity growth in marketing through mySAP CRM

As there were only few extreme scores, the median values are overall near by the mean averages. A 16% increase in productivity for marketing planning and campaign management means that at the time of the interview 16% less hours of work were needed to produce the same quantitative and qualitative level of output as before the use of mySAP CRM.

For *marketing planning and campaign management*, most respondents that reported high values did not have any systematic way of handling campaigns before. The process was completely redesigned once mySAP CRM was introduced to the company. The most impressive improvements observed in that category reached up to a 70% reduction in time spent on campaign management. The interviews took place in January and February – and it may have been due to the timing that several respondents used the mailing of Christmas cards to customers and business partners as an example of tremendous timesavings. In marketing planning, another positive effect mentioned was the use of a single IT tool instead of many inconsistent planning instruments. In one case, campaigns were planned by Excel tables that were handed to and collected from each sales representative, leading to clumsy and time-consuming changes or progress controlling. The planning of events was mentioned three times as a major improvement; one participant achieved a 45% productivity enhancement. Coordination among the diverse internal groups involved and the external service providers was achieved significantly faster.

Marketing analyses improved by about 15%. This figure is plausible, as the improvement of marketing analyses depends mainly on the quality of the customer information, which has increased by 30%. The difference of 15 percentage-points can well be attributed to the fact that productivity gains in the marketing analyses require not only the change in information but also the change in behavior. This apparently takes longer and it will – according to the participants' expectations – never quite reach the same level of enhancement. The identification of target customers and market segmentation were by far the most frequently cited positive effects to explain the productivity increase in the area of marketing analyses. The more sophisticated analyses, such as customer lifetime value, were hardly ever deployed. In one case, price sensitivity of customers was analyzed using mySAP CRM to identify opportunities for price increases up to 5%. Top timesavings in this category are at 50%.

The *lead management* in marketing was typically improved by a relatively simple change: the consistent and systematic following-up on, for example, interested customers at a trade fair. In the past, following-up these contacts depended solely on the individual sales representative's initiative. Now, leads were collected and systematically qualified, in order to then be handed over to sales. So this was more a reactive mode of the mySAP CRM deployment relative to the often-cited active generation of leads from the customer database. The reason is again straightforward: The customer database in most cases was not yet in a state where the analytic lead generation could have worked. But even in this mode with limited information resources, up to a maximum of 60% less time was needed to reach the same level of results as before the introduction of mySAP CRM. Wherever a structured lead management process had not previously existed when the CRM project was started, productivity improvement did not lead to a potential for cost reduction but to a potential for revenue increases instead.

Two additional cost savings were considered to be relevant but not directly related to the marketing processes: *outsourcing of marketing activities* and savings on material costs for market communication. Eight respondents have outsourced direct mails to specialized marketing agencies or a phone-based campaign to external call centers. CRM enables this outsourcing move because it serves as a platform to exchange information in a way that target customer information was delivered to the agency and results were returned. Before, generating the target customer file would have been too time-consuming. One participant managed to reduce the required level of qualification of staff for the mailing of marketing materials by "internal outsourcing". Before using CRM, the marketing department had been responsible for mailing; afterwards the system enabled staff of the marketing materials depot to handle this process. This move reduced the total amount of human resources needed as well as the cost per remaining employee working in this process. In another case, lead generation for a new market region was outsourced and the qualified leads were then directly fed into the CRM system to be tracked by their own sales representatives. The economic effect of all those activities outsourced was rather small as the activities were typically infrequent and limited in size. Total savings were in the range of EUR 10,000 to 100,000 p.a.

Savings on *material cost for market communication* resulted from a higher quality of customer information as well as from a more focused approach to target customer selection. One participant used an external marketing agency for direct marketing. For several years, on average 20% of all addresses delivered to that agency were wrong, duplicated, outdated, and so on – but every call and mail had to be paid for. The use of CRM reduced the amount of incorrect data by more than 80%, thereby directly and immediately reducing the waste of the yearly marketing budget. Another case achieved 30% savings on its marketing materials costs by an improved quality of customer contact data. Again, in comparison to the process-driven productivity improvements, these additional effects vanished in importance.

Figure 20 on the next page indicates that the productivity growth in marketing analyses and marketing planning/campaign management was quite evenly distributed across participants from close to zero to beyond 30%. The productivity effects in marketing are also broad based and not only rooted in the experience of a few participants. Of all those that answered the question, about 75% reported a positive impact. In lead management, however, a polar profile results: Either the improvement of productivity was very high – or it was marginal. Thus predictions based on the average values for lead management will either be too low or too high. So the decision maker on CRM should rather analyze the situation to identify the productivity potential in the specific situation of his or her lead management process.

Results – Productivity Targets

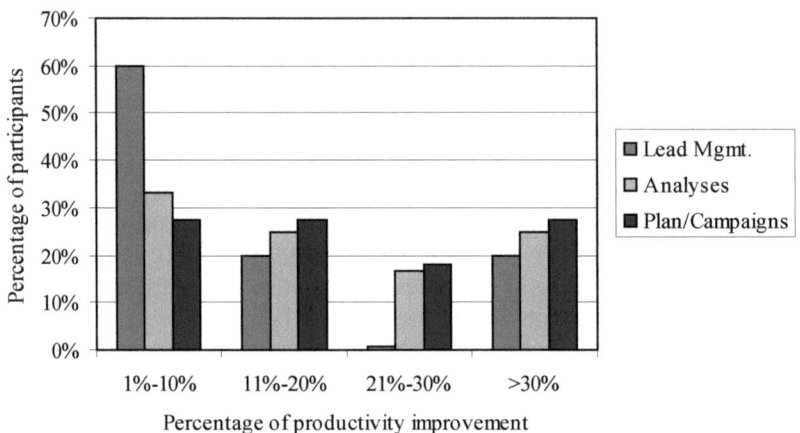

Figure 20: Distribution of present productivity growth in marketing through mySAP CRM

Summing up the key findings about the productivity enhancement through the mySAP CRM deployment in marketing:

- Productivity enhancements for marketing planning/campaign management averaged 15% and were expected to exceed 20% in the steady state, largely driven by the integration of tools and the systematic structure of campaigns
- Marketing analyses improved similarly, owing mainly to the better customer information, not so much due to more sophisticated types of analysis
- Lead management improved by 10% with a future expectation of 15%. A simple consistent following-up on leads was key to the productivity gains
- Marketing outsourcing and cost reduction on marketing material were observed but remained marginal in absolute terms

3.3.3 Sales: Operative Process Improvements

29 out of 35 participants supported their sales activities with mySAP CRM: It is by far the CRM function with the broadest use of the system and the most significant effects. Sales includes the sales representatives in the field as well as the internal sales support processes. The sales function displayed the greatest diversity of all CRM functions among participants: Sales for IT services is an entirely different process than sales for consumer goods or pharmaceuticals.

Therefore, a rather generic scheme had to be used to be applicable to all participants[97]; still it had to be adapted to the individual situation in the phone interviews. The following generic sales activities have been investigated: sales planning, sales lead and opportunity management, customer interaction, reporting, order management, contract management, and internal coordination.

Sales planning is primarily a top-down management activity but it also includes bottom-up contributions from each sales representative. It starts with setting the sales targets and breaking them down to the sales team or to the individual sales representative. Then activities need to be planned on how to reach those goals, for example, sales campaigns to push certain products, to cover specific target customer segments, or geographic regions. As a result, the sales force size and structure, the sales territories, the training schedule and so on, have to be determined. Finally, compensation and budget need to be planned, involving the sales force on all hierarchical levels.

Sales lead- and opportunity management is distinct from lead management in marketing: Marketing's output is sales' input. Marketing does the prospecting and lead qualification. Sales picks up the qualified lead to turn it into a customer. So sales is supposed to only deal with "hot leads" which are also referred to as opportunities. In some cases, marketing did not generate or qualify leads; then the whole process from the "cold" lead to the final signature was driven by sales. The primary objective of opportunity management is to enhance cooperation for specific sales efforts which is especially useful if several sales representatives are working on it, maybe even in an international setting, and if the sales cycles are rather lengthy, for example, when selling complex products[98].

Preparation of customer interaction starts from the pre-approach and ends with the closing. The sales representative needs to prepare for the customer interaction by collecting and analyzing the available customer information, creating the "story", possibly preconfiguring a product, checking out prices, rebates, and the availability of goods. Then he has to decide on the best approach to contact the customer and do the tour planning. He will then approach the customer, arrange an appointment, present and negotiate. Often there is more than one meeting needed to satisfy buying center members' information needs and to overcome all objections. Finally the deal is being agreed on.

---

[97] For the overall process check Kotler (2000) p.620ff.; the process model in the study closely resembles the SAP reference model as outlined in Hauke/Schuh (2002)
[98] These influencing factors on CRM success are analyzed in more detail in Chapters 4.3.1 (complexity of products) and 4.3.3 (internationalization)

CRM potentially has a very strong impact on certain phases of this activity but not on others. So a significant part of the customer interaction time cannot be shortened by CRM, for example, socializing with customers. Other parts may be only marginally influenced, for example, travelling time can be somewhat reduced through optimized tour planning, and negotiations may be slightly shortened as a result of an optimized preparation. The phase hypothesized to be most heavily supported by mySAP CRM is the preparation of the customer visit or customer call. Checking out the customer's history, getting the right address or phone number on first attempt, preparing a proposal, these are the activities where support by CRM is expected to be significant.

Reporting may consume a significant portion of sales time. Field sales has to regularly write a sales report about every customer visit. Additionally, forecasting is required in many organizations. Sometimes, market research is conducted via sales. Finally, the budget allocation requires reporting.

Order management then moves from the first written draft that summarizes the results of a sales discussion, to possible (re-)negotiation of terms, to the required internal and external cross-checks, finalization, and sign-off, to filing the order and inputting it into the system (either in the field, if mobile sales support is available, or in the sales office). The order status then needs to be tracked; potential problems in the delivery must be communicated to the customer. The invoice may need to be reviewed by the sales representative.

In some cases, ***contract management*** is required and carried out by the sales force. For example, when an outline agreement is signed and the customer then starts to order products, the sales representative – supported by the CRM system – has to ensure that the agreed terms are being applied. Furthermore, contract cancellations or non-fulfillment have to be tracked as well as agreed-on sales figures, which then have to be mapped against the contract's agreed volume. When the target values are exceeded, the customer needs to be called to offer better conditions. Potentially, an extension of the contract may have to be negotiated. Customer feedback may need to be collected, and the sales representative might want to find out about the contract's financial success.

The final process that has been investigated is the ***internal coordination***. This consists of the regular sales team meetings, interaction between field sales and the sales support, coordination among sales teams as well as between sales and marketing, production, logistics, accounting, IT department, and so on. This internal coordination can use up a large portion of a sales representative's time.

As with marketing, these processes were considered to constitute sales, no matter which department was responsible in the participant's organization. So in IT services as well as in other high-end service organizations, consultants "sold themselves"; there were little if any sales employees. Vice versa, the Interaction Center sometimes organizationally belonged to the sales department but in this study it was investigated as a separate CRM function.

In almost all of these sales processes, the mySAP CRM deployment led to an increase in productivity – with even higher improvements expected for the future. The following figure illustrates the advantages per sales process:

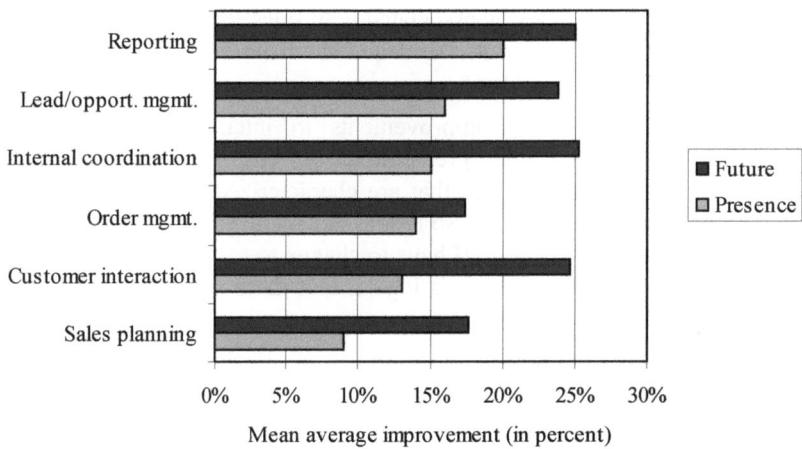

Figure 21: Average productivity gains in sales processes

The mean averages of the present values, that is, those that had been experienced during the productive use of the CRM system until the time of the interview, are spread between 9% and 20%, while the sales productivity improvements expected for the future range between 17% and 25%. These *effects are clearly stronger than in marketing*, but still plausible relative to the customer information improvements reported in Chapter 3.3.1.

It is also apparent, that the *differences between the future and present values vary significantly among the sales activities* under investigation. For some, like reporting, mySAP CRM seems to have quickly reached its maximum impact whereas, for example, impact on customer interaction develops more slowly. Ranking the 6 activities by the difference between present and future values, the rank order follows a plausible pattern:

- The smallest differences are to be found in order management and reporting that measure 3 and 5 percentage-points respectively. These two activities are the ones that are most standardized, repetitive, and therefore the easiest to be supported by an IT system. Often, mySAP CRM replaced another IT supported process in these activities. Thus it makes sense that the mySAP CRM benefits materialize the fastest in this group.
- The next two in the line are lead- and opportunity management (8 percentage-points) and sales planning (9 percentage-points), that is, activities that are most closely associated with sales force management. And as management looks after it, the required changes in behavior will be realized in a short period of time.
- Finally, the differences in improvements to internal coordination (10 percentage-points) and the preparation of customer interaction (12 percentage-points) are activities that are characterized by a high degree of interactivity among individuals. So it does not suffice if one person changes, but (almost) all of the CRM staff have to change to realize the benefits. This takes more time and therefore it is logical that these activities do not show their full potential in the present values.

After the overall results have been checked for plausibility, the results are analyzed by activity in more detail. To do so, ***reporting*** is first, as it scored the highest of all sales activities in Figure 21 with a 20% mean average present improvement of productivity and 25% as expected for the steady state. However, in this specific case, the median is only at 5% (and 15% respectively for the future). So just like in the case of lead management in Chapter 3.3.2, some participants must have had significantly higher results in reporting than the majority of CRM users. Checking the distribution of values, that is the case: A strong group of users with productivity improvements far beyond the 30% high end of the range of predefined answer categories on the questionnaire is offset by 1/3 of respondents who did not experience any effect at all. Overall, a "u"-shaped distribution emerges, as the following Figure 22 illustrates.

Results – Productivity Targets

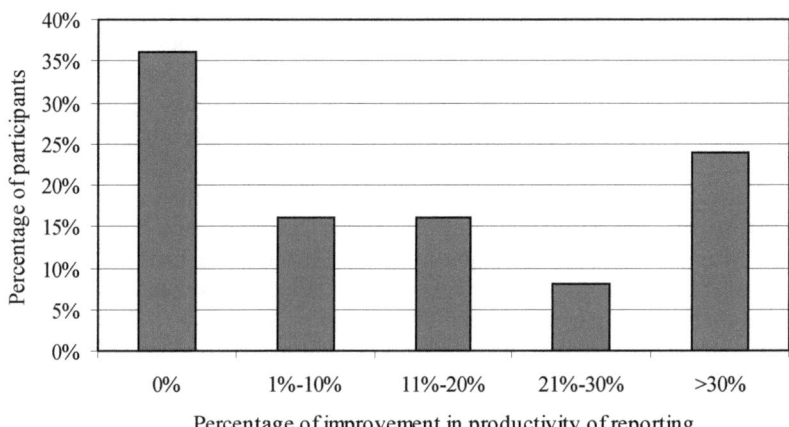

Figure 22: Distribution of present productivity gains in reporting

The top group enjoys an internal group average of 58% productivity improvement, that is, 2/3 of the "unproductive time" spent on reports had been reduced by the introduction of mySAP CRM. A closer analysis of this top-performing group does not reveal any commonality among sectors or company sizes. There is not even a common pattern of how these savings were achieved. In one instance, the former head of sales was fired when the deficiencies in sales became apparent. The new leader "razed the sales organization to the ground – and then rebuilt it on the basis of modern sales principles." – as the respondent put it. In the wake of this turnaround, the reporting was also radically streamlined and standardized based on the CRM system. In the same line, two respondents told that in the past, sales representatives redid a lot of the reporting that had already been done – either because they had forgotten about their own reports or because the coordination with colleagues was insufficient. The introduction of CRM resulted in a massive reduction of duplicate work, as the customer information was now being pooled. One participant argues that two effects were at work: operational improvement of the formerly paper-based process and more trust in the numbers which in turn leads to less cross-checking and extra analyses. Similarly, a top-scoring participant considers the drill-down function for market analyses as crucial for reducing the sales employee's workload of extra-reports.

On the other hand, 1/3 of the participants did not experience any effect at all and another 16% are only marginally positive. Again, a more detailed analysis reveals a multitude of reasons. Some participants said that they do not use SAP

Results – Productivity Targets

for reporting purposes or that the mySAP CRM release that they started out with did not perform in that respect. Several respondents argued that mySAP CRM alone was insufficient for this purpose; they planned to add in the Business Warehouse. Some indicated that they had minimized the reporting effort before – and using CRM did not yield additional improvement any more. Often, it was argued that on the one hand, time spent on reporting had increased due to the extra effort of correcting existing customer profiles and the additional information required in a higher quality now. On the other hand, the reporting process has been slimmed down and the tool helped to speed it up. So they concluded that the net effect was zero.

A comparison of rationales from the top and the bottom group leads to an interesting conclusion about which is the more relevant for the future. The top group has more often implemented the system "by the book" and it builds reported values on "lasting" functional improvements (for example, the drill-down, avoidance of double work). The bottom group mainly cites obstacles that are temporary in nature: an outdated release, a not-yet-implemented Business Warehouse, or a temporary plus in data maintenance. So for the future, the high values are more indicative than the low ones. Therefore, the mean average is more meaningful than the median in this particular case. More evidence for this conclusion can be drawn from the fact that for the future values, the median is at 15% already – and the difference between mean and median is reduced to 10 percentage-points.

Lead- and opportunity management scores second highest in productivity gains through mySAP CRM with a present mean average of 16% (median 10%) and a future mean average of 24% (median 20%). 60% of all participants answered this category; 70% of these realized a positive impact, that is, 30% said that the effect was zero. The average present improvement of all those who had a positive effect was 23%. Interestingly, the improvements in this activity exceed those of lead management in marketing by more than 60%. A possible explanation for this result is that the key factor of success in marketing's lead management has been identified not as analytic brilliance but systematic persistence. Of all the lead management process steps, the tracking was almost unanimously reported to have the most business impact. And the tracking is done in sales rather than in marketing. Moreover, lead management in marketing normally does not see many different people working on the same project whereas that happens frequently in sales.

Internal coordination was improved in ¾ of all cases but with regard to the present values as often in the 1-10% range as above 10%. Only 3 participants exceed 30% in this category. Therefore, despite the large number of positive experiences, the present mean average ranks only third among all sales activities. A different picture shows up when the future values are being looked at. Here, the improvements in internal coordination take the lead with a little over 25% in productivity gains. The main driver of productivity for this activity is the improved interaction between field sales and sales support. Many respondents mentioned that the lack of trust among these two organizations had resulted in double-work, constant double-checking on numbers, delayed information, misunderstandings, and so on. Other frequently mentioned areas of improvement in the internal coordination were the interfaces between marketing and sales, and between different sales teams internationally. As mentioned above: Due to the fact that an improvement in interaction will only materialize when all individuals have changed, it takes time. Consequently, the difference between future and present values is highest in this category.

Order management has only been improved for 9 participants – while 12 respondents stated that they did not realize a positive effect up to the time of the interview. Out of the 9 positive experiences, 3 scored above 30%; they, however, went from 50% to above 90%. Two of the three top performers in this category deployed the mySAP CRM Internet sales functionality to automate the order management process previously only supported by fax or telephone. The reverse is not true though, that is, not all of the e-shop users on the basis of mySAP CRM have significant productivity gains in order management. In fact, out of 10 Internet sales users, besides the three mentioned above, four reported no effect on orders; three others scored between 3% and 20%. The reasons for this discrepancy between high and low impact of the CRM are manifold. Some e-shops were simply used as information tool, not for sales purposes and therefore ordering was not affected at all. Sometimes, acceptance on the side of the user or on the side of the customer was not (yet) there. In one case, only a pilot version of the e-shop had been implemented at the time of the interview.

As expected, ***customer interaction*** proved to be the dominant activity in sales, which on average takes up more then 50% of sales employees' time. Thereof, preparation takes 10%. Again as expected, ¾ of all respondents that provided information in this category had experienced positive effects at the time of the interview already. So mySAP CRM benefits in customer interaction are second only to internal coordination with respect to the breadth of positive impact. However, 2/3 of all participants report an impact of CRM on the customer interaction below 10% at the time of interview. That is surprising because customer interaction is one of the most frequently cited examples of "operative CRM" benefits in literature. The answer lies in the significant gap of more than

Results – Productivity Targets

12 percentage-points between the present and future values for the CRM impact on customer interaction: In this activity, the benefits do not show up as quickly as in other processes – as argued above. The main driver of benefit in this activity at the moment is the significantly shortened time to collect customer information. Before, sales employees had to check several different files with different formats; they had to call other departments to (hopefully) get the information at all. Furthermore, the quality of information was greatly improved, so that the sales representative did not waste time, for example, building an offer based on faulty information. As the time to access relevant information has been reduced by more than 30%, a reduction of 12% for the customer interaction is rather conservative.

In *sales planning,* productivity rose only by 10%; that figure is at 15% if future expectations are included. Until the interview, no participant had experienced a productivity increase beyond 30%. Only 1/3 of all respondents scored above 10%, another 1/3 put down zero impact. As sales planning is a management function, most benefits have been realized after a short period in time, so the future potential is limited. There are several reasons for the relatively low impact on sales planning. A structural reason is that the nature of some participants' business renders sales planning futile. For example, one respondent answered that forecasting did not play as much of a role as in other industry sectors, as their highly flexible production schedule had a very high portion of value added by suppliers, and little to no lead times. Some considered sales planning to be a "back-of the envelope" exercise where no analytic or operative support by a system was needed. Others simply did not use CRM for planning purposes – either because they "plan entirely decentrally" and do not use any supporting system, or because they prefer to use other systems for planning. Several participants did not find enough supporting functionality in their (early) version of mySAP CRM; those that did not use a Business Warehouse in particular, cited this to be the reason for a low impact on sales planning. In several instances, this process had already been supported by prior systems and therefore the difference between the old and new system was not as large as with other processes.

Taking a closer look at those who scored high in this category, they usually had large-scale sales forces, a complex spectrum of products and sizeable sales planning efforts. One respondent explained a high value by the fact that several months of planning efforts had been reduced to one month at the end of the year. 50% of the planning time was impacted by mySAP CRM and thereof 50% have been reduced, resulting in a 25% overall improvement of productivity. On two occasions, top scores in this category were explained by a previously fragmented system landscape that led to a prohibitively high complexity in obtaining an integrated and consistent view across the different sales regions and subdivisions. The introduction of mySAP CRM for the first time provided an opportunity to have a central sales-planning component while investing a reasonable effort. It was not only the size of the sales force and the product scope that made CRM support in sales planning worthwhile, but also a high degree of customization in, for example, solution businesses. When machinery, IT, or chemicals had to be tailored to the specific situation of a customer, CRM in sales planning yielded a higher benefit than in other situations.

One sales activity was missing in Figure 21, the *contract management*. Out of 13 respondents in this category, only 2 have experienced a positive effect of 5% and 30% respectively. Even for the future, only three participants expect an impact here. This is too slim of a basis to report any effect, therefore it is left out of the chart. There are several reasons for this low result. First of all, some of the sectors in the study simply do not apply outline agreements and therefore do not need contract management – namely pharma/medical or IT services. If contract management was a task at all, it was mostly handled by accounting rather than sales – and in accounting, it was not supported by CRM. Moreover, renegotiations and contract cancellations were reported to be extremely infrequent. Therefore, the potential for an impact of CRM was considered to be insignificant. Finally, there was not a single case in which the collection of customer feedback or the tracking of financial results per contract was considered to be relevant parts of sales activities. This is fully consistent with the results of a survey conducted by the VDI in 1999: Only 17% of 51 large and medium German companies that participated classify customers by their value potential[99]. As customer lifetime value management increasingly gains popularity, potentially the contract management will become more important in the future.

The assessment of mySAP CRM impact per sales process only sheds light on one side of the impact. The second aspect is the importance of the different processes relative to the overall mix of sales activities. Even a strong impact on a marginal activity has limited potential for value added. Therefore, as outlined in the CRM Value Metric, impact per process needs to be weighted by the proportion of time spent on the process. The resulting range of time weighted productivity gains in sales is rather limited as Figure 23 indicates: More than 80% of all participants range between 1% and 20% improvement with regard to this category.

---

[99] These results are reported by Rapp (2001) p.96

Results – Productivity Targets

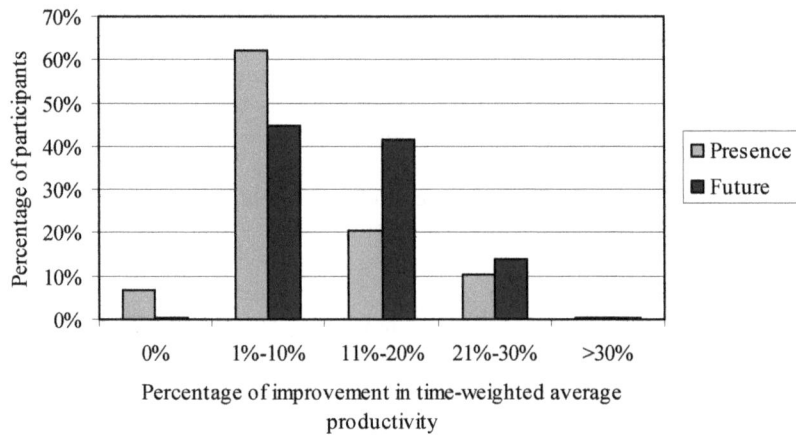

Figure 23: Distribution of time-weighted average productivity gains through mySAP CRM

The weighted average productivity in overall sales, that is, field force and sales support, had increased by 8% from the point of going live to the interview. An average improvement of 12% is expected for the future. Top values are in the 25%-30% range. But even in the future, no participant expected the improvements to surpass 30%. To further understand which processes have the most impact, the 12% of expected productivity increase in sales in the steady state are decomposed to its constituting elements in Figure 24:

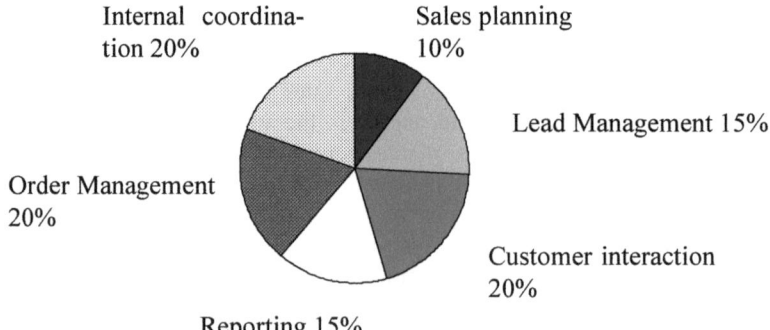

Figure 24: Contribution of sales processes to overall productivity improvement in sales through mySAP CRM (values rounded)

Results – Productivity Targets

Order management is one of the top contributors to the weighted average productivity, although it only ranks fourth in impact per process as depicted in Figure 21. But a significant portion of sales time was allocated to this process before the introduction of CRM. On the other hand, lead- and opportunity management ranks fourth together with reporting in Figure 24, down from second place in the impact per process statistic.

To summarize key findings from productivity increases in the sales function:
- The highest impact by CRM is on *reporting* with currently 20%, expected to grow to 25%. Productivity improvements are driven by reduced frequency and higher efficiency of reports. As it constitutes only a small part of overall sales activities, the total contribution to higher sales efficiency is only 15%.
- *Lead management* has been improved by 16% (24% expected) by a more consistent following-up on interested customers, again only adding 15% to the overall sales benefit
- *Internal coordination* has a broad base of support from participants, also ranges from 15% to 25% in improvement over time, and makes up a higher portion of sales time, thus adding 20% to the overall benefit from CRM
- 15% less FTE on *order management* is largely due to Internet sales. This time-consuming sales activity adds 20% to the overall CRM benefit
- Timesavings in *customer interaction* materialize more slowly, from less than 15% today to 25% in the steady state. They are largely due to faster access to quality customer information. Although only the time for preparation was taken into consideration, this activity belongs to the top three in value-added from a productivity point of view.
- *Sales planning* only sees a 10% to 15% improvement applied to a rather small proportion of overall time, thus ending at 10% value added
- Finally, *contract management* has been found to be insignificant

3.3.4 Interaction Center: New Opportunities in Telesales and Help Desk Functions

For the Interaction Center (IC), 6 processes have been investigated as they were potentially impacted by mySAP CRM: the help-desk function, inbound and outbound telesales, documentation, capacity management, and the introduction of new call center staff.

The ***help desk function*** comprises all non-sales-related activities in which the IC supports a user. This may be, for example, the classic hot line, delivering information about the company and its products. It may also be the more service-related task of helping customers put their purchased products to work, including trouble-shooting and taking complaints. In financial services, the call center may be in charge of informing the customer about his account status. This help desk function can be used in B2C as well as in B2B relationships. Another possibility is to deploy the IC in-house only, for example, as a service coordination center where all the service requests are pooled, prioritized, and then sent to the field force.

Telesales may be inbound, that is, the customer is calling, or outbound, where the call center agent calls the prospective customer. In D-A-CH countries, the regional area of this study, outbound telesales require the customer's permission. They were only used in B2B relationships. Outbound telesales include the selection of target customers (which are often leads handed over from marketing or sales), the scripting to lead the call center agent through the customer interaction, the sales call itself, and the follow-up – either the taking of the order, or a second call, or the customer interaction by a sales representative. Inbound telesales consist of the same set of tasks with the exception of customer selection, as this is neither possible nor required.

Calls have to be ***documented***, so that in case the customer calls again, any other call center agent or sales representative is able to build on what had already been discussed in the first interaction. The documentation is often linked to Computer Telephony Integration (CTI), that is, the system automatically loads the correct customer file by recognizing phone number. The CTI as well as the ACD (Automated Call Distribution) functionality is part of an overall CRM perspective – but they are not part of the mySAP CRM software. Therefore they were not assessed in this study.

Finally, two smaller effects were hypothesized to add value. Improvements in capacity management were deemed to be important for call centers. Also improved scripting and guidance for the call center agent was assumed to support the new call center agent in getting acquainted, thus shortening the time-to-productivity of the agent. However, as far as the ***call center agent time-to-productivity*** was concerned, only two participants had experienced positive effects below 10% while five stated that there was no improvement. For those responding positively, the clarity of scripting and the role definition had improved, warranting some benefit for new agents. For those who did not experience any impact, either the fluctuation among call center staff was so low that they had not yet experienced a new agent in training, or the changes that occurred were marginal in relation to the overall call center staff. One participant estimated the net-effect of advantages and disadvantages of the new CRM system to be zero in that respect. Two participants had staffed the call center with highly qualified personnel. They stated that in relation to the overall training cycle, the improvement of scripting was a rather marginal effect.

Improvements in *capacity management* have also been insignificant Again, it was the static nature of the call centers under investigation that led to low values in this category. So one respondent argued that the (small) call center operates constantly at the maximum level of calls with insignificant volatility for the number of calls in a strictly limited B2B environment – and therefore no benefit in capacity management could possibly be achieved by CRM. For another participant, a reduction in capacity was not intended and thus not observed. In a third case, productivity gains were more due to the technical call center optimization than to the Introduction of CRM. Only one respondent saw a reduction of excess capacity by up to 15% because mySAP CRM affords more transparency about agents' workload.

For the remaining IC activities, the following results were reported by the 7 participants who deployed the mySAP CRM Interaction Center:

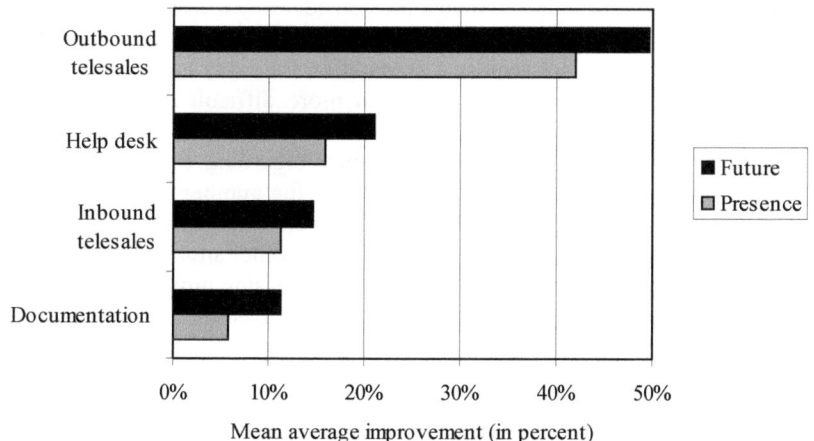

Figure 25: Productivity gains in the Interaction Center

Improvements in the productivity of **outbound telesales** clearly take the lead for present and future values. The high averages are not caused by a single high value so the median is close to the mean: for the present observations it is at 30%, for the future steady state at 45%. 5 out of the 7 users of the mySAP CRM IC function reported in this category and all of them had experienced a positive impact. The two other participants either first started outbound telesales with the introduction of CRM or did not use the outbound telesales at all as the call center was restricted to a help desk function by corporate policy. Those that did see an improvement saw the main benefit in improved customer profiles reducing the time for preparation. Respondents said that outbound telesales in the time before mySAP CRM were a "nightmare" or "not economically feasible" with very long lead times and a large-scale effort to achieve a consistent target customer list. Therefore the frequency of those activities was low, the results mixed.

Inbound telesales differ sharply from outbound telesales with regard to CRM benefit. Only an average increase in productivity of 11.5% has been experienced and roughly 15% are expected for the future. But given, that the main CRM benefit for outbound telesales is in the call preparation, logically inbound telesales are less impacted: Preparation is impossible. So the benefit is restricted to operative improvements, like standardized forms, integrated data formats, and so on. Also access to a higher quality customer profile was confirmed to result in a higher "first-time-right" ratio and thus to a reduced number of callbacks.

In the **help desk function**, improvements are considerably lower compared to the outbound telesales but higher than for inbound telesales. The rationale for a second rank is that it does not require a preparation for every call as in outbound telesales but scripting is more important and more difficult than for inbound telesales. The magnitude of changes in help desk productivity ranges from a 5% reduction to a 70% increase. The top performer regarding the change started from a very low level of productivity. In this case, the number of customers had increased dramatically in a very short period of time. Furthermore, to give sound advice required an in-depth understanding of the customer situation. Because the organization was not prepared to handle the ever-increasing number of calls, they ended up "somewhere in the company". Whoever received the call started to dig up and study the customer profiles, then called back. Also, due to high time pressure, documentation suffered, which in turn again increased the effort in answering the customer's request properly. The mySAP CRM IC sharply turned around the situation. This change led to a 5% increase in employee productivity outside the IC, as more reliable and richer customer information was now readily available. Besides the direct access to customer information, another driver of value for the help desk was the link-up of a solutions database to the CRM system. Two participants confirmed a reduced need for expensive 2nd level support. Sometimes, however, that was considered as the next step. In one case, the company consciously decided against it because even with a system support, the complexity of the products was too high for the low-skilled IC agents.

Documentation finally experienced the least productivity gains of all IC processes. This is a "net result" – as most participants reported positive and negative effects from the introduction of mySAP CRM in that respect. However, not all participants had such a balanced experience. One respondent was very negative and reported a 50% increase in documentation effort relative to the prior system. The increase was due to additional information requirements as well as to more complexity in handling the system. This would by itself not automatically result in a lower productivity because the benefits from richer customer information might well offset the extra-effort. However, in this case, the participant did not use the extra information in any way, so it yielded no benefit whatsoever. Therefore the higher documentation effort clearly needed to be marked as a reduction in productivity. Two other participants had a zero net result. The rest of the participants scored either at 20% or 30% improvement. The main positive effect resulted from the pooling of customer information, which led to a significant reduction of redundant data entry. Furthermore, preconfigured sets of activities and a pre-defined structure of reports saved time.

Summing up the results for the CRM impact on the Interaction Center:
- ***Outbound telesales*** improved by more than 40% on average for most of the 7 respondents that deployed the IC. The value driver was an easier and faster preparation with improved customer information.
- ***Inbound telesales*** only has experienced an 11.5% improvement by the time of the interview. Compared to outbound telesales, this result is plausible as the preparation for incoming customer calls is more difficult.
- Productivity increased for the ***help desk function*** by 15% with 20% improvement expected for the steady state. This is plausible, as it resembles more an inbound telesales situation, but still benefits more from the standardized scripting.
- ***Documentation*** showed rather low and mixed results. Benefits resulted from a reduction of redundant data entry, preconfigured sets of activities, and a pre-defined structure of reports. Often, however, the effort increased due to higher information requirements.
- Improvements in ***capacity management*** and the ***time-to-productivity*** for new call center agents were insignificant.

3.3.5 Internet Sales: Automated Order Management

Electronic Customer Relationship Management ("eCRM")[100], "eSelling"[101], "Internet Sales" – different terminology that indicates a differently scoped focus around the Internet. Most of the participants referred to the function as Internet sales, so this term is chosen in the study as well. Productivity improvements through using CRM in Internet sales[102] can be systematically structured as follows:

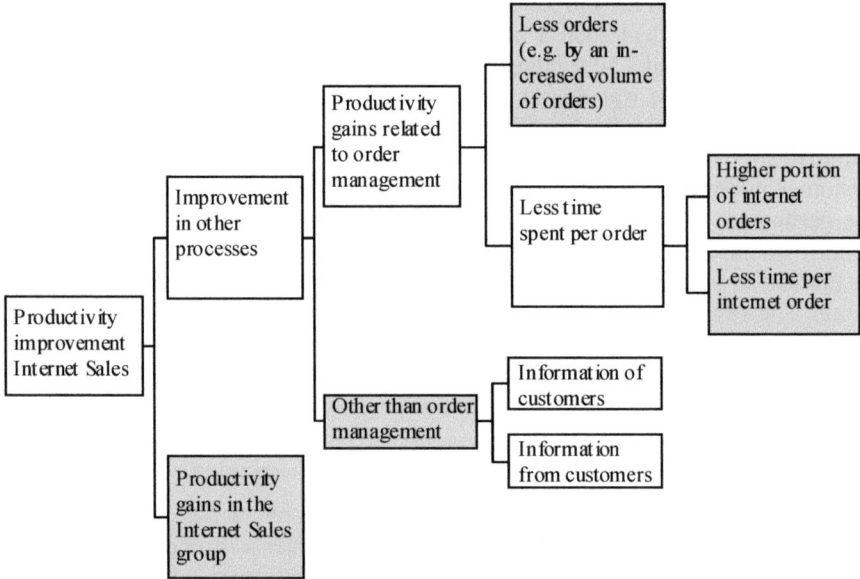

Figure 26: Overview: Sources for productivity improvement in Internet sales through CRM (shaded information assessed and discussed in this chapter)

It might be surprising not to find the familiar distinction between B2B and B2C as it was also used in the questionnaire. 6 out of 35 participants used the Internet sales function of mySAP CRM to operate an e-shop. All of these shops were B2B, so no experience with B2C has been reported in this study.

---

[100] Muther (2002), esp. p. 21 ff.; Dyché (2002) p.291 defines it as "activities to sell to, support, manage, and retain customers who do business through a company's Web channel."; Schmidt (2001) p.236 defines the term broader as the use of IT and telecommunications to support the customer relationship
[101] Hauke/Schuh (2003) p.84 define the topic as "eSelling (formerly: Internet Sales) is a complete solution for selling products via the Internet."
[102] For the revenue impact of Internet Sales check chapter 3.4.4

Productivity improvements through the use of mySAP CRM Internet sales can show up in the department or group that operates the Internet sales, for example, if a former e-shop now requires less maintenance effort. This corresponds to the kind of effects investigated in the CRM functions so far. However, out of the 9 participants who used mySAP CRM Internet sales, not a single one had experienced any benefit for the Internet sales group. This can be explained in part by the fact that only 3 Internet sales users operated an e-shop before they started out with mySAP CRM. So for roughly 2/3 of the companies, there can be no savings. Of the three respondents that had used e-shops before, two used shops from other software providers and the third participant operated a proprietary e-shop solution. However, one of the suppliers went bankrupt during the e-business shakeout; the solution was difficult to maintain and "half-baked" as it still included fax orders. The other supplier's software was not accepted by the customers. Therefore the respondents stressed that the mySAP CRM implementation was a full restart. The proprietary solution was used but it was "stand-alone" and therefore "not-such-a-good experience" as the respondent said. It also had a very limited scope so that support for the CRM system needed to be slightly increased, not decreased upon switching over to mySAP CRM.

So for Internet sales especially, most of the benefit materializes in other CRM processes, especially the automation of order management. Some ***non-order productivity enhancements*** have also been observed. Two respondents reported a significant reduction in customer inquiries due to the improved transparency of prices and products. This effect typically materialized in the Interaction Center. Three participants said that the time needed to identify the right product for the customer was reduced by 50% or above. These findings are fully consistent with results from research by Avlonitis/Karayanni[103]. Analyzing the effects of Internet sales of US and European corporates, they reported a statistically significant positive impact of Internet sales on sales management efficiency, product management efficiency, and sales performance.

Despite these positive effects on diverse CRM processes, the dominant effect was the ***major improvement in the order management process***. In fact, all of the Internet sales users deployed the e-shop primarily for the sake of automating the order process. As Figure 26 illustrates, improvements can be caused by two effects: fewer orders and less time per order. A reduction in the number of orders can be due to a higher volume per order, which in turn may be caused by a higher reliability of the medium compared to fax or phone as no rewriting is required. Another reason for increased order volume may by automated order

---

[103] Avlonitis/Karayanni (2000) p.452 ff.

Results – Productivity Targets

systems fully integrated into the customer's workflow. Not only an increase in the size of the order but also less errors in the order processing reduce the number of orders as less re-orders are required[104]. In the sample, however, order management improvements were not achieved by reducing the quantity of orders but the opposite was true. Many users stated that the size of the order had slightly decreased, the number of orders increased. In one case, divergent effects were observed: the foreign customers reduced the order size and placed more small orders whereas for the national customers web-orders were bigger than regular "fax-and phone" orders.

So the main driver of productivity is time reductions per order. The enormous increase in efficiency for web-orders vs. offline fax orders via sales support is widely recognized and confirmed by the study's results: The mean average present productivity increase from shifting orders online is 70%. A strong cluster of high scores drives these sky-high numbers as outlined in Figure 27:

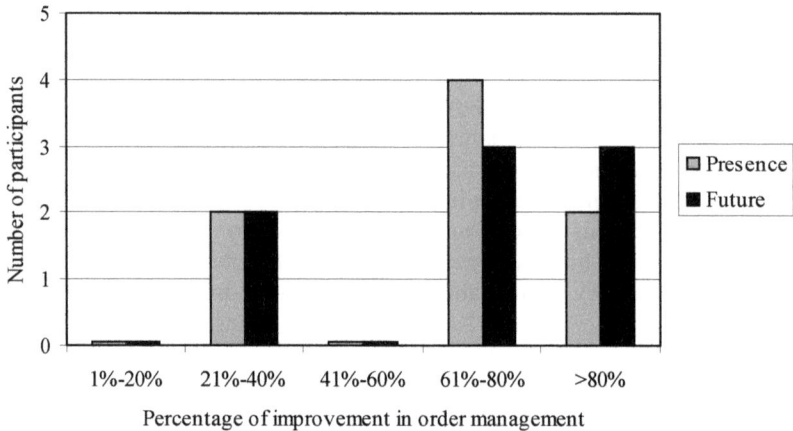

Figure 27: Distribution of productivity improvement in order management through mySAP CRM Internet sales

All of the 8 participants using mySAP CRM powered e-shops have experienced very positive effects. This "right-sided" distribution leads to a future median of 80% that even exceeds the mean average of 70%. Present values are only slightly lower, which indicates that the massive benefits materialize quickly. Given this

---

[104] For a similar distinction check Leek/Turnbull/Naudé (2003) p.122

strong effect, most participants were in the process to transfer as many orders as possible to the e-shop. The implemented shops were nonetheless still rather restricted in scope. In two cases, only spare parts were to be ordered via the Internet. One company had rolled out the system only in one country. Target values for the percentage of orders via the e-shop in steady state ranged from below 5% to 100% with a strong cluster around 20%.

As stated above, the order management effects do not materialize in the Internet sales group but in sales. In Figure 28, therefore the productivity gains for Internet sales users were compared to the mean average of all companies and the mean average of participants without Internet sales:

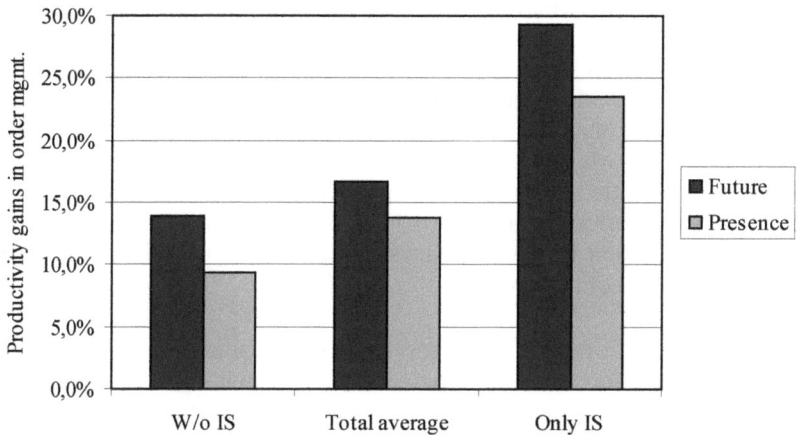

Figure 28: Comparison of productivity gains in order management for users of Internet sales versus other participants

The figure clearly indicates that Internet sales users have achieved on average more than twice the productivity gains in order management compared to the non-users. Combined with the fact that order management is among the top three productivity drivers in sales, the power of this CRM function is apparent.

A short summary of results for Internet sales closes the chapter:
- Participants in the study have used the mySAP CRM Internet sales exclusively for B2B, predominantly to automate the order process. This led to a mean average of 70% time savings per order relative to the offline fax mode via sales support

Results – Productivity Targets

- Compared to non-users of Internet sales, users achieve twice the productivity gains in the important process of order management within the CRM function of sales
- About 20% of all orders were on average expected to come via the e-shop in the steady state

3.3.6 Service: Improvement Potential Not Yet Developed

For the remaining CRM function, the service, there was too little supporting evidence in the study to conduct detailed analyses and maintain anonymity at the same time. Therefore, no quantitative results will be displayed. Several reasons may have caused the scarcity of evidence. Service is extensively supported by mySAP CRM release 3.0 and later but it was not so prominent in earlier releases. As most participants had started out with an earlier version, only three participants used CRM in the service function. However, this does not explain the surprising fact that the improved customer information did not have an impact on service. Maybe it is due to the research method that those benefits have not been detected. Whenever a respondent did not have the CRM function supported by the corresponding mySAP CRM module, impact was only checked by a general question for "other effects", which might have been too broad to remind respondents of this area.

The potential benefit from CRM in service is indeed substantial, for example, in better support for the tele-diagnostic service by providing a customer history. CRM can also improve productivity for service order management, the creation and management of service level agreements (SLA), capacity management, and so on. And in fact, for the three companies that used CRM in service, three processes were improved: the service help-desk, the fulfillment of service orders, and capacity management. Not all of them experienced an effect in all three processes, though.

With respect to the *service help-desk* that takes the service requests and tracks trouble tickets, respondents reported increased transparency of all activities in the service arena. Furthermore, the service staff was provided with a tool to prioritize the customer requests – directly linked to the overall customer profiles. Additionally, one participant added in a solution database to the overall system configuration, thereby enabling service staff to quickly get access to mission critical information. This – in turn – drove up the systems use and user satisfaction. The service function also saw some significant benefit by informing the customer better: Frequently asked questions were answered in the e-shop, which led to a noticeable reduction in customer queries.

Service order fulfillment was supported by mySAP CRM with regard to spare parts management, customer contact, diagnostics, and the coordination among service staff. Increased transparency of the entire service activities was beneficial in this respect as well as with regard to ***optimizing capacity*** in order to boost utilization while ensuring immediate service.

So all in all, it can be concluded that

- Potential benefits of CRM use in services have been confirmed for the service help-desk function, the service order fulfillment, and the optimization of capacity
- The potential of CRM in service has not yet been fully exploited by those to whom it would be available

3.3.7 Other Productivity Effects and Potential Cost Savings

In this chapter, all other productivity effects are summed up. That includes collaborative CRM and additional effects outside the CRM functions. Collaborative commerce "reflects the ability of various partners within a supply chain to share important data about products, inventory levels, and orders"[105]. This ability may also be extended to important customer data in order to coordinate services and offerings more effectively. If, for example, a complex machine is sold by company A while company B looks after the logistics and company C puts it to work in the customer's factory, all three should share parts of the information that was provided by the customer to the sales representative of company A. This way, misunderstandings can be avoided, and the customer's workload in coordinating the different suppliers is significantly reduced, where the quality of service increases. Collaboration does not require mySAP CRM: Some have used SAP R/3 functionality, others EDI, or simply oral or written communication. But CRM can be used to enhance collaboration among companies that jointly and interdependently create value for the customer. This would be an extended version of "***collaborative CRM***", a term which sometimes is limited to denote the interaction between one supplier and its customer[106]. To

---

[105] Dyché (2002) p.289;
[106] The term "collaborative CRM" is defined by Dyché (2003) p. 289 as "specific functionality that enables a two-way dialog between a company and its customers..."; Hauke/Schuh (2003) p.102

cover all these potential effects, the question in the interviews was framed to ask for any productivity gains through CRM in the coordination with business partners.

While few of the participants had experience with collaborative CRM at the point in time of the study, several regarded this form of CRM as a "next step", "strategic decision looming", or "an interesting perspective". Especially in situations when a large number of companies worked in a major project, for example, in building a public edifice like a hospital, this use of CRM was considered to add significant value by reducing mistakes, double-work, omissions, and so on. In the same way, cooperation with freelance partners and subcontractors was named twice as an interesting area to be investigated. When the channel partners act as value added resellers, the coordination of who had promised or delivered what to which customer was considered as a very likely field of collaborative CRM in the near future. Also in the area of channel partners, one participant needed an extensive and complex pre-coordination of campaigns before going to market. In this case, the business partner coordination effort per campaign was reduced by 30% to 60%, depending on the scope. Benefits from collaborative CRM even materialized for participants that regularly needed to cooperate with other divisions – or foreign subsidiaries – within their own company in delivering their products and services to their customers. Although they formally belonged to one legal entity, collaboration was as difficult as in cross-company relationships because they constituted entirely separate organizations.

Additional *savings outside of the CRM functions* have also been achieved. Two effects have been frequently mentioned: outsourcing and the reduction of stock.

- *Outsourcing of CRM activities* has already been described as productivity booster in Chapter 3.2 for the marketing function. In addition, one participant managed to achieve cost savings by outsourcing the service.
- CRM, however, also enabled outsourcing outside of the CRM functions. So one respondent was able to *outsource the entire product warehousing and commissioning* to a specialized service provider, which led to a 30% reduction in cost and a higher level of quality at the same time. He argued that without mySAP CRM, and more specifically without joint access to an integrated, high quality set of customer data via a standard interface and

---

use the term "live web collaboration" ins the same sense as "a complete support solution to assist customers who have queries or have problems while using a Web shop in eSelling".

fully-aligned order processes, the required "real-time coordination" would have been impossible.

- One company reduced its ***average annual inventory of receivables*** by 17%, which represents a net saving of over EUR 6 million p.a. The rationale behind this success is that CRM supported the external sales force to be better informed about customers' dunning levels.
- Another cost decrease has been achieved by the ***reduction of stock levels*** as a result of using mySAP CRM – in the most extreme cases by up to 35%. But only 6 participants had experienced a positive effect of this kind with an average reduction at 16% and 21% when future expectations are added in. Reduction in the average stock would have to be valued with the "cost of carry" which includes depreciation, cost of capital, warehousing, and so on. As these figures were difficult to obtain, only the cost of capital was used to conservatively value those productivity enhancements.

While the findings in this chapter are more anecdotal in nature, they may nonetheless be valuable to identify potential pockets of value in CRM:
- Despite no single "live" installation in the sample, collaborative CRM in all shades of meaning has been widely regarded as an attractive future possibility
- Cost savings have been achieved outside of the CRM functions by CRM-enabled outsourcing of warehousing and commissioning, the reduction of the average annual inventory of receivables, and reductions in the cost-of-carry for inventory. With some notable exceptions, these effects were small in comparison to the overall financial impact of mySAP CRM.

3.4 Revenue Targets: More Customers and More Revenue per Customer

After assessing the productivity benefits of a CRM deployment that translate directly into cost reduction potential, the fulfillment of revenue targets has to be investigated. First, the methodology will be outlined along with the general results. Then the four principal revenue drivers are analyzed in the remaining chapters.

3.4.1 Increase in Revenue: The Basic Logic-Tree and Aggregated Results

The potential to increase revenue is a logical consequence of more customers or more revenue per customer[107]. Additional customers might be new customers, or former customers who, due to increased customer retention, have not been lost to competitors. An increase in revenue per customer can be due to higher quantities or prices. From these basic possibilities, the following logic-tree emerges:

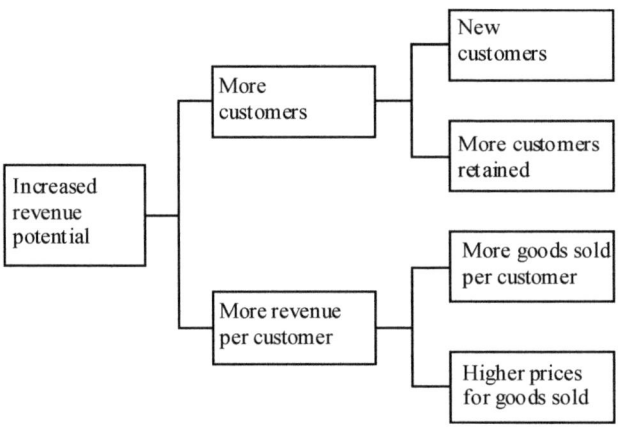

Figure 29: Overview: Drivers of additional revenue through CRM

The end points of the tree are the principal drivers of revenue that will be analyzed in detail consecutively. For each driver, additional "hard" factors are outlined, such as, for example, the number of leads that result in new customers. Also the "soft" factors will be added in where they have the most decisive impact. The allocation of the soft factors to specific ends of the logic tree is nonetheless somewhat arbitrary as they usually influence many of the hard factors at the same time. For example, the reduction of channel conflict potentially explains why customers are more satisfied, therefore possibly more loyal, and why in the end the mySAP CRM user ends up with more customers. It may also add to the effectiveness in gaining new customers. And, of course, there could potentially be a positive impact on the number of goods sold and even the prices. The same ambiguity of effects will be found with most of the

---

[107] Grant/Schlesinger (1995) p.59 also see a "larger duration of contracts" as a source of more revenue. However, that third possibility is not on the same logical level. It is merely one way to increase revenue per customer. Thus it will be dealt with in the context of "More goods sold per customer"

soft factors. To avoid duplicating results, only one major influence of the soft factor onto one hard factor will be highlighted while other links may only be hinted at. As argued for the research design in Chapter 2.2.1, there will not be a complete business dynamics map of soft and hard factor interdependencies.

But before the details of each branch in the basic logic-tree (Figure 29) are unfolded, the overall results for the revenue will be presented:

- Regardless whether present values or experience-based expectations are considered to be the more relevant category: 80%-90% of all participants have reported additional revenue due to the mySAP CRM deployment
- The overall mean average increase in revenue from mySAP CRM was slightly above 12% in the steady state and 5.8% at the time of the interview.

Of course, the range of increases in revenue has been widespread, as the following figure illustrates:

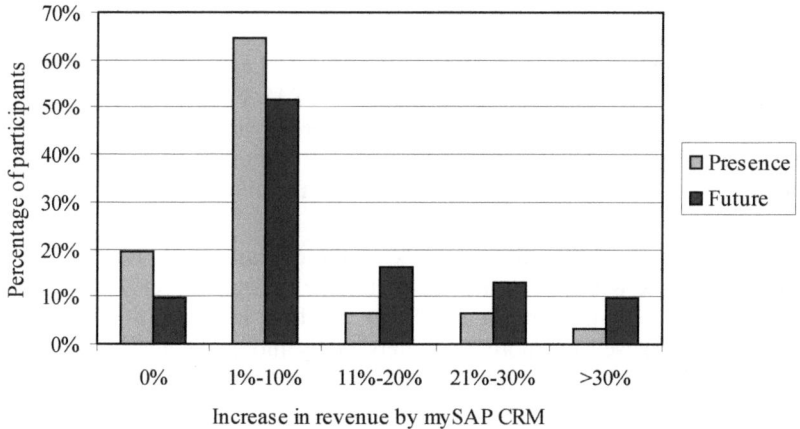

Figure 30: Distribution of increase in revenue

Although most improvements stayed below 10%, almost 10% of the users expect an increase above the 30% level.

Even more impressive than the increase in revenue is the ***value added by increased revenue***. As outlined before, two extreme results were calculated: one based on the increase in revenue and one rooted in the cost savings potential. For

2/3 of all participants, the revenue-based result was higher. Furthermore, participants that yielded a higher benefit on the cost side were on average less successful in the CRM deployment compared to those that had a higher result from revenue. The total sum of NPVs without terminal value based on revenue relates to the equivalent cost-based NPVs 80:20, that is, 80% of the entire value created for the participants in this study originates from an increase in revenue. That finding is supported by the fact that the average NPV based on revenue is at EUR 12.3 m, that is, more than twice the average cost-based NPV of EUR 5.5 m.

A *plausibility check on these figures relates the productivity increase to the enhanced revenue*. To recall: Overall time-weighted productivity increased by 8% (present) to 12% (steady state), revenue by 5.8% (present) and also 12% for the future. That means that the increase in revenue for the time since the productive use of CRM was disproportionate, in other words, participants needed to invest more sales capacity of equal quality for every Euro of increased sales. This is plausible, as sales get tougher in the short term: The law of decreasing returns is fully reflected in those numbers. Also, not all of the productivity gains can be transformed short term to worthwhile activities on the revenue side, as some personnel simply will not have the right skill. This finding also, of course, reflects the strained economic situation in the D-A-CH countries since 2001, that is, the time that the respondents have been using CRM. Finally it is plausible that the gap between productivity and revenue will narrow in the future as more and more of the short-term fixed parameters can be modified, such as, for example, the qualification of personnel and opportunities in the market.

After the overview and plausibility check on the overall results for the revenue impact of CRM, we will now turn to the results by revenue driver. Following the branches of the logic-tree in Figure 29 to the first junction, the increase in revenue may be caused by more customers or by more revenue per customer. First, the additional revenue through an *increased number of customers* is investigated. If the extra-revenue from additional customers is related to the total extra-revenue which was attributed to the mySAP CRM introduction on the basis of participant by participant, the median is at 21% whereas the mean average is 38.5%. That means that the average user gained 38.5% of all extra revenue from additional customers. Nonetheless, in this particular case, the mean average is not a good proxy for the effect that users can expect from using CRM. That is due to the interestingly polar distribution of values which is immediately visible in Figure 31:

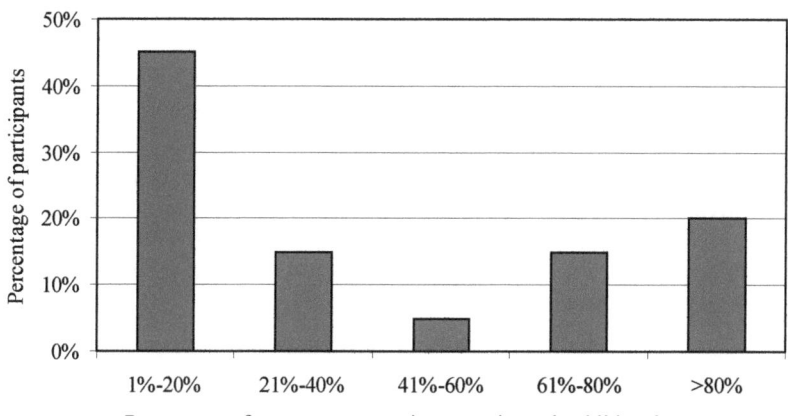

Figure 31: Distribution of the share of revenue increase through additional customers

Additional customers either play only a marginal role – or they are the major source of additional revenue. Especially IT service provider score high in this category which is due to the nature of their business: Every "order" resembles the acquisition of a new customer, no matter if it stems from a company which has been previously served. While therefore "new customers" are key, the order does not significantly rise in volume through CRM, as it is based on a solution for a problem and that problem is unaffected by the quality of the customer relationship. Besides the IT service providers, a great diversity of sectors can be found among the top third of participants in this category.

The values in Figure 31 are not weighted with the total amount of revenue involved. So even if a small participant has seen 80% of extra-revenue coming from additional customers, this may be only a marginal amount compared to a large participant that has only received 20% of its extra revenue from additional customers. Weighting these figures with the total amount of revenue added, it turns out the additional customers contributed 26% to the overall surplus in revenue in the study. This figure does not distinguish between newly acquired or retained customers. As Figure 29 illustrates, the other source of additional revenue, that is, the increase in revenue per customer, must have contributed 74% to make the two possibilities add up to 100%. Whilst overall the additional customers are therefore less important than the additional revenue per customer, the decision maker on CRM needs to keep in mind that additional customers can be the major source of extra-revenue for a CRM user.

Results – Revenue Targets

Moving on in the logic-tree to the next junction, ***the relationship between the newly acquired customers and the retained customers*** needs to be assessed. The following data has been generated from the study:

- 54% of all participants have increased the number of customers through the deployment of CRM. Thereof, 53% report gaining new customers, 83% have reduced customer churn, and 37% experienced both effects. So the number of companies retaining existing customers far outweighs those that acquire new customers.
- The number of additional customers via lower customer churn was three times the number of new customers.
- Revenue via new customers constitutes only 22% of all the revenue by additional customers while reduced customer churn is the origin of 78% of this revenue.

From all these observations it can be safely concluded that customer retention is by far more important than gaining new customers. This also confirms the majority of CRM experts when they locate the value of CRM on the side of an intensified customer relationship instead of new customer acquisition. Supporting empirical evidence is found in an Information Week survey stating that 93% of participants had seen customer loyalty as the main driver of value justifying their CRM investment[108]. A KPMG-survey on "One-to-one Marketing in Electronic Commerce" comes to the very same conclusion[109].

Moving to the lower branch in the logic-tree of Figure 29, the ***increase of revenue per customer*** contributes 74% to the overall extra-revenue. 80% of all participants have experienced higher revenue per customer. Among these participants, the share of revenue through more revenue per customer is distributed exactly opposite to the share of revenue through more customers in Figure 31, as the two distributions add up to 100%. So we find a normal distribution with very few customers reaping above 80% of added revenue – and again few that get less than 20% from higher revenue per customer. So while extra revenue through CRM because of an increase in the number of customers has a polar profile of "either-or", almost every participant reported higher revenue per customer on a significant level.

---

[108] Cited by Dyché (2002) p.6 ff.
[109] Cited by Stojek/Ulbrich (2001) p.195

Results – Revenue Targets

Again, we follow the branches of the logic-tree to the second junction of the lower branch: The revenue surplus per customer can be split up into an increased quantity of goods sold or a higher price:

- At the time of the interview, 20% of all participants saw an increase in prices at an average of 5% while 40% increased the number of goods sold through using CRM.
- In the steady state, almost 30% of all participants will have seen an average price improvement of 7% whereas 80% sell more products or services per customer.

These numbers are also reflected in the contribution to extra revenue. The 74% of extra revenue that originates from more revenue per customer can be divided as follows: 10 percentage-points are due to higher prices, 64 percentage-points result from higher quantities of goods sold to the existing customers.

The diagram below sums up the overall revenue increase in the study divided into the principal revenue drivers:

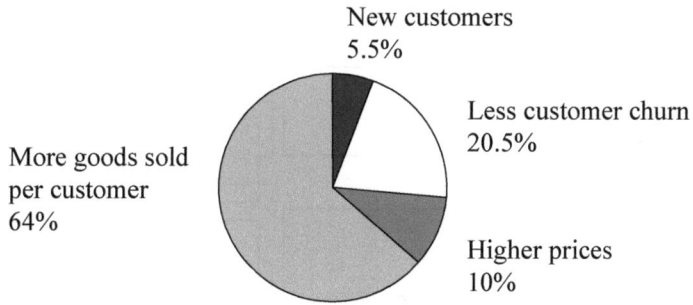

Figure 32: Distribution of sources of additional revenue through CRM

Key findings about the increase in revenue read as follows:
- The deployment of mySAP CRM in the study has increased revenue by 12% in the steady state and 5.8% at the time of interview
- 80% of all participants have experienced an increase in revenue so far, while 90% expect to see more revenue through CRM in the future
- 24% of the additional revenue originate from additional customers, thereof 5.5% from newly acquired ones and 20.5% from retained customers

Results – Revenue Targets

- 76% of the additional revenue result from increased revenue per customer, thereof 10% from higher prices and 64% from more goods sold

After giving an overview of the increase in revenue and its principal sources, the different revenue drivers will now be analyzed in more detail in the following chapters.

3.4.2 New customer acquisition: Leads

The first driver of revenue impacted by CRM is the acquisition of new customers. This has been shown above to be the smallest of all levers – nonetheless important for a number of participants. To follow the research design of a step-by-step build-up of cause and effect, first the causal chain is explained which summarizes the main interdependencies evidenced in the study:

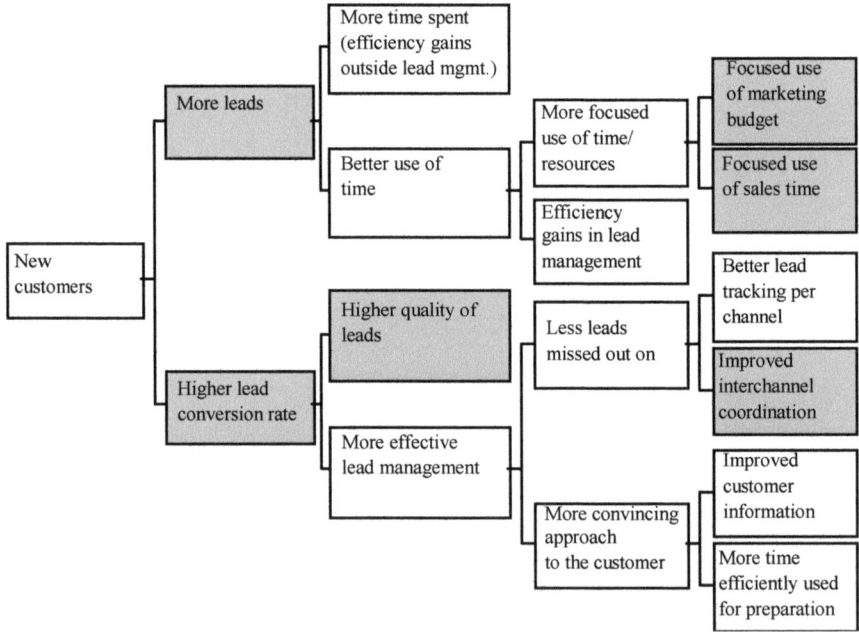

Figure 33: Causal chain: New customers (via lead process) through CRM (shaded parameters explicitly assessed in the questionnaire)

There is a multitude of ways by which a company can gain new customers. Customers can approach the company, triggered by market communication or word-of-mouth. Some companies have a rather simple sales approach of calling or visiting prospective customers at a very high rate. And sales can follow a lead process, the approach that benefits most from CRM support. Except for a very few participants, lead processes had been established before the mySAP CRM project – or shortly after, so it also has the greatest empirical relevance. All of the simple approaches can also be considered as a simplification of the more general lead process. Therefore Figure 33 structures the lead process that will be in focus for the remainder of the chapter.

A "lead" is one of the terms used with utmost diversity in practice. These were the two most frequently witnessed interpretations:

- A lead is a (prospective) sales opportunity, that is, regardless of whether it is a former or a current customer who has voiced an interest in one of the company's goods or services, this opportunity is referred to as a lead[110]
- A lead is a new, prospective customer that has not been a customer before (at least not for a long time)

Literature supports the first version, however, only few respondents – mainly from the IT service sector – used the term correctly in the sense of the first version. Therefore, the second version of "lead" is used in this research project. Another term that is frequently used synonymously with "leads" is "opportunity". Then again, "leads" and "opportunities" are defined as two consecutive stages in the development of a customer from attraction through to interest and then desire to action, that is, the purchasing of the good or service[111]. In this more refined use of terminology, leads are potential customers at the stage of interest. As an "opportunity" they reach the level of desire, and are handed over from marketing to sales. This refined distinction has also not been followed here for the simple reason that very few users were familiar with the concept.

If leads are defined as above, new customers can be the result of more leads or a higher lead conversion rate – which describes the first junction in the logic-tree of Figure 33. These alternatives are then mutually exclusive and collectively exhaustive. In order to systematically measure the impact of CRM on the generation and conversion of leads, a model of the lead process is needed. In this study, a simple model of a lead process has been deployed: Leads are generated

---

[110] Kotler (2000) p.657 f. avoids the term altogether and talks about "prospects" by which he denotes a sales opportunity; Hauke/Schuh (2003) p.25 ff. consider the lead to be the early stage of a sales opportunity
[111] Hauke/Schuh (2003) p. 50ff.; for the AIDA response hierarchy model Kotler (2000) p.554 ff.

Results – Revenue Targets

by either marketing, sales, or service, then handed over and "transformed" into customers by either sales or the Interaction Center. As there are just not enough observations of CRM support in service in the sample, only marketing, sales, and the Interaction Center were analyzed and indeed, the number of leads generated as well as the lead conversion rate have changed under the influence of mySAP CRM as the following figure illustrates:

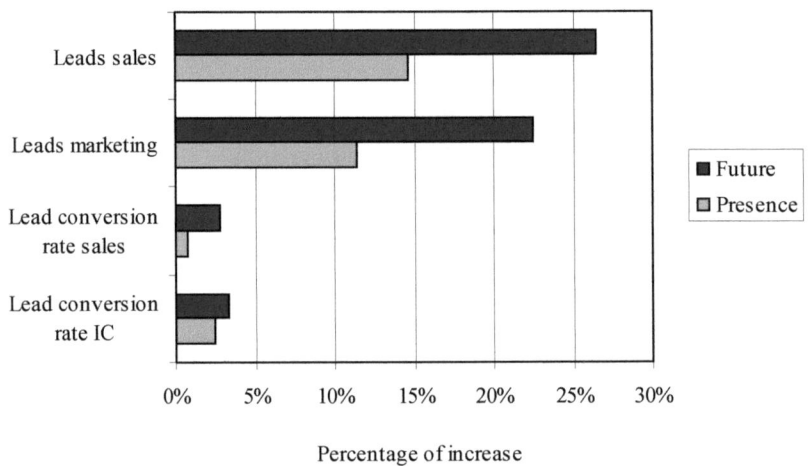

Figure 34: Mean average increase in the number of leads generated and the lead conversion rate in sales, marketing, and the Interaction Center

By far the most support through using mySAP CRM has been evidenced in the **number of leads generated** whereas the conversion rate was hardly impacted at all. In sales, almost 70% of all 19 respondents that answered this question had experienced a positive impact. If only these respondents were considered, the mean average increase would even be above 35%. There are four top scoring participants from a variety of different sectors above 40% - and up to 180%. They all reported very poor lead management processes before the introduction of mySAP CRM. The figures are on the conservative side, as all of the participants who did not have a lead process before CRM are not contained in these numbers: Here, a before-and-after comparison does not make sense on a percentage change basis.

In marketing, the results concerning the generation of leads are similar compared to sales – except for the number of positive experiences. Only four participants managed to raise the number of leads in marketing with the support of CRM at the time of the interview – and seven expected a positive impact for the steady state based on the observed changes at the time of the interview. This results in a success rate of 35%-50%, so in the present, a third of all answers regarding this question have been positive.

It is also interesting to observe that the ***gap between the steady state and the time of the interview*** is rather large in relation to the productivity figures from Chapter 3.3: The increase in the number of sales leads outright doubles until the steady state. This confirms the hypothesis discussed in the context of the companies' project targets in Chapter 3.1: First, internal processes need to be changed, then the customer interaction yields better results. The more automated the process, the less time is needed. Consequently, the gap between present and future results is much smaller in the highly automated Interaction Center compared to the sales or marketing functions.

Contrary to the number of leads, the ***increase in the lead conversion rate*** is insignificant, regardless of whether sales or the Interaction Center are concerned. Only about a quarter of all participants that answered this question expect an improvement – and even for the future, the magnitude is marginal. That is surprising, as a number of CRM effects potentially drive the lead conversion rate – and as the results will show, the root parameters are a lot stronger than the result. A respondent who got his figures from sales gave another potential explanation. He assumed: "A sales person can easily confirm that CRM helps to generate more leads – but he has a hard time admitting that it increases the success rate which he believes is due to his own skills in selling". As most answers in this category relied on assessments from sales or sales support, the numbers may well be too low if this hypothesis should prove right.

Following the branches of the logic tree in Figure 33, an increase in the number of leads can be caused by more time spent on lead generation and/or by a better use of the time. The better use of time may again result from an ***improved efficiency in the lead management process*** itself or from a more effective use of time. All of the efficiency aspects have already been covered in the context of an enhanced productivity. These productivity improvements can be "reinvested" to, for example, simply follow-up on more customers than before. As a reminder: Lead management productivity was improved by 10% in marketing and 24% in sales at the time of the interview, supported by 70% of respondents in this category. So the efficiency gains alone would already suffice to explain the increase in the number of leads.

Besides the efficiency boost, however, ***effectiveness in the use of time*** has improved by more focus. This is driven by a more focused use of the marketing budget, as well as by focusing more on allocating sales time to the key customer segments. All of these value drivers have been positively impacted by mySAP CRM as illustrated by the next figure, which also already contains parameters that potentially improve the lead conversion rate:

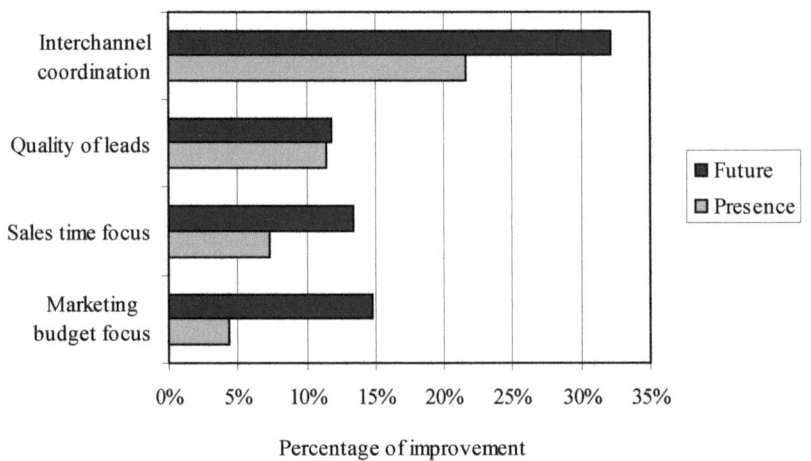

Figure 35: Improvements of influencing factors driving new customer acquisition (mean average percentage of change)

At the time of the interview, 10 out of 23 respondents to this category had raised the portion of sales time allocated to A- and B-customers; the mean average improvement across all 23 participants has turned out to be 7%. This increase was expected to have doubled upon reaching steady state. Also, in the marketing budget funds are already more focused on A- and B-customers than before – with an even bigger future potential. Nonetheless, the efficiency gains – as cited above – are far greater. Therefore, the main driver of the significant increase in leads has been and will be efficiency – not the effectiveness of a more focused time allocation. In other words, CRM on average supports sales staff to spend more time on lead management and to spend less time per lead, but for the participants in this study, focus did not make the difference. Another observation points in the same direction. The question of an increase in quality of market communication leading to, for example, a higher recollection of the goods or services on offer, has been confirmed by one participant only.

Moving to the second branch – the increase in the lead conversion rate – the quality of leads has to be explored as well as interchannel coordination. All the other parameters outlined in this branch in Figure 33 have already been analyzed and discussed above. ***Interchannel coordination*** refers to the alignment between marketing, sales, service, and so on, but also between field force and sales support as well as between different (international) sales teams, and of course, the coordination between the CRM functions of the company and the business partners. Coordination among these channels is regularly cited as one possible positive effect of CRM – and this assertion is confirmed by the study's results. 23 participants have reduced the frequency of interchannel friction, misunderstandings, incorrect or belated information, double work, omissions, and so on, by an average of 32% by the time of the interview and almost 40% in the steady state. The mean average across all participants is 20% and above 30% respectively. There is strong support for this effect across the respondents:

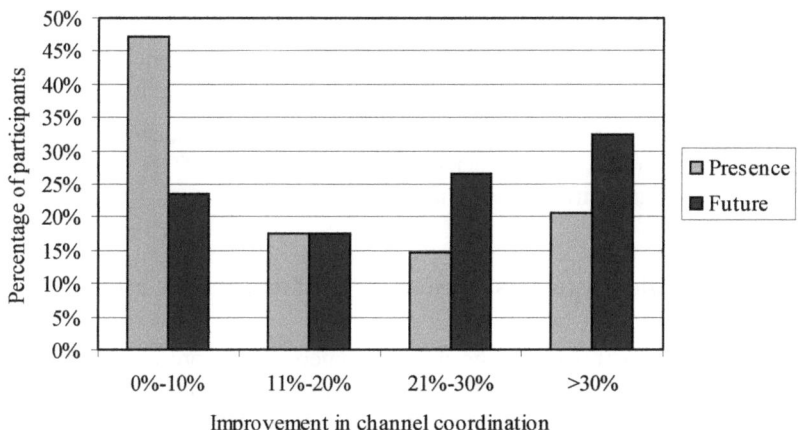

Figure 36: Improvements in channel coordination (percentage of reduction in channel friction)

A third of all participants expect an improvement beyond 30% in the steady state and out of the 46% in category "0%-10%", only half marked no effect. So about ¾ of all participants already had a positive impact in this respect at the time of the interview. Together with the fact that leads are more thoroughly tracked, less leads are missed out on. This was also confirmed again and again by respondents' remarks. The more convincing approach to the customer described above, combined with less leads missed out on can be described as a more effective lead management as Figure 33 does. Finally, even the *quality of leads* generated had improved, although only by a mean average of 10%. This parameter was operationalized as the number of leads mistakenly added to the lead list. Only 11 participants were able to provide an observation-based assessment; of these, half stated a positive effect.

Summing up the findings concerning the attraction of new customers:
- An increase in new customers has been attained predominantly through a 10%-15% increase in leads generated (beyond 25% for the steady state). This in turn was largely driven by higher efficiency in the lead management (24% in sales), and more focus on sales time allocation to A- and B-customers and by a more focused spending in the marketing budget (both below 5%)
- Besides the quantity of leads, their quality had improved by a mean average of 10%
- The numbers from this study show the lead conversion rate largely unaffected by CRM; measurement problems may however be the cause
- Friction in channel coordination had already been reduced by 20% at the time of the interview, expected to rise to 30%. ¾ of all respondents had experienced a positive impact in that category.

3.4.3 "New" Old Customers: Customer Satisfaction and Customer Retention

Additional customers need not be new customers. The more important aspect is to keep the existing customers. This point is stressed fervently in CRM literature and has been proven right in Chapter 3.4.1. Often, proof resorts to quantified business dynamics models. Even without those models, non-linear effects come into play as customer loyalty yields not only a one-time return – but benefits that accumulate over time. This explains the importance of this source of additional revenue in this study.

As for the new customers, a logic tree of cause-and-effect is displayed below as a blueprint of the revenue effects for this section:

Results – Revenue Targets

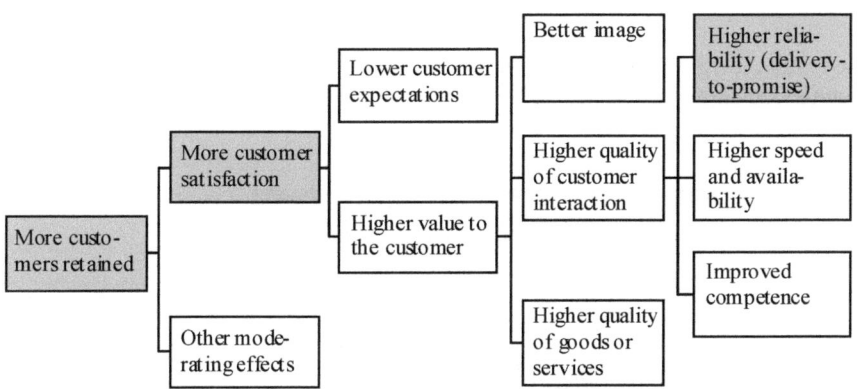

*Figure 37: Causal chain: Reduced customer churn through CRM
(shaded parameters explicitly assessed in the questionnaire)*

"The key to customer retention is customer satisfaction"[112]. Other effects have an influence on the strength of the link between satisfaction and retention, such as, the level of competition[113]. But as these "moderating factors" are not directly influenced by CRM, they have not been investigated in this study. So the focus is on customer satisfaction, which is defined by the difference between customer expectations and the customer's perception of value. As customer expectations will be barely influenced by CRM, customer value comes into focus. Customer value results from the quality of the good or service, the quality of customer interaction, and the image[114]. The quality of customer interaction[115] again depends on the staff's competence and the reliability and speed of reacting to a customer's request. Indeed, competence in terms of better customer information has already been proven as a result of the CRM deployment in Chapter 3.3.1; a higher speed will be covered in Chapter 3.5. Thus only three concepts were to be investigated and are discussed here:

- Customer retention
- Customer satisfaction
- Reliability, a component of the quality of customer interaction

---

[112] Kotler (2000) p.48; reconfirmed in the context of the Internet Economy by Reichheld/Schefter (2000); in the context of Internet Marketing by Bauer/Grether/Leach (2002) p.159
[113] Giering (2000) on "moderating factors" influencing the relationship between customer loyalty and customer satisfaction
[114] Kotler (2000) p.35 on the model of customer delivered value refers to "customer interaction" as the "personnel value" – but the contents is identical
[115] The "quality of interaction" that is used here needs to be distinguished from the far broader concept of "quality of relationships" as conceptualized by Naudé/Buttle (2000) p.351-355

The results for the first two parameters indicate that indeed the participants have experienced significantly positive effects:

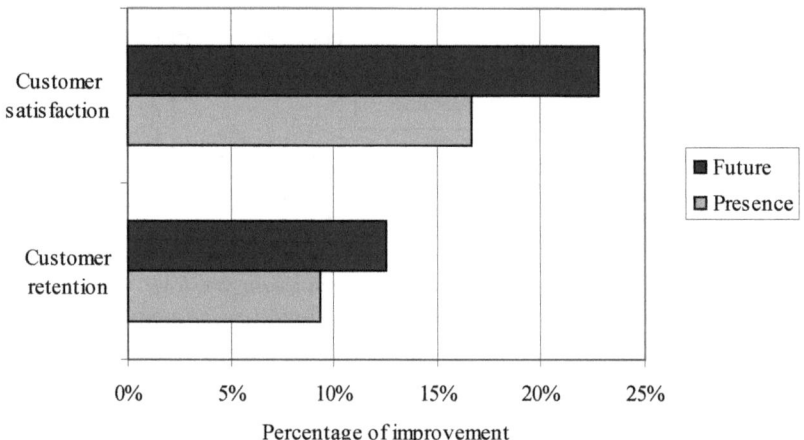

Figure 38: Mean average improvement of customer satisfaction and retention

Customer satisfaction has risen on average by almost 17% while it is expected to grow by above 20% until steady state is reached. Of the 26 respondents in that category, 70% had experienced a positive effect by the time of the interview and a record 85% expected a positive effect at steady state. The mean average of all the positive answers is 25% for the experiences so far and 27% for the future. The basis for these impressive numbers was either concrete measurements of customer satisfaction, or at least a structured form of customer feedback that could be built upon. In 10 cases, neither alternative applied, and so the answer was left blank in the questionnaire. While more than half of the respondents measured customer satisfaction, only a few had measurements that were indicative of the effect of CRM. Some had measured satisfaction up to two years before the CRM introduction – and the next observation was a long time after going live: It was therefore impossible to filter out the impact of CRM. Others changed the service provider that conducted the customer satisfaction survey – and thereby also changed the measurement approach, which again rendered the data incomparable. So most of the 26 answers were based on feedback from customers, aggregated to one number by the respondent. To this end, he or she was asked to position the customer satisfaction on a scale of 1-5 before – and to judge from the feedback where the customer would score now. Then the improvement was calculated from these two points of data.

Satisfaction and retention show a very different profile when it comes to the distribution of values among participants, even in the steady state, that is, regardless of the speed of development:

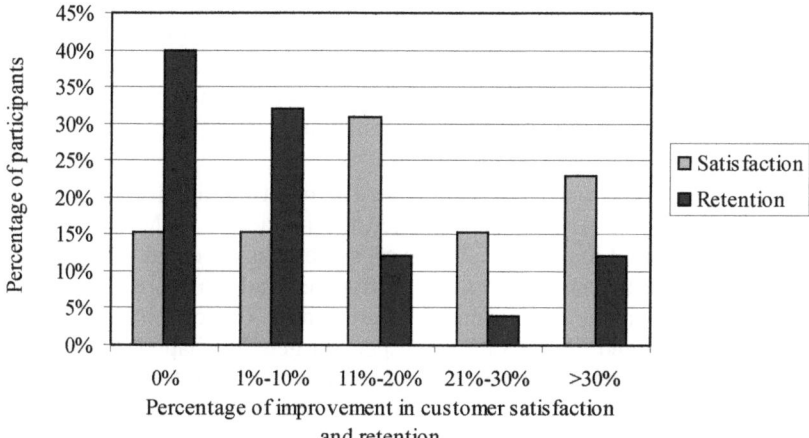

Figure 39: Distribution of increases in customer satisfaction and customer retention among participants (steady state values)

An increase in customer satisfaction is a widely-observed phenomenon with an almost uniform distribution across the different levels of change whereas customer retention is only experienced and expected by fewer participants – and only by very few respondents to a high degree. This distribution of scores for the **customer retention** from Figure 39 underpins the lower mean averages shown in Figure 38. A lower impact on retention also was to be expected, because satisfaction drives retention, and on the way, some will get lost. Although the increase in retention is lower than satisfaction, still 60% expect a positive impact in this respect – and 48% had already experienced a reduction in customer churn at the time of interview. Taking the mean average of only the positive answers at 20%, it means that year after year, 20% of all customers that would otherwise leave, stay with the company as a result of deploying CRM. Viewed from this perspective, the high impact on revenue shown in Chapter 3.4.1 is easily understandable. Participants verify that even minor changes in a customer relationship have major repercussions, especially for companies operating in a tight market where losing customers has dire financial consequences.

Results – Revenue Targets

As to the drivers of customer satisfaction according to Figure 37, abundant anecdotal evidence was collected, though not statistically relevant data. Although it was hypothesized that *image* was not affected by CRM, five respondents had image-driven targets like "we needed CRM to make us look more modern" or "CRM was needed for the e-shop that was requested by our customers". One respondent measures success of the CRM project (among other observations) by stating that "the customer press-coverage was enormous". One may think that image is the wrong reason to implement CRM – but it could potentially even yield a return through improved customer satisfaction.

The ***quality of the product itself*** was indeed explicitly excluded by the vast majority of participants when they explained the impact of CRM on customer satisfaction. A potential impact was, however, sometimes expected for the steady state, as more in-depth knowledge about customers leads to more focused and forward-looking product development efforts, and consequently to better products – as mentioned in the context of speed targets in Chapter 3.5. Such an effect has been reported as statistically significant by Li and Calatone, when analyzing the impact of customer and market knowledge on new product development from 236 software companies in the US[116].

The third factor influencing the value to the customer, ***quality of customer interaction***, was also not measured directly in the questionnaire. However the factors driving the quality of customer interaction have been measured:

- ***Improved competence*** has already been outlined in the context of better customer information in Chapter 3.3.1.

- An ***increase in availability*** was noted primarily by those participants that deployed the Internet sales or Interaction Center functions: an increase in availability of service for customers of over 50% on average with peak values beyond 80%. Furthermore, the productivity increase in the marketing, sales, and service functions can, of course, be used to increase the speed of information and transaction processes[117]. And, indeed, constant availability of information and efficient information transfer have been confirmed in other empirical research to have a significant positive impact on customer commitment[118].

---

[116] Li/Calatone (1998) p.24 ff.
[117] This is the third alternative for the use of productivity gains in the CRM Value Metric (Chapter 2.2.2) which will be outlined in more detail in Chapter 3.5. (for example the shorter time-to-volume is relevant in this respect)
[118] Bauer/Grether/Leach (2000) p.159 f.

- Finally, the customer interaction not only needs to be good and fast – it also needs to be reliable. Reliability was measured by *delivery-to-promise,* a measurement that denotes the portion of all deliveries on time with 100% quality (right products, no damage). This ratio relates the fulfillment to the promised and therefore expected products or services. As customer satisfaction has been defined as the difference between the expectation and fulfillment, the impact of delivery-to-promise on customer satisfaction is obvious. Delivery-to-promise has been investigated in the interviews and about 1/3 of all respondents that answered this question saw a positive impact of CRM. So supported by the CRM deployment, the delivery-to-promise ratio had already risen a mean average of 19% at the time of the interview, and that increase was expected to climb up to 24% in the steady state.

To conclude the mySAP CRM impact on customer retention:
- Customer retention – responsible for 20.5% of the entire revenue increase witnessed in the study – has risen by roughly 10%, and is expected to end at a plus of 12% in the steady state
- The main driver, customer satisfaction, has increased by 15% by the time of the interview (expected to end between 20% and 25%)
- Customer satisfaction is positively impacted by a higher customer value through a better image, mid- to long-term better, more customer driven products, and especially by an improved quality of customer interaction.
- The quality of customer interaction has been driven by higher competence, speed of processes and availability of information, as well as more reliability, which has been measured by a rise of the delivery-to-promise ratio of an average 19% (and 24% expected for the future).

3.4.4 Increase in Goods Sold: Larger Quantities and Cross Sales

Since additional sales to existing customers are by far the dominant revenue driver, contributing 64% of all extra-revenue witnessed in the study, it pays to take a closer look – again by analyzing the structure of cause and effect.

The principal distinction is made between the customer buying more of the regular product spectrum he is used to – or his choosing products that are new to him, which is referred to as cross selling. It should be noted that cross selling does not require "new products" in a sense that they need to be new to the market or new to the company. The following impact of CRM on the two sources of extra revenue has been recorded:

- For 12 out of 32 respondents, cross-sales have risen by close to an average of 10% - and that corresponds exactly to the figure that 18 of the 32 expected for the steady state
- Regular sales have increased by "only" 5% on average by the time of the interview for 14 participants, but they have the potential to grow to an average increase of 7% for 19 respondents in the future

These results seem to imply that cross sales should be more important to users of CRM than the increase in regular sales. However, the percentages reported above are not yet weighted by the absolute amount of revenue in question. The overall 64% added revenue by more goods sold split up into the two sources of revenue as

- 18% for cross-sales
- 46% for revenue from the regular product scope.

So whereas "cross-selling is all the rage nowadays"[119] and literature stresses the strong impact of CRM on increasing cross-sales, the CRM decision maker should normally focus on improving the regular sales as they turn out to be the more important lever for extra revenue. It has to be admitted, however, that this general rule does not always apply. For example, in situations when the CRM deploying company is already a customer's preferred provider or even his single source, the only possibility to expand sales with this customer is to focus on cross-selling.

As the next step, the plausibility of these figures is to be checked by analyzing the CRM effect on the drivers of cross-sales and additional regular sales. This also enables us to understand how to influence these two sources of revenue through CRM. Therefore, a logic tree is presented in Figure 40, outlining the cause-and-effect chain with respect to higher sales:

---

[119] Dyché (2002) p.31

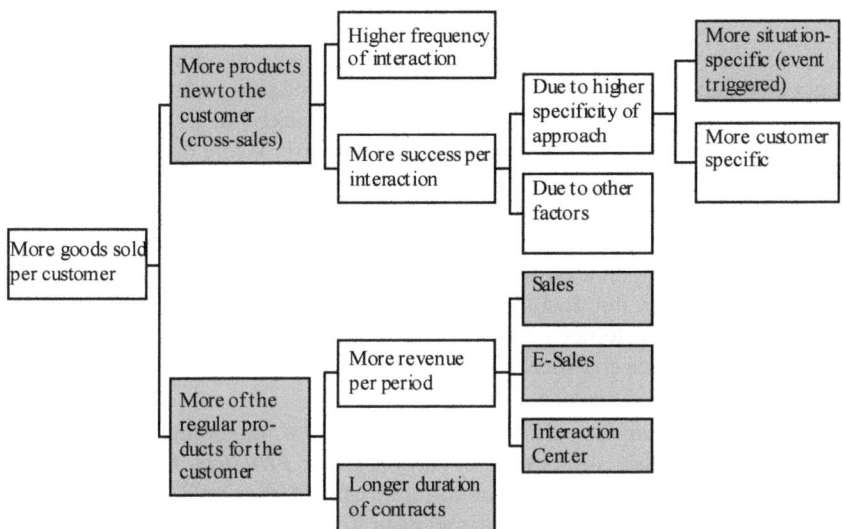

Figure 40: Causal chain: Increased quantity of goods sold per customer (shaded parameters assessed in the questionnaire)

To **cross-sell** systematically to a customer, one can either see the customer more often, or each customer interaction can be more persuasive. A higher frequency of customer visits is of course possible through higher efficiency of the entire sales process as outlined in Chapter 3.3.3. However, the potential to increase cross-sales this way has been confirmed by respondents to be small, because the "airtime" for the sales representative – especially with respect to unusual proposals – is normally limited. So the focus should be on the quality of interaction which may rise due to higher specificity or other factors, such as sales skills, the right timing, and so on, which are hardly influenced by CRM. Therefore only the specificity has been further investigated in more detail. The sales approach can be more specific to the customer or to the situation he is in. The improvement of customer information as outlined in Chapter 3.3.1 already provides evidence for a more customer specific preparation of customer interactions. So the ability to identify "gaps" in the way customers exploit the range of products and services offered opens up more potential, which can result in more-targeted sales communication.

This leaves the question open, as to which extent a more situation-specific selling through CRM has improved the specificity of the sales approach. Maybe the purest form of situation specific customer interaction is an **event-triggered customer contact**. So when, for example, a pop star comes to town, the local music store may send a targeted push e-mail to all who purchased a CD of this category of music before (and who have given permission to be contacted upon such events). This way, the music store cross-sells tickets to CD customers who may otherwise not have been aware of the opportunity. While only about 40% of the 17 respondents to this question saw an impact of CRM on the frequency of event-triggered customer contacts, they experienced an impressive almost 20% increase in this type of customer interactions. Of those who saw no impact, many considered event-triggered customer contacts as unattractive, as "unethical push marketing", or simply not doable in their respective industry sector and specialty. So event-triggered customer interaction does not apply to all – but if it applies, CRM helps to produce significant improvements.

By reinvesting freed-up sales capacity into more or better sales pitches, participants have also sold *more of the regular products to their regular customers*. Again, two effects can be differentiated: Either each customer spends more per period – or the duration for each contract increases, provided that revenue is related to time and given that the regular influx of new customers remains at the same level. The hypothesis was that service providers would see longer running contracts due to an increased customer satisfaction and customer loyalty, and that other companies could have longer running outline agreements which are then executed step-by-step via sales orders. Ultimately, neither the service hypothesis nor the one on outline agreements was supported by the evidence. Not a single respondent had seen any change in the *duration of contracts*. All of the effect recorded in this branch of the logic-tree is therefore due to an increase in the revenue per period of time.

The extra-revenue has been analyzed by channel, that is sales, Internet sales, and the Interaction Center. Marketing and service were not thought to directly generate revenue. Only a single participant had experienced extra-revenue via *Internet sales*; all other respondents only used the channel as a convenient and cost-efficient order management tool without any extra-revenue – neither in the present nor as an expectation for the future. Although this result may be surprising if contrasted with hyped Internet expectations, it is fully consistent with research by Avlonitis and Karayanni[120]. Also Leek et. al. find that "IT is still being used by companies to automate what they currently do, rather than to do new things"[121]. This aspect of order process automation via B2B Internet sales has already been described in Chapter 3.3.5.

---

[120] Avlonitis/Karayanni (2000) analyzing benefits of internet use of 130 US and European industrial businesses; for the conclusion mentioned, check p.456
[121] Leek/Turnbull/Naudé (2003) p.122

By contrast, the ***Interaction Center*** has indeed seen some significant increase in revenue on the basis of CRM, although far less than the productivity increase. But here too, the extra revenue was cannibalized to a large extent from sales. The causal chain for extra-revenue in the IC, which should be seen as an extension to Figure 40, has been conceptualized as follows:

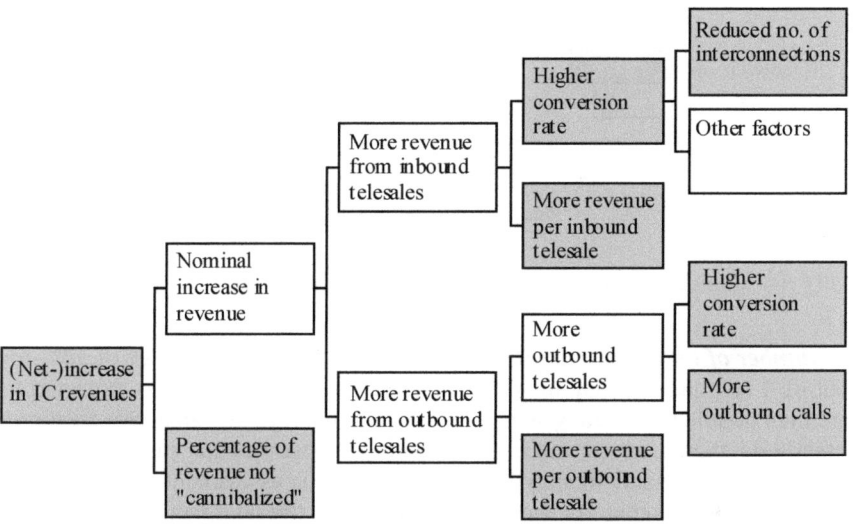

Figure 41: Causal chain: Extra revenue from the Interaction Center (shaded parameters assessed in the questionnaire and in this chapter)

Only a ***net increase in revenue*** from the Interaction Center is of interest; therefore the nominal increase in revenue needs to be multiplied by the percentage of revenue which has not been cannibalized from the other channels, namely from sales. The next steps in the logic tree are straight forward: Additional revenue may only come from in- or outbound telesales, and for each branch, the extra-revenue results from either more revenue per transaction or a higher number of transactions. Surprisingly, only one single respondent had additional revenue beyond the rechanneled ones, and even for the future, one single participant with expectations of additional revenue remained. To analyze potential causes for this result, the revenue drivers in the logic-tree of Figure 41 have been analyzed to come up with the following findings:

Results – Revenue Targets

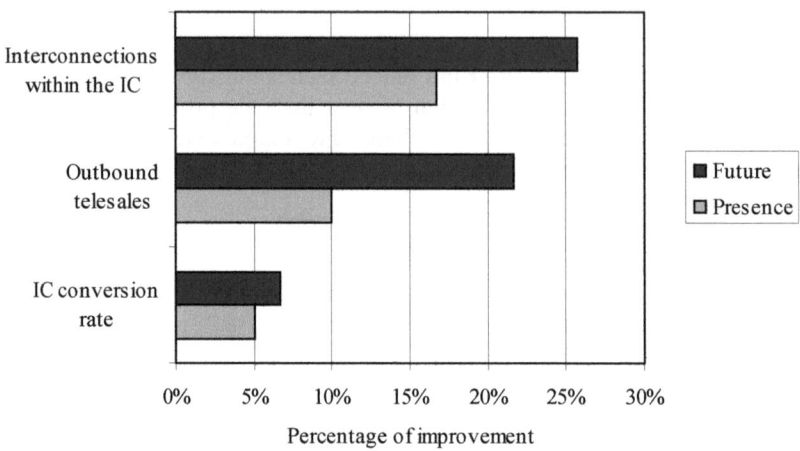

Figure 42: Change of revenue drivers in the IC through CRM

The **number of outbound telesales** calls has increased by an average of 10% for 4 out of 4 respondents that answered this question. This number is expected to more than double until steady state. As outbound telesales are an active customer contact, one should expect more net revenue increase but that just was not the case. Possible explanations may be the very cautious assessment of this hard to test figure "extra-revenue" or the fact, that outbound telesales were only used in a B2B environment as a substitute for former sales visits – thereby reducing cost but not leading to extra-revenue.

With respect to the **telesales conversion rate**, 50% of all respondents providing information on that question saw on average a marginal 5% increase. Again, this number is disappointing, given the claim that a CRM-supported call center agent should be able to convince a customer more easily to buy more or more expensive products (up-sales). Again, this may be due to the specific B2B-environment, where ordering depends on a often complex buying center decision and where rational choice based on a current demand is more likely to happen than in the B2C arena. So the targeted offer in the telesales phone discussion does not lead easily to additional sales. Furthermore, two Interaction Centers (ICs) were only open to branches of the own company or to resellers, a very narrow market environment. Furthermore, it should be borne in mind that the basis for this evidence is rather slim and therefore none of these results is representative of the entirety of CRM deployments in interaction centers.

The strongest confirmed effect has been a *reduction of interconnections* within the call center: So if a customer calls, he would now get a full answer from one CRM-supported agent without having to repeat himself as he is being handed over to other levels of the call center. The number of such interconnections has been reduced by more than 15% and is expected to be reduced by more than 25% in the future. The main driver behind this rate of improvement is the fact that now every call center agent has access to the customer data as well as better information about the specific product configurations. The result of this "soft factor" is a higher customer satisfaction, which in turn may then influence the likelihood that the customer will close the deal.

As Internet sales have not contributed to the overall increase in revenue, and the IC has only marginally improved the situation, *almost all increases are due to more sales per customer through the sales force*. That also corresponds to the fact that in the study sample most participants by far used the Mobile Sales module of mySAP CRM. An increased "share of the customer wallet" in the regular product scope may be due to the same effects that were already analyzed with respect to cross-sales: more sales visits or a more effective sales approach.

To summarize key findings on extra-revenue from more goods sold:
- The 64% of the entire extra revenue, which comes from more goods sold, is divided into 18% from cross-sales and 46% from more sales in the regular product spectrum
- Cross-sales have, however, seen the higher percentage of impact from CRM of about a 10% increase, mainly driven by a more customer-specific sales approach, as well as 20% more in event-triggered customer interaction
- An increase in regular sales is due almost in its entirety to the sales force. The IC and Internet sales have only contributed marginally to an increase in net-revenue. While gross-revenue has been somewhat raised by a 10% increase in outbound calls and a 5% higher conversion rate, almost all revenue was suspected to be just purchases transferred over from sales. This finding may, nonetheless, be strongly influenced by the specific setting in which participants in the study deployed IC and Internet sales.

3.4.5 Higher Prices: Absolute and Relative Price Increases

The use of CRM may support increases in price. This has been frequently mentioned in literature and some case study evidence has been provided[122]. Here, we distinguish between an *absolute and relative price increase*. An absolute price increase means that the company has established strong customer ties so that even when the prices of goods or services are increased, customers do not reduce the order volume and do not defect. In contrast, a relative price increase denotes an increasing price delta relative to the competition. So if the competition is forced to lower its prices while the CRM user is able to withstand price pressure, the resulting difference between the new price level and the competition is, in part, due to CRM. If nothing had been changed but CRM, then the entire amount could be attributed to CRM. However, in most cases the influence of CRM had to be distinguished from other influencing changes in the company or in its environment. In order to assess the CRM impact, the question was asked: "To what extent would your price level be affected if you switched off CRM".

Absolute price increases as a result of mySAP CRM have not been confirmed – though the sluggish economic circumstances must always be borne in mind. This was also the no. 1 reason cited by respondents: At the time of the survey there was no room for price increases at all. Pharmaceutical and medical suppliers furthermore stressed the point that price increases will also be impossible in better times as legal barriers in D-A-CH would not allow for such a step in the medium term.

On the contrary, 20% of the participants have seen *relative price increases* of a mean average 5%: Due to cut-throat competition in a stagnant economy, direct competitors had to cut their prices by 10% – 30%, while participants' prices have remained constant or had to be reduced by a significantly lower margin. 28.6% of all participants expect relative price increases of 7% for the steady state. The main rationale put forth for these increases were similar to those for increases in quantity: higher customer satisfaction and loyalty, better and more targeted service, and so on. Another suspected driver of price potential by CRM has been confirmed by two participants only: a better segmentation of the market leading to a more distinguished understanding of the price sensitivity of different types of customers. Not a single user had experienced such an effect – and only two were concretely planning to carry out such an analysis in the future with very

---

[122] Rapp (2001) p.130 ff. argues the possibility of price increase through CRM and underpins his conclusion with case examples from Heinz Pet Food, EBay, Letsbuyit.com, and Ludwig Könemann publishing; the example of Miele is cited by Wehrmeister (2001) p.68

modest expectations as to the benefit of it. This once more reinforces a finding stated in the context of marketing: operative improvements, not the sophisticated analytics were at the heart of benefits so far. As the "low hanging fruit" may be picked soon, the analytical side may come into focus later.

While the overall increase in prices seems negligible, the ***contribution of price improvement to value added by CRM*** is very high. The seven participants that experienced price effects until the time of the interview enjoyed a median 3-year-CFROI of 112% (a mean average of 210%) compared to an equivalent figure of 48% (a mean average of 103%) for those companies that did not have price improvements. So companies that managed to raise relative prices supported by CRM had more than twice the CFROI relative to those without higher (relative) prices. To exclude the possibility of coincidence, the percentage of value added by the relative price increase has been computed: 75% of the entire added value for these companies originates from the price effect. This surprising effect can be explained by the fact that price increases do not create additional costs. So while the additional goods sold only create value by the EBITDA-margin, price changes impact the bottom line directly. Therefore, even small increases in relative prices of less than 1% happened to turn out as major value creators.

In conclusion:
- Deploying mySAP CRM has opened up potential for 20%-30% of participants to increase relative prices, that is, prices relative to the direct competitors by a mean average of 5% (expected to rise to 7% in the future)
- Participants who raised relative prices enjoyed more than twice the 3-y-CFROI on their CRM investment compared to those that did not; 75% of the value added for these participants was due to the price increase
- So despite marginal percentages of increase by CRM, price effects are a key driver not of revenue but of value added

3.5 Speed Targets: Time-to-Market, Time-to-Volume, and Time-to-Delivery

Productivity gains are measured in terms of volume of work (for example, man-months), and speed in terms of time elapsed (for example, months). The translation between the two is straight forward: If, for example, two sales representatives worked for 10 days to complete a complex proposal in the past, that is 20 man-days, CRM may help to reduce the volume of work to 10 man-days. If the two still work on the proposal and if there are no other reasons that require the full original time frame, the proposal will now be finished in 5 days. In this example, cost savings will only materialize in the future if one of the two is laid off – or an increase in revenue will result, as twice the amount of proposals will be written in the same amount of time. Therefore, as indicated in the CRM Value Metric, speed effects are dealt with as a third way to use productivity gains, which ultimately result in cost-savings or revenue-increasing effects for the future.

In principle, all processes can be speeded-up. Here, however, only four processes and their respective indicators were investigated in more detail:

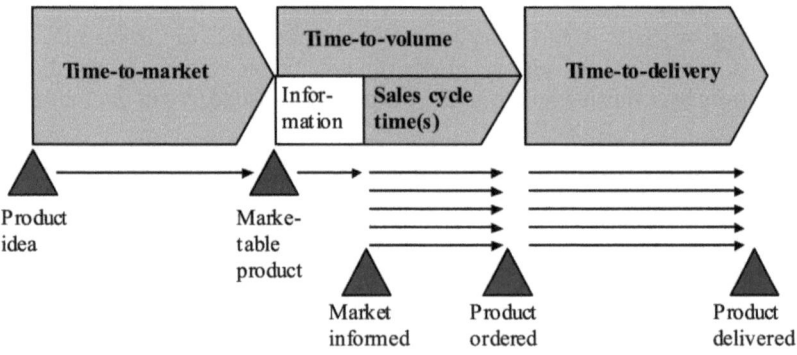

Figure 43: Speed target concepts and indicators

The new-product development process, that is, the time from the idea to the marketable product is measured by the time-to-market. The second step is the introduction of the product to the market. This starts with the information of the market about the new product. When all potential customers are informed, the sales force convinces a customer to order it. The time elapsed that is needed to complete a deal is called the sales cycle time. From the point in time of the customer order to the time of the order fulfillment is frequently referred to as the time to delivery.

25% to 40% of participants reported that they have saved time in one of the four areas, and 35% to 55% respectively expect such speed effects for the future. The average amount of time saved per process is depicted below in Figure 44:

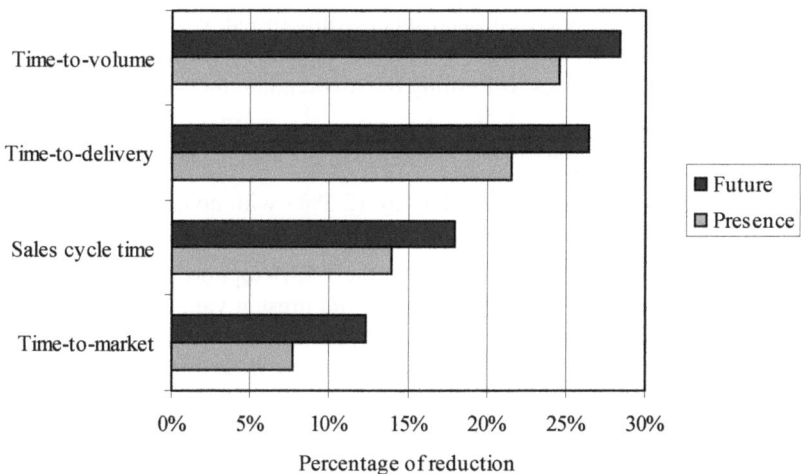

Figure 44: Acceleration of CRM processes as a result of mySAP CRM

Most participants have not yet reduced their ***time-to-market***. Other than most benefits of using IT in new product development[123], advantages through using CRM will not be felt in this process until companies have gathered sufficient information about their customers' preferences and motivation, and they are thus in a position to recognize trends more quickly and focus on the development of new products and services on actual customer requirements. As the average time of productive use for CRM was 14 months, these preconditions were not met in most cases. Nonetheless, seven participants had shortened their time-to-market by less than 10% and one respondent confirmed a 15% improvement. On the one hand, one participant explained an improvement in this category by a better

---

[123] For an overview of IT benefits in product development check Ozer (2000), who mentions increase in speed, productivity, collaboration, communication, coordination, decision quality, and consequently product quality among others

Results – Speed Targets

market insight leading to a more focused research and development approach. On the other hand, a better coordination among the different departments involved in the new product development process was seen as crucial for the success. The remarkable effect in his case was not so much the reduced time-to-market, but an improvement in the quality of the new products. Before CRM deployment, 50%-60% of all new products were among the 30 top-selling products, afterwards, above 90% were among the top sellers.

Once a new product or service has been successfully tested, it must be introduced to the market, a phase that is measured in terms of ***time-to-volume***. This time-to-volume consists of two phases: Informing the market, and the sales pitch:

- The sales cycle time was reduced by an average 12% at the time of the interview with an expected 16% reduction in the steady state.
- Informing the market has speeded up by 12.5% - with no difference between future and present values

This result is highly plausible. First of all, the CRM-support for informing the market quickly displays its potential as future and present values are identical. In comparison with the individual sale, it is the more technical process and therefore it is impacted directly and immediately by a technical CRM-system. The sales cycle, which requires a change in the behavior of the sales representatives and maybe even that of the customers, lags considerably and therefore sees a much higher future upside potential. Another observation that reinforces the plausibility of these results is the comparison of productivity gains and the increase in process speed. One major means of informing the market about new products are marketing campaigns, which experienced a productivity increase of 15% (present) to beyond 20% (future). As has been pointed out before, productivity gains may be reduced by reinvestment in speeding-up processes – and 15%-20% are fully consistent with a 12%-16% increase in speed. Finally, the sales processes of customer interaction and lead-/opportunity management dominate the sales cycle. Both have seen productivity gains of 13%-16% for the present and close to 25% in the future – again more than the sales cycle speed increase but still within a plausible range.

Of all the speed targets, time-to-volume and sales cycle reduction were the ones with the broadest base of experience: 40% of all respondents had already observed a reduction in the time-to-volume and 50% expected it to be positively impacted by CRM. While the range of improvement on the time-to-market was rather narrow, time-to-volume has a polar distribution, as illustrated below:

Results – Speed Targets

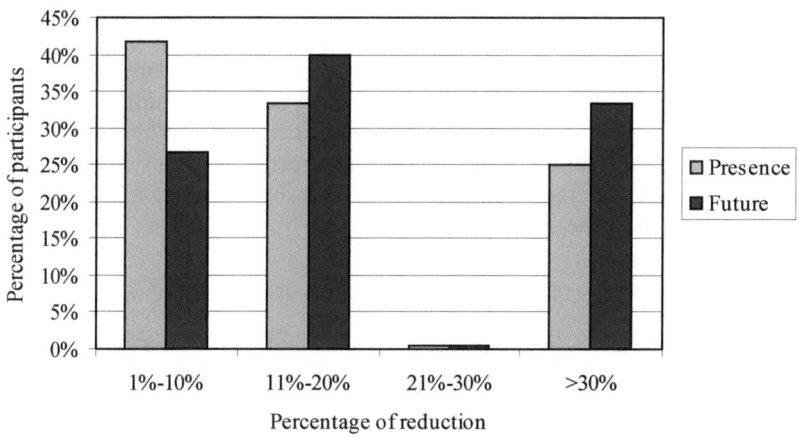

Figure 45: Distribution of reduction of the time-to-volume

So participants either had either marginal effects in this category or they scored high. The peak value was a 90% reduction in the time taken to introduce a new product to a large number of customers around the world. Catalogs were previously used for this purpose. However they often arrived late and were quickly out of date. An e-shop based on mySAP CRM has reduced the market introduction phase from approximately one quarter to less than one week – and given customers more information at the same time. While not all respondents in the top group experienced this tremendous improvement, it is obvious that typically companies with a very broad base of customers were in the top third. Another driver of value in this category seems to be the complexity of goods or services: Most of the IT service providers in the study are in the top-performing group. As IT services have a rather complex service, they benefit from an increased transparency of customer solutions and avoid reinventing the wheel with every new customer.

The **time-to-delivery** has been reduced for 11 out of 26 participants who answered this question. Contrary to time-to-market and time-to-volume, the time-to-delivery is distributed almost evenly among those that see a positive effect (grouped in the categories of 1-10% to >30%). The reduction of time-to-delivery is a result of orders being entered and processed more quickly, errors and misunderstanding being avoided, especially between the field sales and sales support, and activities being coordinated better between departments and across the company. All of these effects have already been underpinned with data from

Results – Speed Targets

the survey[124]. Additionally, improvements in the time-to-delivery have been strongly supported through integration with other SAP software components. Participants who did not notice a shorter time-to-delivery mainly argued that CRM would not impact this process in any significant way as the order process only took a marginal fraction of the overall time needed to satisfy the customer. Others claimed that they had optimized the process before to such an extent that CRM resulted in no further improvements.

Summing up the findings on speed effects resulting from mySAP CRM:

- Time-to-market, the time to deliver a new product or service has not shortened for most participants, because the necessary customer information for analysis was not yet fully developed. So 7 participants have experienced an average 7.5% improvement

- Time-to-volume has been shortened by 24.5% at the time of the interview, and is expected to rise to 28%. The main drivers are: a shortening of the sales cycle time of 12% (present) to 18% (future), and a reduced time to inform the market of 12.5%

- For 11 out of 26 participants, time-to-delivery was reduced at an average rate of 21% at the time of the interview, and 26.5% expected for the future. Efficiency gains in order management and sales coordination added to this effect, as well as the integration with other SAP system components

---

[124] Productivity gains in the order process have been covered in chapters 3.3.3. (Sales), and 3.3.5. (Internet Sales), reduction of failures in coordination have been reported in 3.4.2. (new customers)

4 Key Factors of Success: Industry Sector, Situational Fit, and Proficient Project Management

While Chapter 3 provides an overview as well as in-depth analysis of financial success through CRM and its operational drivers, Chapter 4 answers the question concerning the factors of success in CRM deployment. Results are first distinguished by sector. However – as will be shown – the spread of results within a sector is huge, thus "the sector" is not a good predictor of CRM success. Therefore a structured framework of potential factors of success is developed. Chapters 4.3. to 4.5. then investigate empirical evidence for the influence of these factors on the success of CRM. Finally, a sector-by-sector analysis outlines, which influences are crucial to explain the performance difference. This way, "the sector" is no longer seen as an inevitable fate – but opportunities and threats through using CRM within an industry sector are made visible to enable more informed and therefore better decisions on the use of CRM.

4.1 Financial Results by Sector

For many participants, the industry sector was considered the crucial influencing factor for CRM success. Therefore, the study starts and ends with a sector analysis. The concepts of the financial indicators of CRM success, that is, the CFROI, NPV, and the break-even period, have already been detailed in Chapter 3.2.1. The groups of sectors have also been introduced in Chapter 2.2.6. Thus the base is set. Before the numbers are displayed, however, a few important aspects need to borne in mind to avoid misinterpretation:

- If a sector "wins" in the ranking, it may simply be due to the fact that the state of CRM before the system's implementation was so far behind best practice that a very large improvement potential was simply tapped. "Losing" sectors might have had a better CRM practice from the start.
- Whenever a sector "wins", not all of the sector companies enjoyed the same high values – and vice versa: The participant with the highest CFROI of CRM does not come from the top sector. The spread of values within a sector has regularly been huge.
- Finally, the reader is reminded that these numbers are not representative for all mySAP CRM implementations in the respective sector – and even less so for all CRM applications.

In that sense, the results of a comparison of median CFROIs, which are illustrated in Figure 46, should be read carefully:

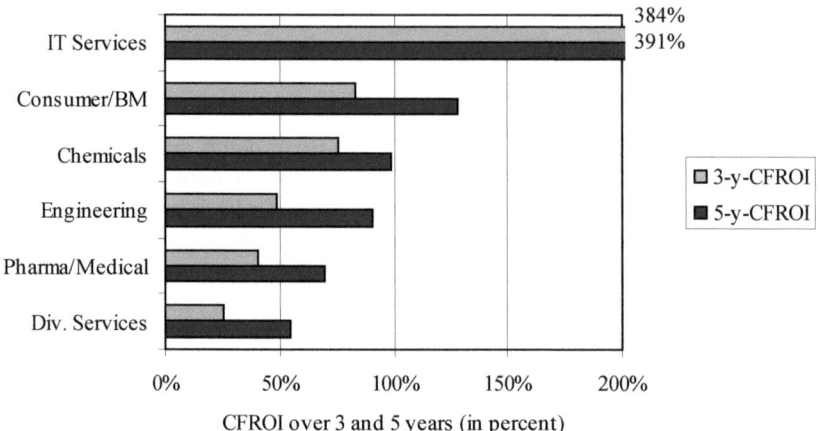

Figure 46: Distribution of median CFROI (3 year and 5 year) across sectors

The median 3-y-CFROIs range is between 21% and 384%, the median 5-y-CFROIs is between 54% and 391%: So the leading IT services have 7 to 18 times the benefit from mySAP CRM compared to the worst performing group of companies in the group of diverse services. Also, the leading IT service providers were fast to realize benefits: There is hardly any difference between the three year and the five year values, while the heterogeneous group of diverse services did not achieve half of their 5-y-CFROI after 3 years. These numbers compare to a median value of all participants at 53%. Thus, IT services, consumer goods/building materials and chemicals enjoyed a higher than average CFROI while engineering, pharmaceuticals/medical supplies, and especially the diverse services sector underperformed on their CRM investment.

The question is: How good of an indicator is the industry sector's average as a predictor of CRM success for the single company? If the spread of values within one sector group is narrow, the quality of the average as an indicator is high and vice versa. The spread of values is usually expressed by their standard deviation, that is, by the average distance of the values from the sample's mean average value. As this is an absolute measurement, a comparison of standard deviations from different distributions is meaningless. Therefore, the spread of values within an industry sector group will be expressed by the coefficient of variation, which is defined as the standard deviation over the mean average of the sample.

While the coefficient of variation is in principle well suited to the purpose, statistic theory requires all single values of the distribution to be positive. Therefore the negative CFROI-values from the sector sub-groups were abolished, the positive ones factored into the coefficients of variation as displayed in the following figure:

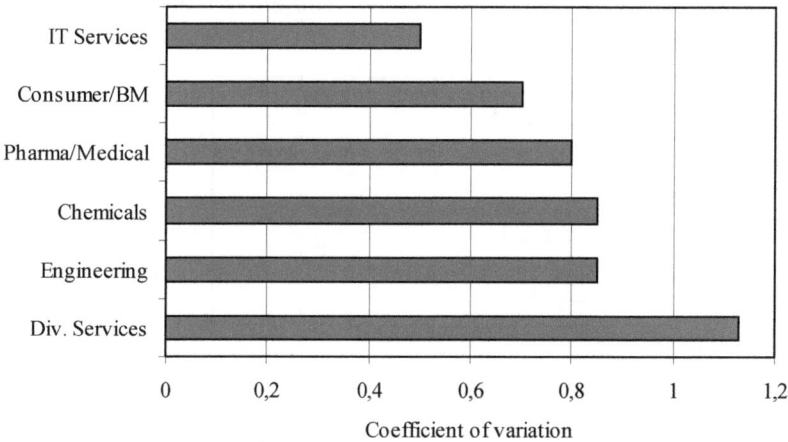

Figure 47: Distribution of coefficients of variation across sectors

A coefficient of variation of 0.5 for IT services means that the average deviation of values from the sector group's mean average measures 50% of the mean average itself. The "normal" range of a coefficient of variation is 0 to 1.0; any value above 0.3 is already considered to be high[125] for all practical purposes. None of the sectors however stays below a value of 0.3; the diverse services sector even exceeds the "normal" range of 0 to 1.0. And this huge spread within each sector group has already been narrowed by taking out all negative values.

For the group of diverse services, this result is not surprising as it represents a broad variety of sectors. However, the high values on chemicals are as surprising as for pharma/medical and also for the very homogeneous sector group of engineering. By comparison the rather heterogeneous group of consumer goods and building materials has one of the lowest coefficients of variation. The

---

[125] The value of 0.3 is generally considered to be limit for the use of normal distribution before changing to a lognormal distribution to approximate a group of data

consequence of these surprising results is that the "sector" does not seem to be a good predictor of CRM success, measured in terms of CFROI.

However, potentially NPV is well predicted by the industry sector's average; therefore it is the next measure of success to be investigated. The following figure displays NPVs by sector – first shown with the terminal value and then without a terminal value:

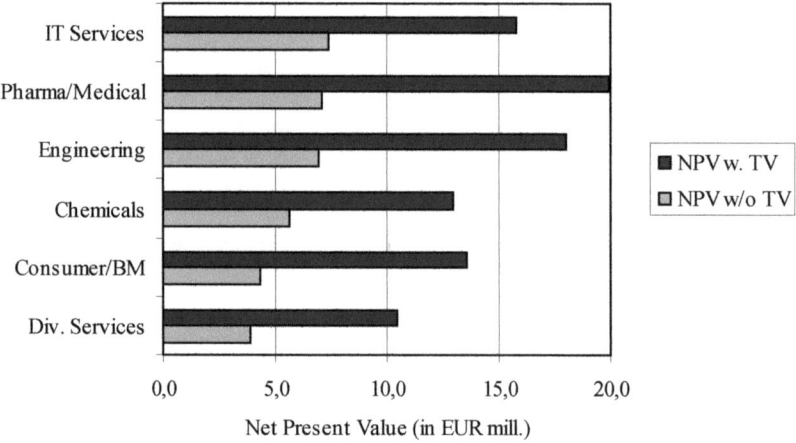

Figure 48: Distribution of median NPVs (with and without terminal values) across sectors; in EUR millions

The NPV expresses the absolute value added to the user of CRM. On average, all sectors are positive. Contrary to the CFROI, the median NPVs do not differ significantly between the sectors: The highest sector median is only 1.5 to 2 times higher than the lowest value. The respective median NPV without a terminal value for all participants is EUR 5.8 m.

Another interesting observation is that the range of sectors differs from the CFROI perspective: While IT services still lead, engineering and chemicals changed places as well as pharmaceuticals/medical supplies and consumer goods/building materials. An explanation for this difference is the absoluteness of the NPV vs. the relative character of CFROI: The more revenue and cost are impacted by the CRM implementation, the higher the NPV, even at a low CFROI. Some pharma/medical have huge CRM implementations that drive up the NPV. The same effect is at work for consumer goods/building materials –

just in the opposite direction. They are rather medium sized companies, so that their high CFROI was achieved on the basis of a relatively small investment, leading to a lower than average NPV. While the chemical companies in the sample are larger by far than those participants from engineering in terms of revenue, they typically had only limited CRM implementations, such as, pilot projects in one country and/or one division. What counts, however, is not the total amount of revenue but the revenue (or cost) impacted by the CRM implementation. The engineering companies had mostly rolled out the CRM to the entire company, and thus were at an advantage for NPV.

No only do sectors change place when moving from a CFROI to a NPV perspective, but terminal values, again, change the ranking of sectors entirely, raising pharma/medical to the top, followed by engineering, and the absolute CFROI leader, IT services, ends up in the third place. To understand this phenomenon, one needs to go back to the formula used for the terminal value as outlined in Chapter 3.2.1: It is the perpetuity of the average historic operational cash flow. So, a higher average cash flow leads to a higher terminal value. The NPV can still be low if the majority of payback accrues towards the end of the 5-year NPV period. In this case, the "late" values carry a heavy discount while fast-to-implement sectors enjoy little discounted cash flows early on. This is exactly the case with IT services and pharma/medical. While IT services are fast to implement, their NPV without terminal value is higher than for pharma/medical while the latter wins out in the long run on the basis of much higher average operative cash flows. The same is true for chemicals and consumer goods/building materials. As we will show in the break-even analysis (Figure 49), chemicals have a shorter time to break even relative to consumer goods/building materials – and therefore they lead in NPV without terminal value. However, because the producers of consumer goods rolled out their CRM applications to the entire company within 5 years, their average operative cash flow is higher than the one for the limited installations of the chemicals – and so is the NPV with terminal value.

As for CFROI, the question is how well these sector results predict the individual CRM success for a company. The coefficients of variation based on NPVs without terminal value – which are the smaller ones relative to NPVs with terminal value – even exceed those of CFROI: Only IT services and pharma/medical are below 1.0. The higher range is easily explained by the fact that the coefficient of variation for NPVs is influenced not only by the relative success of CRM but also by the absolute company size. Although the explanation is easy, the consequences are serious: The sector is an even less suitable predictor of value added by CRM.

Finally, the break-even period will be analyzed by sector. To recall: The break-even period is an indicator of investment risk as a long break-even time means that a lot may happen until the investment turns a profit:

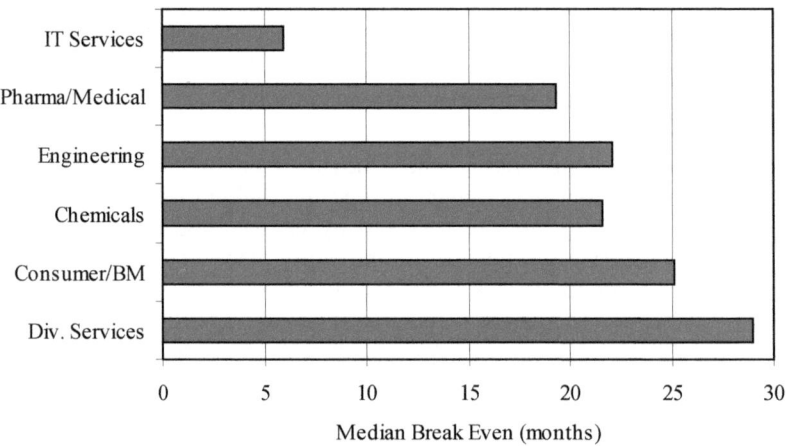

Figure 49: Distribution of median break-even periods across sectors; in months

The break-even periods of four out of five sectors are within a range of a little more than 5 months. Just as for CFROI, services are the major exception with the IT services leading and the group of diverse services lagging. IT service providers managed to drive their CRM investment to value added on average within 6 months – compared to 23 months for all participants.

Coefficients of variation[126] for the break-even period range between 0.3 and 1.0 across the sectors. So, sector values on the break-even period are somewhat more useful for the individual participant relative to CFROI or NPV. Still – the range is high and therefore the "sector" will be substituted by an analysis of potential underlying factors of success before in Chapter 4.6, the question will be taken up again to explain why the differences between sector performance are as high as they have been shown.

---

[126] As there are no negative values here, the correction needed for the CFROI and NPV was not required here

Summing up the findings on financial results across sectors:
- The predominant result is that "the sector" is not a good predictor of CRM success as the spread of CFROI or NPV values within a sector is too large, no matter how homogeneous or heterogeneous the individual companies are
- Differences in CFROI abound between sectors, covering a range from above 380% in IT services to 21% for diverse services
- NPV for the leading sector of IT services is twice the NPV of the last sector, diverse services – so the spread is lower than for CFROI. The ranking of sectors depends not only on the relative performance of CRM, but also on the absolute size of revenue or cost impacted, and furthermore on the timely structure of paybacks.
- Break-even periods have a rather narrow spread of 5 months for 4 of the 6 sector groups. Again the IT services lead with 6 months; diverse services need almost 30 months to break even.

4.2 Systematic Framework for Key Factors of Success

Two approaches to the topic of "success factors" can be distinguished in literature and practice. On the one hand, authors and consultants build on their personal or their firm's experience, on common sense, or on interviews to generate a "to do list" of CRM implementation. The focus is on *"rules for good project management"* because these "recipes for success" build on the implicit hypothesis that CRM success is always doable. While the rules may be helpful in managing projects, their empirical base often remains elusive, their structure is arbitrary, and the question remains unanswered: Are all of the listed rules needed for success – and are all rules needed for success really listed. This is doubtful as, for example, Wessling claims to have identified "the 17 basic rules for successful CRM projects" while Rajola posts a list of 16 "critical success factors" differing from Wesselings, Homburg/Sieben come up with 12 "success factors for CRM", Stokburger/Pufahl with the "10 principles of value based CRM", and Stengl/Sommer/Ematinger boil it down to 6 bullet points – none of these lists is related to each other[127]. Despite taking the opposite perspective, enumerations of "perils of CRM"[128] display the very same profile of strengths and weaknesses. A notable exception from the rule of intuitive prioritization is

---

[127] Wessling (2001) p.167 ff., Rajola (2003) p.153 f., Homburg/Sieben (2000) p. 26 f., Stokburger/Pufahl (2002) p.35, Stengl/Sommer/Ematinger (2001) p.49
[128] Rigby/Reichheld/Schefter (2002); for other lists of potential problems in CRM projects also see Kehl/Rudolph (2001), Stengl/Sommer/Ematinger (2001) p.39 ff., Dyché (2002) p.256

Key Factors of Success – External Situational Factors

the result of a survey conducted by Wilde[129]. He identifies 15 factors of CRM success that cover the project management and preconditions within the company.

On the other hand, especially those responsible for the introduction of CRM often search for answers to the question of success in *"the situation"*, that is, those factors, which from the point of view of the CRM project manager, cannot be changed in the short term. No common definition of the situation exists. Rather it "is an open concept which we will fill with concrete contents depending on the questions and the current knowledge at hand"[130]. The openness of the situational concept and the implicit "excuse for failure" by blaming the situation for being inevitable are weaknesses of this approach as indeed, a lot can be done right to succeed in CRM.

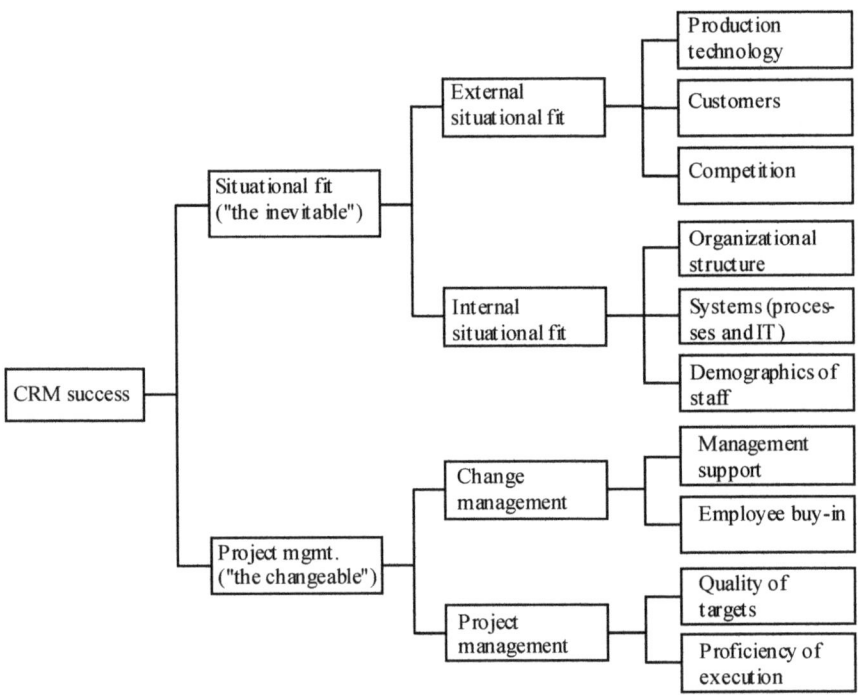

Figure 50: Overview of factors for CRM success

---

[129] Wilde (2002) p.43
[130] Kieser/Kubicek (1992) p.205

The "manageable" and the "unmanageable" make up the first split of potential factors of success. The "unmanageable situational fit" has to be established externally and internally, while the boundary between these two is more intuitive than clear-cut[131]. Here, ***external factors*** are considered to be all CRM-relevant market forces that influence the companies in one sector alike. External forces determining a sector's profitability are outlined in Michael Porter's well-known 5-Forces Framework[132]. Therein, he identifies 5 distinct forces on a sector's profitability: current competitive pressure, new competitors, new technologies, and customer and supplier power. Of these factors, only three are considered to be relevant in the context of CRM: technology, customers, and competitive pressure[133]. The others are neglected: Suppliers are naturally not directly affected by CRM, nor do they directly influence the success of CRM deployment. The arrival of new competitors may possibly be prevented by a CRM-strengthened customer loyalty that scares away potential rivals. This scenario however is a rather speculative indirect effect that lacks observability in the time frame at hand. Therefore it has not been included in the list of explanations for CRM success to be investigated. One other potential external situational factor, which is not explicitly dealt with in Porter's framework, is the influence of distinct national cultures on CRM. This aspect has not been researched in this study as it was excluded with the sample structure, consisting only of the relatively homogeneous German-speaking central European countries (D-A-CH).

Internal situational factors include all CRM-relevant influences from within the company. They are, in the narrow sense of the word not "inevitable" or "unchangeable" as change management addresses many of these elements. However, they are characterized by substantial inertia and are often out of reach for the CRM project manager – so from his or her perspective a given which needs to be adapted to. Again, a known framework has been deployed to structure the potentially relevant factors, the 7-S-framework by Peters and Waterman[134]. The study only produces evidence on some of these factors, namely structure, systems, and staff. All other factors, strategy, skills, style, and shared values have not been investigated as this would have required an even more in-depth analysis incompatible with the primary purpose of the study. The influence of the selected internal situational factors on CRM performance will be outlined in Chapter 4.4.

---

[131] Kieser/Kubicek (1992) p. 209 f.
[132] Porter (1989) p.26
[133] For a similar customization of the Porter framework to the specific situation of CRM Wehrmeister (2001) p.78-89
[134] Peters/Waterman (1982); for a different framework on "preconditions" for CRM Homburg/Sieben (2000) p. 22-25 whose factors have been taken into consideration in this study

CRM project management finally comprises all factors that can be directly determined by the CRM project manager. Good project management in a narrow sense is to design and build the CRM system "high quality, in time, in budget". In a wider sense, it also includes all required change to convince those who are supposed to use the CRM system – change management. Change management can be again distinguished by hierarchical layer: management in a broad sense and those employees that are affected by CRM. Good project management again has simply been structured by two phases: good planning and good execution.

The ***purpose of Chapter 4*** is to generate some initial empirical evidence on those possible success factors for CRM. As research on the profitability of CRM is still in its explorational phase, it is not intended to rigorously test hypotheses. As explained at the outset (Chapter 2.3.1), the goal of this study is not to produce large-scale superficial results with spurious statistical significance, but to go deeper in understanding how CRM success can be measured and how it comes about.

4.3 External Situational Factors of Success: Technology, Customers, and Competition

Starting with the external situational factors, the potential influence of the following factors will be investigated: production technology, customers, and finally competitive pressure.

4.3.1 Influence of Production Technology: Service Character and Complexity of Goods and Services on Offer

Here, production technology is understood to characterize the processes of production as well as the result, the main goods or services that the company has on offer to the market. In this sense, it has a major impact on how a company functions. Two dimensions of production technology and goods and services on offer will be explored: its service character and the complexity of the goods and services on offer. ***Services*** can be operationalized by a set of characteristic attributes[135] such as immateriality, synchronous production and consumption, interactivity in the production process, singularity of process and result, as well as the importance of contributions from the customer. Furthermore, the potential

---

[135] For an in-depth empirical analysis of service attributes and their influence on organizational structures in professional services Selchert (1997) with further reference to service literature

for professional services especially, is inseparable from the service provider in person and their quality and value is difficult to determine. This is a gradual service concept – the more of these factors are given, the purer the service character of a company's offering.

These *service attributes have a major influence on a service provider's* internal organizational structure, processes, skills, and so on – but they also heavily impact the customer relationship. If a customer not only purchases the final product, but also has a hand in making it (for example, the customer has to provide information to the auditor so that he can do his job), then CRM is important for understanding the scope of the possible solution relative to the customer setting. And if the customer is unable to see and test the product beforehand, which requires him to trust in the company's information, CRM is crucial to make all CRM staff speak with one voice. So service companies should see a very strong impact from CRM. And indeed, that effect is clearly visible in the sector group of IT services – although it is not the only cause of the outstanding benefit reaped from their CRM deployment. Three out of four IT service providers have their highest value potential not in cost reductions but in the increase in revenue – and all stressed the fact that the coordination of and cooperation among employees and teams in approaching the customer is essential for business success. One respondent saw the main benefit in a rapid prioritization of opportunities based on fast access to customer data. Surprisingly, the diverse services group comes in last on all dimensions of success. This may be explained by the fact that other factors interfere, as Chapter 4.6 clearly illustrates.

Besides the dimension of service character, the offer to the market may also be classified by its *complexity*. Two aspects of complexity have been distinguished: the number of different goods sold and the level and frequency of customization[136]. As hinted at in Chapter 3.3.3, the more complex the product, the more a sales representative benefits from automated order processes, a product configurator, and so on. Furthermore, when selling complex products, customer interaction is a lot higher than for simple products. Changes in the product configuration benefit from support. Customer self-service via, for example, e-shops requires CRM if the spectrum of alternative products is huge, whereas a static product catalog is sufficient for a narrow product scope.

---

[136] Wehrmeister (2001) p.99 f. describes similarly the "complexity of the customer demand" and the "frequency of customer interaction" as drivers of value from CRM

To check this line of reasoning, the sector groups are plotted into a complexity matrix, with the number of products on the one axis and the degree of product customization on the other. The CFROI rank is characterized by shadings: the darker the shade, the higher the sector in the ranking:

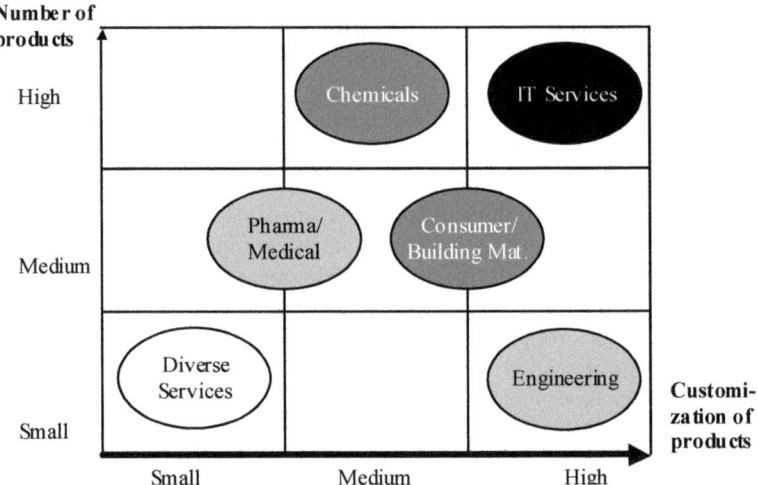

Figure 51: CFROI according to sector complexity

Clearly, the hypothesis is supported: The most complex sector takes the lead on CFROI of CRM, the least complex takes the last place – and all the others are placed accordingly. Attention should be paid to the fact that the positioning of sector groups is based on the participants from the study, not on an overall market view. So, for example, consumer goods/building materials in the study contain a high portion of companies that tailor-make products, for example, furniture or doors and windows for building sites; this is different from a Nestlé or Procter & Gamble type of consumer goods company. The positioning can thus be argued as follows:

- Participants in the leading sector of ***IT service providers*** are predominantly professional services – as opposed to operational services – and therefore their business is mainly customization with a very broad range of software and hardware products used to build solutions for their customers. This places the sector in the upper right corner.

- While the participants from the ***consumer goods and building materials sector group*** have a lower number of products relative to chemicals, they rank higher with regard to customization.
- ***Producers of chemicals*** generally have a huge number of products. Moreover, in the sample, the chemical products belong to the category of specialties that require consultative selling to exactly assess the customer's needs[137]. Some customization takes place when different basic substances are blended to meet the customer requirements, such as when their equipment is used to process raw materials.
- In relation to the other sectors, the ***engineering companies*** had only a small number of basic products – but these were then customized to a large degree to meet the customer needs.
- ***Pharma/medical*** is the exact opposite to the engineering companies in relation to the sources of complexity: While the number of goods is moderately high, customization does not take place – except for the suppliers of medical equipment.
- The ***diverse services***, finally, have predominantly standard goods or services with standard prices and hardly any customization: for example, a local utility or a health insurance company.

If the two axes of the complexity matrix were equally weighted, the chemicals and consumer goods/building materials as well as engineering and pharma/medical would be on the same level of complexity just with a different profile. However, the ranking of sectors according to median CFROI in Figure 46 indicates that consumer goods lead chemicals and engineering is ranked higher than pharma/medical. In both cases, the leader scores higher on the customization. Thus, it is evident that the customization of products is the dominant dimension with regard to influencing the success of CRM. So, in general, businesses with a high level of customization have a high likelihood to reap a rich benefit from the CRM deployment.

---

[137] Empirical evidence on the special needs of specialty chemicals providers is reported by Wiedmann/Greilich (2002) p.285

4.3.2 Customer Influence: Insignificance of Large Numbers

Besides the production technology and goods and services on offer, the number of customers has been hypothesized to influence the value of CRM[138]. It is unclear though, if a small or a large number of customers drives CFROI. For a large number of customers, the sales representative greatly benefits from CRM keeping track of all the contacts, following-up on leads, and so on. Furthermore, analytical CRM displays its strength, by identifying trends and changes that would have otherwise gone unnoticed. Also, for a large number of customers, a large number of sales representatives would be at work, so coordination problems grow exponentially, which may call for CRM support. However, in a very narrow market with only a few current and potential customers, again CRM may become important. The loss of a single customer could then already potentially impair the company's value. Therefore, CRM support for the intense multi-level cooperation with key customers may yield an exceptional benefit.

To investigate the empirical evidence, three groups were formed according to the number of customers impacted by CRM – not the total amount of a company's customers. The limits to the groups have been set so as to attain an equal amount of the 25 complete data sets per group:

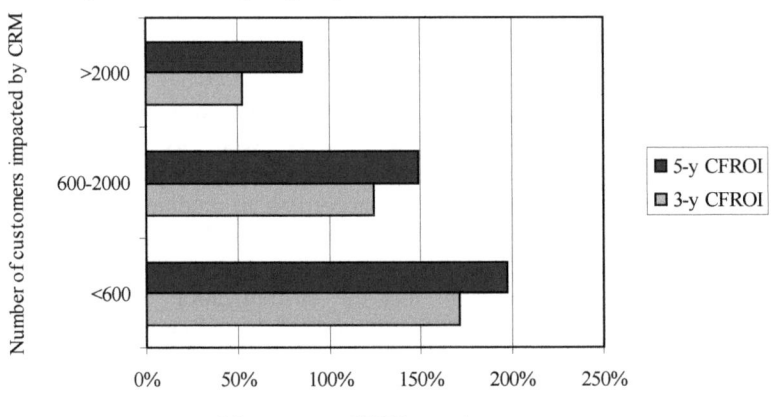

Figure 52: Mean average CFROI (in %) from participant sub-groups distinguished by the number of customers

---

[138] The Porter 5-forces-framework also names other determinants of customer power but they are considered to be less important in the context of CRM

Clearly, the companies with less than 600 customers experienced the highest CFROI – no matter if it was for the 3-year or 5-year horizon. This consistency across time horizons refutes the potential objection that a smaller CRM implementation only wins because it is faster to implement, compared to the more complex implementation projects with many customers and sales representatives. So, at least in this sample of companies, the rationale to tie in the very few but precious customers outweighs the operational efficiencies and analytical benefits of CRM in a wide customer base.

This finding – higher benefit for smaller users – however, cannot be applied to the overall population of mySAP CRM users in D-A-CH. The measure of linear relation between two variables, the Bravais-Pearson correlation coefficient, abbreviated as "r". As this measures ranges between a perfectly inverse relation ($r = (-1)$) and a perfect positive relation at $r = +1$, the result of $r = (-0.28)$ shows the right sign in relation to the hypothesis that the larger the company, the smaller the benefit. However, the negative correlation is so weak that it is statistically insignificant. So not even with a 95% certainty can it be claimed that there is a relationship between the two variables at all[139].

Often, size of a company is not expressed by the number of customers but by the overall revenue. So this measurement has also been analyzed, but the correlation between the amount of revenue impacted by CRM and the 3-y-CFROI is just as feeble and insignificant ($r = 0.19$). Although the slightly positive correlation could imply that larger companies benefit more from CRM, only 8% of participants above EUR 200 m in impacted revenue have achieved a CFROI above 150%, whereas almost 40% did so below EUR 200 m. So again, a large size of a company is not necessary to achieve a high CFROI of CRM. Of course, if NPV were considered instead of CFROI, the result would be reversed: Then the absolute amount of revenue (and customers) comes into play giving larger CRM operations the lead.

4.3.3 Influence of Competitive Pressure: The More the Better for CRM

The impact of competitive pressure on the benefit of a CRM implementation is ***inconclusive on a theoretical basis*** as there are conflicting arguments. On the one hand, a stiff competition allows for no mistakes with regard to the customers – and therefore CRM helps reduce breakdowns in coordination, gains operative

---

[139] Based on the 2-tailed t-statistic, the correlation is insignificant at the 5%-level; also the visualized scatter chart is inconclusive as to any other than linear functional relation between the two parameters

efficiency in CRM processes and ties in the customer on a relationship basis, instead of on the basis of rebates at arm's length. So benefits from CRM should be high[140]. On the other hand, in such a competitive environment, efficiency and effectiveness may have been already high before the CRM implementation. Then the gains from CRM would be small – but nonetheless important to the user. Under conditions of low competition, inefficiency is more likely to exist – but there is less pressure to abolish it. Thus again, CRM benefits may be small, as simply no need is seen to change processes and to cut back on resources used.

To check for empirical evidence, the different sectors in the study can be grouped into *three classes of competitive pressure*:

- A fierce competition rages in IT services with a shrinking market (since 2000, the year of most CRM project start-ups) and severe price reductions. The same is true for consumer goods and building materials – at least in D-A-CH, the home market of all participants. The construction industry has been shrinking for several years, and as a result, the building materials and furniture sector are shrinking as well.

- The medium group constitutes chemicals, engineering, and pharma/medical. Competition in these mature industries is high – but not as fierce as in the top group.

- Finally, five out of six companies from the group of diverse services are governed by the public sector or have at least a strong link into the public arena. Regional monopolies in utilities, publicly-regulated health insurance and quasi-public service agencies have by far the lowest competitive pressure relative to the field of sectors under research.

Taking a look at Figure 46, these three groups follow without exception the ranking according to CFROI: Participants from sectors with the highest competition yield the largest CFROI while those with the lowest competitive pressure realize the smallest benefit from their CRM engagements. This finding is further confirmed when the different situations within one sector group are analyzed. Within the diverse services, the only participant that does not have a direct public sector impact has a significantly higher CFROI. The reverse is true within the sector of pharma/medical. For one company, mySAP CRM was just a centrally-deployed controlling tool to monitor the CRM activities of different branches and departments but with no immediate involvement of the central staff in operations. This central staff did not feel much competitive pressure inside the company and consequently the benefit of CRM turned out to be close to zero.

---

[140] This line of reasoning is being followed by Wehrmeister (2001) p.91 f.

The reasons for the ***high benefit in highly-competitive industries*** are as cited above. The question remains; why did public sector participants yield a lower benefit from their CRM investments? The dominating commonality among those companies is severe problems in project management caused by a diversity of interests. Four out of the six participants in this group suffered from seriously troubled projects. In one implementation, the different organizational units that wanted to cooperate at the beginning, departed one after the other as they found out that not only was software to be implemented, but a full change in processes, structures, and culture was needed. Diversity of interest in another case caused many loops and delays as requirements changed frequently. The result was finally a compromise that no one really supported; benefit remained slim. Problems were caused not only by the difference between units, but also between management and employees. So in one case, top management backed off when employees started to resist as they realized that jobs may actually be at stake. Without top management support, the project was still finished but the acceptance rate was low, and so are usage and benefit to the present day. Therefore, it seems as if the absence of competitive pressure triggers badly-defined projects and hampers the willingness to follow-through.

Summing up the impact of external situational factors as evidenced in this study:
- The service character and the complexity of the market offer, as determined by the number of different goods sold and the degree of customization, have indeed been evidenced to influence the CFROI of CRM
- Companies that used CRM to tie-in a smaller base of (potentially more important) customers experienced a higher CFROI compared to large scale implementations
- All supporting empirical evidence from the study points to the fact that the higher the competitive pressure, the higher the benefit from CRM

4.4 Internal Situational Factors of Success: The 7-S of CRM

Applying the 7-S framework to CRM, three factors have been investigated and will be dealt with in the following chapters: organizational structure, systems, and staff.

4.4.1 Organizational Structure: Dynamics Breed High CFROI of CRM

Organizational structure typically characterizes a set of lasting formal rules to direct the activities of the organization's members towards the organization's targets[141]. The impact of the static organizational structure on CRM performance has not been investigated in this study. However, structure also changes. It does so constantly. In this study, by structural change we mean the phases of rapid and fundamental rearrangement of organizational rules.

Several participants had undergone this kind of ***major structural change***: They originated from a merger, just acquired another company, were spun out from their former mother company, radically reorganized their processes and/or structures in the area of CRM, or recently undertook a major repositioning effort in the market. From a CRM point of view, these phases of radical change are very interesting. Old habits and rules are abandoned, and as one respondent put it: "chaos reigns". So the potential for improvement is huge and it is being felt by the individual employee seeking orientation. This in turn potentially leads to a higher willingness to adapt to the new system, so CRM has a chance to be quickly adopted and used. Furthermore, the new processes are more easily optimized compared to gradual modifications of a historically grown process. Finally, the IT infrastructure in these situations often starts from zero base, that is, data is cleansed, legacy applications are migrated, and so on, so that from a technical perspective, optimal conditions prevail for introducing CRM. Thus, it may be expected that companies "in motion" have a higher benefit from the CRM implementation.

This line of argument is supported by the ***empirical evidence*** of this study. Seven participants had undergone major structural change within less than a year before the CRM project started. This subgroup displays the following characteristics:

- The median 3-y-CFROI is 77.5% compared to 50.5% for the rest of the companies in more stable situations

---

[141] Kieser/Kubicek (1992) p.4-24

- The break-even period is 28 months compared to 22 months for stable companies

So indeed, the *CFROI* is somewhat higher. However, within the group of participants in motion, the spread is large, reaching from a negative CFROI to more than +400%. This shows that a change situation alone does not guarantee a high return on CRM investments. In the case of the lowest performer, CRM had not been used to overcome the differences in CRM approaches to the market that had arisen from a previous merger. For the top-performing CRM implementation in that group, almost all of the positive effects came true that were described above: A highly disorganized sales force resulting from a merger with a weak go-to-market approach was radically reorganized to unleash the full potential, which had previously been hampered by faulty structures and processes. Interestingly, however, companies "in motion" *break even* later than those in stable environments. This may be caused by the "creative chaos" which requires more time to overcome than situations of incremental change.

4.4.2 Systems: No Impact of IT Proficiency Before the Implementation

The term "*systems*" not only encompasses IT systems, but even more importantly, the processes that were in place when CRM was implemented. Every participant has been asked to describe the situation before the mySAP CRM project. Of course, it was expected that companies which had streamlined CRM processes and already used some IT applications to support their CRM staff would see a lower return on their CRM investment, compared to those who had no systems in place at the outset.

However, the data only partially supports this hypothesis. After abolishing one far outlying value from the top end as well as one from the bottom end, all remaining answers to the question of the "situation before" were codified and grouped into three distinct categories:

- Category 1 comprises participants that had neither structured CRM processes nor applications to support CRM functions before the mySAP CRM project. An example would be companies with a high degree of departmental specialization that did not coordinate activities between, for example, sales and marketing. 20% of all data sets were in this category.
- Category 2 describes companies that used one or diverse local or even privately purchased applications, where few if any were connected to each other, and none of these had been integrated to the back-end systems. Roughly 35% of all participants fall into category 2.

- Category 3 includes companies that already had streamlined their CRM processes before the mySAP CRM project and that used one integrated tool. A surprising figure of almost 45% of all participants has been classified as category 3.

The following median and mean average values show up for the different classes of "CRM sophistication" before the start of mySAP CRM:

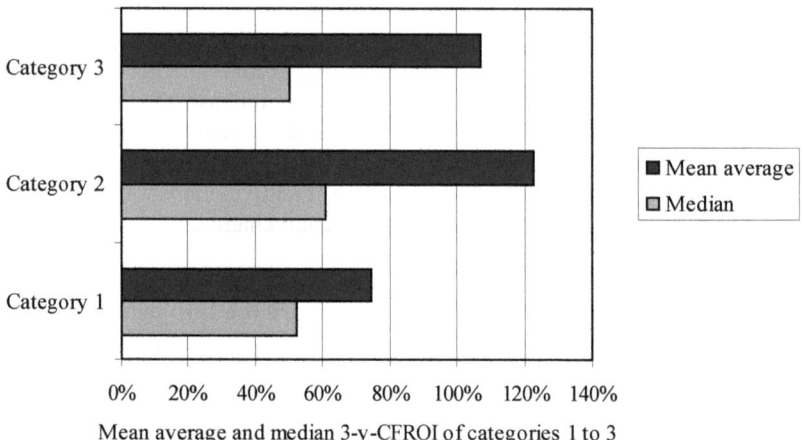

Mean average and median 3-y-CFROI of categories 1 to 3

Figure 53: Mean average and median CFROI (in %) from participant subgroups distinguished by the situation before the mySAP CRM implementation

First of all: the differences in Figure 53 are marginal at best. Median values range from 50% to little above 60%; the difference between category 1 and 3 measures an insignificant 2 percentage-points. So surprisingly, the level of CRM proficiency in processes and IT support is not a good indicator for the gains that can be expected from implementing mySAP CRM.

A second observation is also counter-intuitive: Contrary to expectations, the companies with the least developed CRM systems and thus the highest potential show the smallest mean average return on mySAP CRM. This may be due to the specific nature of these businesses not warranting high yields on CRM. A closer look, however, reveals that this is not the case: Participants in category 1 spread evenly across all sector groups except for IT services. It may be that these companies have a longer way to go, as they start from the back of the field. This is again not the case: On the basis of the 5-y-CFROI, category 1 takes the last place not only in the mean average but also in the median. Furthermore, the distance to the leading category 2 roughly quadruples. So any explanation for the finding remains speculative: It may be due to a perceptional problem that those who did not experience the productivity gains from process redesign and IT support in CRM functions before are somewhat more cautious in their assessment. It may be that the CRM skills were underdeveloped from the outset and could not catch up within the 5-year period. Whatever the explanation, it can be concluded that there is ample room for improvement by implementing CRM no matter how proficient the company is at the outset.

4.4.3 Staff: Specific Skills and Internationalization Matter

Finally, the factor of staff is investigated. "Staff" refers to the demographic structure of the employees at large, not single individuals. Four aspects were considered: the overall qualification of staff, its age and IT proficiency, the tenure, and internationalization.

The *overall qualification* of staff could be expected to have a positive impact on the CFROI because highly-skilled staff is more expensive, therefore efficiency gains are worth more than with cheap labor. Furthermore, top qualified staff may be quicker to comprehend the system and more disciplined in using it, therefore getting more out of the system. As it is difficult to assess qualification from the outside-in, and as it is even more difficult to compare different levels, the fully loaded weighted average yearly expense per employee has been taken as a proxy variable. The spread is huge, ranging from EUR 35' p.a. per employee for low qualification call-center staff, to EUR 210' for top qualified specialists also working in a call center. 85% of all participants are, however, between EUR 50' and 100' with a median of EUR 85'. Correlating the average weighted yearly expenses per CRM employee with the 3-y-CFROI, the correlation coefficient is r = (-0.04), that is, the two parameters are entirely uncorrelated in the sample. The top-paying participant experiences a CFROI well above the average but is still far off the top returns. The lowest paying participant's CFROI is only 1/3 lower than the top paying ones – and also far above the average. One company with exactly the median pay level is the worst performing in terms of 3-y-CFROI while the top performer has a weighted average pay level of EUR 95', that is, only EUR 10' above the median. These observations reinforce the finding that pay levels do not have a major impact on the CRM's success.

While the overall qualification seems not to matter, some specific skills do, for example, the *ability to cope with change, and proficiency in IT*. Three out of four IT service participants are among the top 5 companies with the shortest break-even period and the shortest time-to-implementation. Naturally, their staff is used to working in projects, to fast changing processes, and rapidly altering skill requirements, as the technology evolves at such a fast pace. Furthermore, IT skills abound and the willingness to use IT to solve problems can safely be assumed to exceed the average. IT savviness does not, however, preclude resistance of staff: In one case, the solution was not accepted at all and now modifications concerning the look-and-feel are sought to finally make the rather lengthy implementation project become a success.

The *average age of CRM staff* was not assessed in the questionnaire but it was frequently alluded to in the interviews, especially when it came to the readiness to change. On the one hand, most respondents mentioning the topic used it as one explanation for a low acceptance rate. On the other hand, several participants explicitly mentioned that age was not a good predictor for a total rejection of the CRM system. Among their "last 5%" of non-users, all ages were present in an equal distribution. Also youth does not automatically imply acceptance. In one case, almost the entire sales organization had been newly recruited and still the CRM system had a very low rate of acceptance, mainly due to problems on the project management side.

Finally, *internationalization of staff* is not a differentiator among the participants, as almost all were active internationally. However, it can still be considered as one situational element that drives value from CRM as most respondents argued benefits with the fact that coordination was especially difficult across worldwide locations. Frequently, the case was cited that sales teams from different countries pitched for the same global account before the introduction of CRM. This led not only to wasteful double work but also to lower prices as the customer took advantage of the competition between the sales teams. Account planning was frequently not pooled, and neither was the knowledge about offers; several respondents described the situation before CRM as "reinventing the wheel in every country". In one example, changes in prices or product configurations were not transparent to the outpost in Asia which led either to the time-consuming extra effort of double-checking each proposal back-and-forth between Germany and Asia – or to the embarrassment of withdrawing faulty offers. This kind of efficiency boost was frequently cited. In one situation, it constituted the main benefit from the CRM implementation as a significant amount of time was saved for each of the many international sales offices.

Not only was efficiency positively impacted by CRM, but also *effectiveness* of efforts, for example, with regard to the goal of an improved customer relationship. One respondent explained an exceptionally strong benefit from

CRM by the fact that now their sales staff was better informed about the internal operations of a worldwide customer than the customer's employees themselves. So one of their sales representatives in London hinted at the fact that the products ordered for the UK differed from the order in Germany and asked if that was ok; it was not and the customer's purchasing department explicitly appreciated the excellent customer care of the CRM user.

These are the key findings for the internal factors of CRM success:
- Participants that had undergone a major structural change, such as a merger, took longer to break even, but then achieved a much higher CFROI from their CRM activities
- Proficiency of participants in CRM processes or systems before the mySAP CRM implementation did not impact CFROI in a meaningful way
- The overall level of qualification of CRM staff is not a good predictor of CRM success. Willingness and ability to change, IT proficiency, and young age support the acceptance of a CRM system although neither one of these characteristics guarantees success, nor does their absence preclude a high CFROI of CRM. In international settings, CRM is especially beneficial by improving efficient coordination and enabling one voice to the customer.

4.5 Good Project Management: a Necessary but Not Sufficient Condition for Success in CRM

Four factors of success were identified in the context of good project management: management involvement and support, employee buy-in, the quality of targets, and the proficiency of execution. These four factors, which are further divided into several observations, will be analyzed in detail in this chapter.

4.5.1 Management Support and Involvement

Management involvement clearly is one of the most consistently cited preconditions of CRM success – and moreover the no. 1 factor of change efforts in general[142]. So each respondent was asked to which extent management

---
[142] For example check Campbell (2003) p.379 f. for that assertion and compiled evidence from literature; in a survey by Wilde (2002) p.43, the management commitment only ranges mid-field in the top 10 factors of success but it still scores at 4.23 of a maximum 5.0; Kehl/Rudolph (2001) even go as far as to claim that management is one of three major sources of CRM project failure

supported the project – and to which extent they were involved in it. Support refers to all activities that can be performed without actively participating in the project, such as, providing a sufficient project budget, adequate staffing, public and outspoken support for the team and project when problems arise, or communication of the project's progress inside the company. A second question referred to the involvement of the management in the project, that is, active participation in the team's problem solving, controlling milestones as steering committee members, and so on. Management was defined as the leaders responsible for the CRM functions impacted by the CRM project - the head of marketing, sales, service, no matter at which hierarchical level inside the company. If CRM was only to be introduced to one of several divisions, then the division's CRM leaders were considered to be the relevant management.

The *empirical findings* from this study fully support the hypothesis of higher success with management support and involvement. The strongest correlation of r = (- 0.4) was found between the NPV (without terminal value) and the management support measured in terms of German university grades[143] with the possibility to express any decimal between 1 = very good and 5 = insufficient[144]. The correlation coefficient was expected to be negative as in German grades the best is 1 and the worst is 5, so a negative correlation coefficient means that the better the support, the higher NPV. Even if the two observations with the lowest university grades were removed, the correlation coefficient would still not be reduced. So this finding is robust against outliers, that is, the end values do not change the result. Furthermore, it is significant at the 5% level, that is, with a probability of 95% this relationship exists for the entirety of mySAP CRM users in D-A-CH. The implication of this result is, however, not that more support automatically leads to more value. Several participants with good and even very good management support only achieved medium or low results. By comparison, none of the participants in the study with less than good management support (less than grade 2.0) achieved a NPV above EUR 5 m. So it may be concluded that good management support (grade 2.0 or above) is a necessary but not sufficient condition of CRM success.

---

[143] The "German grades" are used in Austria and Germany while the Swiss use the reverse order, that is, 1 = insufficient and 5 = very good; the Swiss grades were therefore transformed to the German system to ensure compatibility

[144] Given the possibility to also use any kind of interim decimal and with only the two extreme values being named, the ordinal metric of grades can be read as cardinal numbers that are required to use correlation analysis

If not NPV but ***3-y-CFROI*** is chosen as the measure of success, the correlation coefficient is lower at an insignificant r = (-0.25)[145]. The main difference between NPV and CFROI is that the former is impacted by the total size of the CRM operations. The higher correlation coefficient for the NPV therefore means that management support is even more important in large CRM operations compared to smaller ones, a highly plausible finding.

Management involvement – the active participation in the project – has scored lower, on grades as well as on the correlation coefficient. The average grade for management involvement is a 2.7 compared to a 2.3 in management support. The very low correlation coefficient for NPV is r = (-0.19), for the CFROI it is r = (-0.1); both relations are statistically insignificant. The lower impact of management involvement on success was also confirmed by comments from respondents who frequently did not consider it to be management's job to become "operative"[146]. This finding is fully consistent with recent research by Campbell from the introduction of CRM at five Canadian financial institutions. She concludes that management "is more seen in a role as to providing the necessary funds and resources to support the project"[147]. Also the CRM vision was seen as a required management input to the project.

After providing evidence for the fact that management support is important, the question is: what ***kind of support*** has been successful. From the participants with low CFROI two patterns emerge that characterize bad support: backing-off when it came to problems and weak follow-up. ***Management backed-off*** at different problematic phases of the CRM project – but no matter when they did, it resulted in a poor economic benefit. In one case, the project team was explicitly forbidden to plan for efficiency gains after the works council had complained about these activities. The project then was implemented without a clear focus on high value added improvements and consequently ended up being longer and more expensive than expected. It also did not yield much benefit by the time of the interview. In another case, management withdrew support from the team after technical problems hampered acceptance of the system among CRM staff. The other pattern of bad support is a ***weak follow-up***[148]. One participant described it as a "laissez-faire" style management: Upon the completion of the project, the employees were asked to please use the new system. No incentives were given, no role modeling, and there were no consequences if some

---

[145] t-statistic not significant at either the 1%- or the 5%-level
[146] In the same way as "advice from a practical perspective" Stojek/Ulbrich (2001) p.200
[147] Campbell (2003) p.380
[148] This is one of three main reasons for the failure of CRM projects cited by Newell (2001) p.262

employees openly declared they would not use the system. The result was that acceptance was low from the start – and dropped over time to marginal values. The dynamics of the negative information feedback loop described in Chapter 3.3.1 were in full swing at the time of the interview. This pattern was observed in very much the same way from at least seven participants – although not all ended in a downward spiral. In two cases, management was replaced and the new leaders implemented a more rigid regime, with a consistent follow-up on all employees who did not use the system to the extent desired.

For the extremely positive examples of management support in CRM, the exact opposite behavior was mentioned as noteworthy: Planning of the project was by-the-book, with clear-cut and measurable targets. A business case was drafted and used as a steering device, and not just as an instrument to get management approval that was no longer followed once the project had been approved. In one case, an elaborate business dynamics analysis had even been carried out. Respondents told of full support and commitment to the team in change management efforts, role-modeling the use of the system to convince employees about the potential benefit. Teams were openly supported in a radical redesign of processes; consequences of the CRM deployment were communicated openly and defended against criticism. Management followed-through on the project progress, in particular on the acceptance and the benefits, sometimes with an elaborate measurement system to exactly assess improvements.

So in conclusion:

- The common wisdom of management support leading to CRM results finds evidence in this study. However, management support is identified as a necessary, not sufficient condition.
- Management involvement is less important than management support.
- The key to good support is steadfastness in times of trouble and a consistent follow-up with a focus on managing acceptance and reaping the benefits.

4.5.2 Employee Buy-In

When faced with the challenge to change processes, values, and behaviors in the wake of a CRM project, employees face significant change barriers: fear of losing one's job, anxieties about the new skills required for the new technology, habitual behavior, unwillingness to share knowledge as know-how is seen as a

Key Factors of Success – Good Project Management

driver of ones own value to the company, and so on.[149] In a survey by Forrester Research, the "adoption phase" has empirically been identified as the most problematic in the CRM implementation process: 45.9% of 111 CRM-experienced participants said that "resistance to process change" represents the most significant obstacle in the entire CRM effort[150]. Overcoming these barriers is crucial, as employees need to use the CRM system and processes if the investment is to bring added value. However, employees will only overcome the barriers to using CRM if they have the skill and the will to do so. Two methods may be distinguished to gain the needed employee buy-in: conducting a distinct change management effort and/or directly involving a large number of employees, key users, and so on in the implementation project team itself.

Several parameters were assessed in the study to check the employee buy-in and potential influencing techniques:

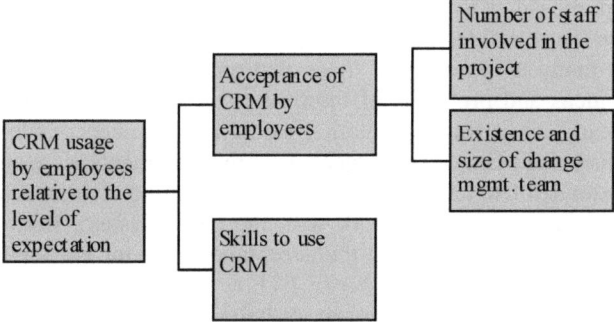

Figure 54: Overview: Parameters influencing CRM usage as a target of change management

The first link – the relationship between ***CRM usage and acceptance*** – has been confirmed as highly significant (at the 1% level): In fact, acceptance is strongly correlated with the usage of the system relative to the level of expectation (r = - 0.77). The "usage" was operationalized by asking for the level of use (in percent) among employees relative to the initial expectation. Acceptance was rated according to the German grade system, which again explains the negative sign of the correlation coefficient.

---

[149] For change barriers in the context of CRM also check Chapters 2.1 and 3.3.1
[150] Temkin/Schmitt/Herbert (2003)

The alternative explanation for acceptance, ***the skill*** was not directly assessed but the number of training days/employees was taken as a proxy variable: The more days of training were spent, the higher the level of skills. The number of training days and the acceptance rate are nonetheless entirely uncorrelated (r = 0.06). This may be due to the measurement because the inverse argumentation is also plausible: CRM-proficient staff needs fewer days of training. However, only in the four cases of IT services, are the chances of having more IT-savvy employees higher than average. Another explanation may be that the training days really do nothing but provide some initial start-up support. The number of days only spread in a small range: 70% of all participants spent 3 days or less on training with a median of 2 days per employee. So one day more or less of training may not really result in the notable difference in skill level needed to influence the acceptance rate.

As a next step, measures to influence acceptance were analyzed. The ***size of the extended team*** was considered as a proxy for the question if the participant tried to involve as many as possible of those that are affected by the CRM effort. Thereby, the ideas and problems of future users would be identified and taken into account early on so that the solution would be more acceptable than if just the IT specialists had planned the project. Two measurements were analyzed: the FTE on the extended team and the number of FTE on the team in relation to the total FTE that was supposed to work with the CRM system. Both parameters however are almost uncorrelated to the acceptance rate: for the total number of FTE, r = 0.16, for the relative number of FTE r = 0.13[151]. So it is still plausible that an early-on involvement of key users helps to generate a solution that is more acceptable, but there was just no empirical evidence in the sample under research.

The other factor to influence the acceptance rate is a ***distinct change-management effort*** targeting the change in attitudes and behavior of employees. The importance of a conscious change management effort is well recognized in theory and supported by strong evidence[152]. For the case of CRM, research by Speier/Venkatesh[153] implies that the implementation of a CRM-system without an explicit adaptation of the sales representative's self-perception leads to failure in the adoption of the system. Their longitudinal study reveals that the negative attitude only develops over time but that it ultimately leads to the loss of many skilled sales representatives who are increasingly unsure of their role in the

---

[151] Neither one of the two is statistically significant at either the 1% or the 5% level
[152] Stengl/Sommer/Ematinger (2001) p.41
[153] Speier/Venkatesh (2002) esp. p. 109 ff.

organization in relation to the technology. In a CRM Forum survey, 87% of respondents whose CRM projects had failed, blamed inadequate change management[154].

In our study, 14 participants said that they had either used a separate team for that purpose or that one or several team members of the implementation team were entirely dedicated to the change management task. Change management had a strong effect indeed:

- The 14 participants who had a distinct change-management effort alongside the CRM implementation achieved an average acceptance rate of 2.3 and a median 3-y-CFROI of 82%. Comparatively, participants without change management[155] only reached a 3-y-CFROI of roughly 50% and an acceptance rate of 3.0. The difference of 0.7 seems small – but it is equal to the standard deviation of the acceptance rate.

- The median NPV without terminal value for the group of companies deploying change management was EUR 9.3 m, for those without change management, the NPV was only EUR 2.1 m.

Finally, it was also analyzed if the *organizational unit that initiates the CRM project* has an impact on the project's CFROI. If, for example, management drives the project without involving the sales department, it is possible that employee buy-in may be low. The same may happen, if the IT department initiates the CRM project without getting buy-in from the CRM functions, that is, sales, marketing, service, and so on. In a survey by Wilde, the early-on involvement of users is ranked among the most important factors of CRM success[156]. The CRM project's initiator was explicitly asked for in the questionnaire. Only in 11 out of 32 complete data sets, was a single department considered as the driver. In the other 21 cases, a combination of departments was cited. The departments mentioned more than once were sales, marketing, IT (including specialized SAP coordinators), and top management. All participants were grouped three times by involvement:

- Top management as initiator (14 cases) vs. no mention of top management (18 cases),

---

[154] Rigby/Reichheld/Schefter (2002) p.104
[155] n = 18 as 3 data sets were incomplete on this topic
[156] Wilde (2002) p.43

- Marketing/sales as initiator or co-driver (17 cases) vs. no leading involvement of marketing/sales (15 cases), and
- IT as (co-)initiator (11 cases) distinguished from no initial impulse from the IT department (21 cases).

For each of these groups, the mean average 3-y-CFROI has been computed as follows:

	Initiator	Not mentioned	t-statistic[157]
Top Management	112.7%	137.6%	-1.8
Marketing/Sales	131.2%	122.3%	0.63
IT	91.3%	140.3%	-3.9 [158]

Figure 55: Mean average 3-y-CFROI for sub-groups according to leadership in the CRM project

The results fully support the aforementioned hypothesis, that top-down driven projects get less buy-in than those that are initiated by the future users; the mean average 3-y-CFROI for marketing/sales leadership in those projects is highest. Nonetheless, the differences between the first two groups' mean averages are rather small and statistically insignificant. In the case of IT, however, the IT-initiated CRM projects have a 50 percentage-points lower CFROI performance; this is not only the case in the sample, but a difference that almost certainly exists for the entirety of mySAP CRM projects in D-A-CH as the gap is highly significant. This result can be considered as empirical evidence for the widely-held belief that CRM is much more than IT, and that technology-driven projects do not get as much buy-in as initiatives by those who later have to work with the system[159].

To sum up the impact of employee buy-in:
- In the sample under research, usage of CRM has been largely driven by the acceptance rate, not by the number of training days

---

[157] The t-statistic was computed as $t = ((\text{mean average group 1} - \text{mean average group 2}) - 0) / (s * \text{sqr}(1/n_1 - 1/n_2))$ whereby n_a = number of values in group a and $s = \text{sqr}(((\sum_{i=1 \text{ to } n}(x_{1i} - \text{mean average group 1})^2 + (\sum_{i=1 \text{ to } n}(x_{2i} - \text{mean average group 2})^2)/(n_1 + n_2 - 2))$ which is also referred to as the pooled estimate of the standard deviation; the test statistic has a t-distribution with n_1+n_2-2 degrees of freedom on the null hypothesis. CFROI values are approximately normally distributed as visible from Figure 11, so that the t-statistic can be used

[158] Statistically significant at the 0.1% level

[159] Check for that line of argument also chapter 2.1.

- The acceptance in turn has been influenced by dedicated change-management efforts, less so by the size of the extended implementation team
- IT-initiated and driven CRM projects show a significantly lower CFROI compared to those initiated and driven by top management or marketing/sales

4.5.3 Quality of CRM Targets

Another frequently-cited and plausible potential factor of success in CRM project management are clear targets adjusted to the specific situation of the company. The diversity of targets has already been analyzed in Chapter 3.1. Here the impact of the quality of targets on participants CRM success is to be analyzed. Two parameters were seen as indicative for this quality of targets.

First, the ***quality of the CRM concept at the outset of the project*** was rated by respondents on the scale of German grades (1= very good, 5=insufficient). Clarity and quality were evaluated relative to the lessons learnt in the project. This indicator has a feeble correlation coefficient with respect to NPV ($r = (-0.14)$), and it is entirely uncorrelated with CFROI, regardless of whether it is on a 3-year or a 5-year basis.

The same holds true for the correlation between the second measurement, the ***time spent on choosing the product, feasibility study, and blueprinting***. This period of time was considered as a proxy for the quality of preparation. However, it is uncorrelated ($r = 0.06$) to either NPV or CFROI. Here, as with the number of training days in the previous chapter, it may be a measurement problem. Companies that are absolutely focused and clear about what they are trying to achieve may not need to spend a lot of time on the project planning without reducing the quality of targets.

So despite the fact that it is plausible to expect a better result from a clear and correct concept, the missing evidence from the study and some of the narrations from respondents also hint at a possible other explanation. Several times, respondents reported that despite a major effort to plan the CRM investment, their assumptions concerning the sources of value were wrong, the time and effort of the project were miscalculated, the quality of the customer data was not correctly assessed, and so on. Therefore, they had to constantly and quickly adapt to an ever-changing situation. Many iterations on the concept lead to a poor grade on the quality of the initial targets but without the concept, it was agreed that the project would have experienced even more difficulties to stay on track. Thus the initial concept may still be an important factor of CRM success, while the ability to adapt and quickly change the concept is needed as well.

4.5.4 Proficiency of Project Execution

Besides project planning, the follow-through on the project is also regarded as a factor of CRM success. Keeping "in time, in budget" and delivering the requested changes of processes, as well as keeping the system up and running are common criteria for project success. Furthermore, most participants were supported by implementation partners, professional IT service companies that provided skilled manpower as well as methodology and knowledge about the software. These factors were also investigated in the study.

The *time of the CRM project* has been explicitly assessed in the questionnaire as time elapsed, that is, not the FTE but the months spent on making CRM happen. Different phases were distinguished along a generic software implementation model: the decision about the software, feasibility study, blueprint and process reengineering, the core phase of software implementation, testing and modifications, and finally the migration of data. Not all participants went through all of these phases. Sometimes the decision about the software was obsolete, as top management had already made a strategic decision for SAP. Some participants did no blueprinting or process reengineering. Data migration was also sometimes substituted for complete re-inputting of customer data, because the original data was so bugged that it did not pay to modify. Also, many projects – especially in the early phases – frequently stopped, as the project manager was waiting for decisions from top management. Therefore, only the core phase of software implementation is taken as the relevant indicator for the project duration. It normally constitutes the longest phase of the entire project and once started, it runs without breaks.

The shorter the time-to-implementation, the higher the CFROI – that was the hypothesis. On the one hand, a short time to implementation indicates proficient project execution, focus on the main value added features, no or few technical difficulties, skilled project management with commitment to milestones, which may also continue after the project through collecting the accrued benefit for the company by raising revenue targets or reducing cost. The value of CRM may also rise by the simple fact that due to a shorter project, the positive effects will materialize earlier. On the other hand, a shorter implementation also reduces the expenses for third-party support as well as own staff in the project. Participants recorded the following implementation times:

Key Factors of Success – Good Project Management

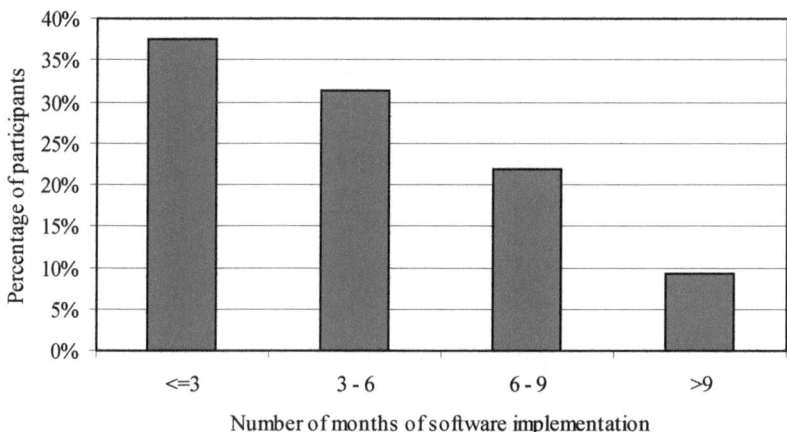

Figure 56: Distribution of the number of months of software implementation

Only three participants needed more than 9 months for the implementation of mySAP CRM software, most stayed well below half a year. As predicted, the correlation coefficient of r = (-0.27) shows that right sign, although it is too weak to be of any statistical significance for the entirety of mySAP CRM users in D-A-CH. So only in the sample can we state that speed in the project matters, not as an end in itself but as an indicator of numerous elements of good project execution.

Project execution can be judged on the basis of the process, but also with regard to the result. The result of the implementation project phase is twofold: changes in the relevant CRM processes as well as a CRM application that is up and running. Changes in process speed, sequence, and so on, are the basis for many of the efficiency and effectiveness gains, described in Chapter 3. Therefore it can be expected that the more profound changes in processes yielded higher project results. So two measures were applied:

- First, the ***project time spent on blueprinting and process redesign*** was correlated to NPV and CFROI. The idea behind this was to check if more time spent on the project's concept would yield a higher benefit afterwards. However, both coefficients of correlation were close to zero.
- Then, respondents were asked to assess what ***percentage of a workday's activities had significantly changed due to the CRM implementation per CRM employee***. If no change in processes took place, CFROI of CRM was expected to be low if not zero or negative. Thereby it must be noted that the

Key Factors of Success – Good Project Management

measurement only covers the breadth of change in processes, not its depth. So few processes may have been impacted but these few activities may have been fundamentally changed. In this particular case, the correlation would be low even if the change in processes does affect profitability of CRM. The following distribution of values somewhat hints in exactly that direction:

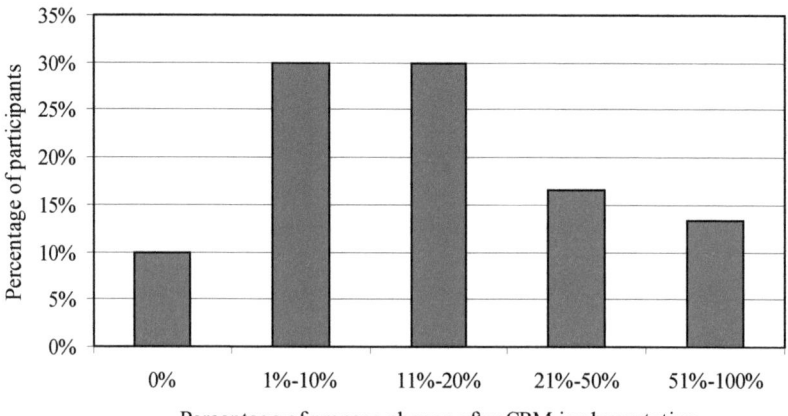

Figure 57: Distribution of the percentage change of processes upon CRM implementation

70% of all participants had seen a change of less than 20% of all activities per employee on average. So change, indeed, was focused on a few processes and activities therein. Therefore it is not surprising that the parameter of the percentage of processes changed per employee was not correlated at all to either NPV or CFROI. As the depth of change per process was not assessed for reasons of time constraint in the interview, the question remains unanswered to what extent this is a factor of success.

Then, the **quality of the implementation partner** could potentially influence CRM success. Therefore, this quality was explicitly assessed using German grades[160]. Overall, respondents were quite satisfied with the support they received from third parties: The median grade is a 2.0, the mean average a 2.3. The worst grades are 3.5 (two times), and four times the partner was rated at 1.0.

---

[160] Ranging from 1.0 = very good to 5.0 = insufficient; as any decimal was allowed to be given, the measure can be considered to deliver cardinal values of which mean average and correlation can be computed

However, the impact of the implementation partner on the project's economic success does not show in the numbers: The coefficient of correlation between the partner's grade and the project's CFROI is r = 0.06; for the NPV it is r = 0.13 – so these variables are uncorrelated. The higher value for the NPV may be due to the simple fact that for larger projects more qualified implementation partners were sought.

Another potential factor of success may be the *project's progress before going live*: Some project managers favor a "rapid prototyping" kind of roll-out with only a limited set of functionality and users at first, whereas others do not go live until almost all functionality is available – but then they start with a large number of users. Both parameters were explicitly asked for.

The *available functionality at the productive start* of the application was assessed by the respondent as a percentage of the functionality planned for in the steady state. Possibly due to the fact that the participants came from German-speaking countries, which are notorious for their tendency to drive everything to perfection before going to market, the median value is high at almost 85%, that is, before going live, 85% of the planned functionality was available. Nonetheless, for the participants in the study, this parameter is entirely uncorrelated to either CFROI or NPV.

The same is true for another parameter, which was deemed important for CRM success by many a participant: the *number of CRM functional modules live*. Only one participant had all 5 possible modules live: marketing, sales, service, the Interaction Center, and Internet sales. 5 participants were live with 3 CRM functions, 13 with 2 functions and 13 with only one function. However the breadth of applications live is totally uncorrelated with the 3-y-CFROI (r = (-0.09)) or the NPV (r=0.0014). So one can earn a return on the CRM investment on a broad set of functionality as well as on a focused use of one or two CRM functions.

The *number of users with whom the participating companies went live* ranges from 2 to 500 with a median of 30 and a mean average of 63 employees. This figure shows some slight though statistically insignificant impact on the 3-y-CFROI with r = (-0.22). The negative sign means that the smaller the number of staff in the beginning the higher the economic return on the investment. This may be explained by smaller implementations simply paying off faster; it may also be due to the fact that some of the very successful CRM implementations in IT services as well as Internet sales installations only require a very small number of staff to generate a significant payback. Finally, it may also mean that the "small productive start – then roll-out" tactics in CRM project management is more successful.

> To sum up the findings on the value impact of proficiency in project execution:
> - While a short implementation time somewhat correlates with CFROI, it is more an indicator than an operational lever, signalling several characteristics of good project execution
> - In the same line, some evidence has been provided for the "start-small" tactics in CRM roll-out.
> - All other plausible parameters that might influence the CFROI or NPV, that is, the conceptual depth, breadth of processes impacted, initial functionality available, or the quality of the implementation partner have not been confirmed as success-critical in this study. Nonetheless, the study's statistical basis does not support a statement, that these factors are not important!

4.6 Value Drivers by Industry Sector

In Chapter 4.1., results were differentiated by sector. In the following Chapters 4.2 – 4.5, a broad variety of possible influences has been analyzed in their relative importance to the CFROI of CRM. In this concluding chapter, the question as to which sector displays which characteristics that may explain the difference in the CRM performance for each sector, remains to be answered. For this purpose, a matrix has been constructed[161]. On the left hand side, all the factors of success, which have been evidenced in the sample are listed, grouped according to the external and internal situational factors and the project management factors as a third category. Two factors are missing: the "systems" as one of the internal factors, as no evidence was found, and the quality of targets in the category of project management. At the top, the sector groups are listed in the order of their 3-y-CFROI median values – starting from the IT services with the highest and ending with the diverse services group as the lowest. For each cell of the matrix, a valuation has been given as to which extent the factor applies to the sector group, indicated by "moons". A full moon signals that the factor fully applies, an empty moon means that no impact of the factor was evidenced – and the other moons gradually map between the two extremes. On the bottom, a

---

[161] The same technique is deployed by Wehrmeister (2001) p.93 ff., just with a different set of hypothetical success factors and sectors; the findings are not based on empirical research.

total "impact score" was calculated by valuing each quarter moon with 1 point and summing up the partial values.

● Factor fully given
○ Factor absent

	IT Services	Consumer/ Build. Mat.	Chemical	Engineering	Pharma/ Medical	Diverse Services
• Production Technology	●	◐	◐	◔	◔	◕
• Customers	●	◔	◔	◔	◕	◕
• Competition	●	●	◔	◔	◔	○
• Organizational Structure	◔	◕	○	◕	◔	◕
• Demographics of staff	●	◔	◔	◔	◔	◔
• Mgmt. support	●	◔	●	◐	◕	◕
• Employee buy-in	◔	●	●	●	◔	◕
• Proficiency of execution	●	◐	◐	◔	◐	◔
	28	21	20	18	15	9

Figure 58: Overview: CRM value drivers by sector

Before the different valuations are explained in detail, one observation should be stated up front: The sequence of impact scores is equal to the ranking in the 3-y-CFROI. So, indeed, the factors analyzed one-by-one in Chapters 4.2 to 4.5 are indicative of the differences in CFROI by sectors. Thus it can also be expected that these factors provide an initial checklist for each individual company that has to decide on whether to invest in CRM or not. However, it should also be noted that the relative distance between the "impact scores" differs from the difference of CFROI results. The equal weighting that was implicitly assumed may therefore be incorrect. Furthermore, non-linear effects may come into play. So if a critical mass of favorable conditions is given, the results may develop exponentially.

First the *IT service* sector is investigated as its participants achieved the highest economic return on their CRM investment in almost all dimensions. From

Figure 58, it is already visible that the factors for economic CRM success identified in this study are nearly perfectly given. In terms of the *production technology*, the IT services take all the benefit from the service sector as well as the advantage for a highly complex and customized offer to the market. They typically depend on a few *customers* to which they enjoy multi-layer relationships, which need to be coordinated, often across international boundaries. In two cases, one customer made up more than 50% of the entire revenue. With regard to the customers especially, IT services also display one special aspect that massively drives value: Their CRM skills are not only employed in relation to their customers, – they are even sold to their customers. CRM implementations in-house have been cited in three out of four cases as a major gain in credibility with customers in selling CRM implementation services. Thus the revenue side of IT services has seen a major boost as a direct result of their CRM investments and, in three out of four cases, the revenue side was the one that created most value.

Two to three years back, *competition* was low in the sector – given the breathtaking e-business rally leading to fully employed capacities to cope with the flood of projects. There was no time to care for optimized internal processes. Right after the hype, the dehype set in, leading to a frenzy of activity on the sales side – again without spending time on optimization. Therefore, now that the competition is cutthroat in a shrinking market, the improvement potential is high at the same time – ideal conditions for CRM to create value.

With regard to the *organizational dynamics*, two of the four IT service companies in the sample resulted from a merger, a situation, which in itself is a source of inefficiencies and change. Furthermore, IT services are project-driven businesses that are used to rapid change and fast reactions to market requirements. IT services *staff* naturally understands and uses technological innovation relatively quickly and easily. This bears fruit in terms of short implementation times – and a short time-to-use. They are professionals in project management, coupled with an intimate knowledge of their own company, which leads to high *proficiency in CRM projects*. Management support was highest in the sample. There is the only one caveat in an otherwise almost spotless record: Acceptance among employees varied drastically. For two participants, the acceptance rate was at 100%, for one 50% and for another close to zero. Also, employee usage of the system was far from best practice. Change teams had sometimes not been installed – which may have been due to the mistaken assumption that IT staff would adapt anyhow. Despite a somewhat mixed picture on employee buy-in, the projects were implemented in record time of less than 6 months. Thus it is not surprising to also see a break-even period that is 25% of the average with respect to all participants. All in all, the abundance of positive influencing factors well explains the outstanding position of IT services within the entire spectrum of participants.

The "runner-up", *consumer products and building materials*, already takes a steep drop in the overall "impact score". For most participants from this sector group, *customization* of their products to the specific customer situation is paramount, as well as cooperation with several other companies in delivering to the customer. At the top, they have a large variety of products and services to offer. The amount of *customers* is higher than for the IT service providers and customer interaction is shorter and easier to manage. *Competition* is fierce though, since the market for consumer products is stagnating and producers of furniture as well as building materials have to survive in a shrinking market – which makes a strong customer relationship even more valuable. Only one company in the group had undergone major *organizational change* recently; the other ones were more or less stable. Thus only a quarter "moon" was attributed. *Demographics of staff* – as for all other sector groups – do not display any special characteristics that are either favorable or disadvantageous. So the internal situational factors are rather weak, contrary to the high *proficiency in project management*. Management support is rather mid-field with an average score of 2.0. Employee buy-in, however, is top of the league. The usage exceeds 80% on average, and many participants had a separate change management team in action. Also, the project duration is second only to IT services. So fast and focused implementations with great emphasis on the "human side" of CRM seem to be characteristic in this sector group and lead to high profitability.

Chemical producers are on the same level in the "impact score" – and differ little in economic success. The pattern is also very similar: External situational factors of success and very good CRM project management drive CRM performance. Compared to consumer goods and building materials, *many more products* are under management – but the need to customize is not as high. Still, a medium level of customization is nonetheless needed as no bulk chemicals were produced, but rather substances that meet the requirements of the customers' machinery exactly. The number of *customers* is on average not very high, again for the same reason that rather specialized products were produced for a relatively stable, narrow, and demanding market niche. *Competition* in this narrow market is strong – however, the overall market volume is stable, and due to the high specialization, changing suppliers is not so easily done, at least for some of the participating companies. So overall, competitive pressure was only set at a medium level.

All of the chemical producers were among the stable companies – so the factor of *organizational dynamics* did not apply. On the contrary, two respondents talked about the rather slow pace of change in their companies with regard to altering the product scope or organizational processes in the area of CRM. On CRM *project management*, the chemical producers took the lead of all sector groups – even topping the IT services sector. Management support was rated as either very good (1.0 in German grades) or good (2.0 respectively). All companies had dedicated change-management efforts, resulting in the highest employee acceptance rate with a group average of 2.1 (again in German grades). Also the usage of the CRM system relative to expectations was above average – although not quite as strong as it would have been expected given the high level of acceptance. In terms of project duration, there was almost no difference to the consumer products and building materials – and had the exact same figure as for pharma/medical to the decimal.

Slightly down on the "impact score" are participants from the *engineering* group on average – although, of course, within that group some companies exceeded the average as they showed more favorable characteristics for a high CFROI on CRM. The *need for customization* is also very high in this group, but less so the number and diversity of products. The breadth of market and the competitive pressure score mid-field. One company originated from a spin-off, then entered into a merger that created one of the highest levels of organizational change of all participants. However, this was an exception in an otherwise rather stable setting of companies. The score on *project management* is somewhat mixed. On the one hand, engineering is in the top league for employee buy-in. The system's usage is second highest of all sector groups and so is acceptance. Four of the eight participants in this group had dedicated change efforts. Compared to the leading sectors, management support scores only marginally lower: Four of the eight participants give the highest possible grade of 1.0. In terms of project execution, it is striking that projects run the longest of all sector groups. This may be sensible to more thoroughly convince staff and thus get a higher payback. Then engineering companies would be ill-advised to cut back on project time of a few months thereby jeopardizing the high employee buy-in. Projects should be screened, however, for nice-to-have features that may not be as profitable as the core functionality and which may thus dilute overall CFROI.

Participants from the *pharmaceutical industry and medical supplies* were comparatively heterogeneous with regard to their economic benefit from CRM whereby it is not the two sectorial sub-groups that differ but rather companies within these sub-groups. The number of substances of a pharmaceutical company is huge – but the number of marketable *end* products is comparatively much smaller. Furthermore, the products are not customized. Then, the sales representative in pharma sees a dozen *customers* a day, but due to the legal setting, does not sell but rather introduces new products to the "customer", the physician. This requires adaptation to the "customer's" preferences, for example, the sales representative needs to recall the last discussion. So CRM still creates a benefit in this special customer relationship. Nonetheless, it is much more difficult to achieve a quick return via increasing revenue. The medical supplies are somewhat more straightforward, in the sense that sales representatives still see many customers relative to other sectors, but they are allowed to sell to physicians and hospitals. Finally, *competition* is at a level comparable to engineering or chemicals – all are active in mature but still growing markets.

Surprisingly low is the *management support* in the pharma/medical-group. With an average grade of 2.5 (between good and satisfactory according to the German system) and only one participant viewing management support at a very good level, this sector group is second lowest of all. Also, *acceptance by employees* is far lower than with, for example chemicals, despite the fact that three out of 6 participants had a dedicated change-management effort alongside their CRM implementation project. The usage is nonetheless at the level of chemicals or engineering. This high level of usage coupled with a small acceptance could be explained by the rather standardized approach to sales in this industry: So CRM staff uses the system without being convinced. This attitude certainly is not the recipe for success. As far as the *proficiency of the project execution* is concerned, the pharma/medical is in the top group second only to IT services.

Finally, the *diverse services* are analyzed, the one sector group with the largest diversity in terms of sectors but also in terms of economic success. Overall, this group scores last on the CFROI, NPV, and break-even period. The reason can be seen immediately in Figure 58: This group takes a serious drop in the "impact score" in relation to the other clusters. Except for one bank, the *services* under investigation do not require a high degree of customization and the number of services available is rather limited as well. So the rationale of higher CRM benefits in services applies – but not the more important aspect of complexity and customization of the market offering.

The number of *customers* is large on average; the importance of each single customer is rather low. For a local utility, customers do not have a choice (yet). For a health insurer, new customers are not necessarily bliss, but potentially even a problem – especially when they are healthy and young. This paradoxical situation can only be explained by the German legislation, requiring health insurers to pay a predefined amount of money for their "good risks" to the entire community of insurers (to cover for their "bad risks"), and that amount is so high that the health insurer is disincentivized to seek "good risks". The problematic situation that raising revenue is difficult or even impossible is true for 4 out of 6 companies in the group, the reasons being that they are owned by their customers, or their prices are regulated by legislation. The strong public influence in this sector also shields largely from *competition*. Many companies in this group are monopolies or quasi-monopolies by internal regulation – so competition is frequently non-existent. The companies in this field are relatively *stable* – only one underwent major change.

Most of the *highly problematic implementation projects* were located in this group – for several reasons. First of all, management support is the lowest of all sectors – in one case reaching down to the worst grade, a 5.0 (=insufficient). This can in part be explained by the fact that frequently management consisted of a group of decision makers on the same hierarchical level who had to agree. So it is not surprising that several respondents reported difficult projects with ever-changing requirements from all sides. Where there was conflict, the solution was not always sought on a rational basis but on the basis of politics – which reduced the economic benefit of the CRM investment considerably. Only one of 6 projects entailed a dedicated change effort. Changing requirements, compromise solutions, and a rather mechanistic focus on the technical side – coupled with some technical problems – led in many cases to a low employee acceptance, in fact the lowest of all the sector groups. Also, some respondents told of a weak management follow-up on benefits: As there was no necessity felt to increase efficiency, the protest of employees made management quickly back-off and leave the system's use to volunteers – which then ended in a downward-spiralling information dynamics loop as described in Chapter 3.3.1. Consequently, the usage of the system by employees was only at a little over 60% of what had been expected at the outset of the project.

From all these observations it is apparent that

- The differences in sector return on CRM investment can well be explained by the existence or absence of factors of success
- The "sector" is **not** an "inescapable fate". But every company should check to which extent external and/or internal situational factors of success apply, and should try for a highly proficient CRM project management. It can then far outperform its sector's average.

5 Closing Remarks: Strengths, Limitations, and Best Use of Results

The study's strengths and limitations are highlighted so that the reader can draw adequate conclusions. The best way for decision-makers to use of the results are outlined.

5.1 Strengths of the Study: Neutral, Quantitative, and Systematically In-Depth

Strengths of the study on "CFROI of Customer Relationship Management" can be summarized as follows:

- *Neutrality through the trustee model* supports openness of participants and provides independence from third party influence. To obtain a realistic picture of the effects of CRM is extremely difficult, and one of the most severe obstacles is the unwillingness to make public quantitative results – whether they are positive or negative. The chosen trustee model, where only the author receives the raw information, which is then analyzed and published to protect the anonymity of participants, solves this problem and therefore enhances the quality and depth of the information given. Also, the independence of the research is guaranteed, as no third party – including SAP – had or will have access to the raw data.
- *Quantitative financial results* have been calculated as CFROI, NPV, and break-even period, instead of producing just another list of potential plausible benefits through CRM. The openness created by the research design made full-circle quantitative results possible, instead of just qualitative statements or small, quantified aspects, which do not add up.
- The ***study is more than a simple survey*** as it does not simply ask for ROI, but it interactively builds business cases with the participants, to come up with systematic and comparable results. It has been discovered in the study, that respondents knew of less than 1% of the benefit before going through the study process. So naturally, simple surveys that directly ask for ROI of CRM do not come up with correct result. If the identity of the survey participants is not validated, as in some recently run Internet surveys, the validity of the results is even more doubtful. The individual in-depth business cases stand in sharp contrast to these practices.

- A step-by-step **CRM success metric** starts from a phase-by-phase process analysis and moves onto cost and revenue impact, to highly aggregated figures of financial performance. Therefore, only those effects caused by CRM are taken into consideration, and double counts are avoided.
- Not only is the metric sophisticated – it was also filled with **high-quality input data**. This point is illustrated by the following observations:
  - More than half of the NPV and 70% of the CFROI are based on *observed effects*, not on expectations. Evidence speaks against hype in experience-based expectations.
  - Furthermore, *sensitivity analyses* were conducted for 29 of the participants' business cases. This gave rise to some important data being systematically varied to analyze the impact on the target values like CFROI or NPV. The sensitivity of the most critical variable varied tremendously among business cases: For a 50% reduction of the most sensitive parameter, the CFROI was reduced by 17.5% up to 150% (median: 58.5%), while the NPV suffered a 19% and 74% reduction (median: 49%). In 23 cases, however, that is almost 80%, a 50% misassessment of the most sensitive parameter did not result in a negative 3-y-CFROI, while only a single NPV turned negative after reducing the most sensitive parameter by 50%. This clearly shows that the results are robust in that even gross misassessments would not lead to a different conclusion – which speaks for the quality of the data.
  - The *time of being live with mySAP CRM should be uncorrelated to the CFROI or NPV* if the respondents were able to assess the situation correctly. And that is the case: The correlation coefficient between the time live with the longest running CRM functional module and the 3-y-CFROI is $r = (-0.11)$; for the NPV it is $r = 0.0029$.
- Potentially influencing *factors of success have been systematically conceptualized and measured* in the study. Although the empirical results need to be interpreted given the limitations as outlined in the next chapter, they refute the myths that success is "doable" for all or that CRM is irrelevant for some companies, for example for small and medium enterprises.
- Finally, the study's design ensures that the criteria for measuring quality of an empirical study are being met.
  - *Objectivity* is achieved when intersubjective measurements come to the same conclusion. The study's objectivity is achieved through the CRM value metric and unambiguous measurements, and the fact that

interviews were carried out over phone - ensuring that any uncertainty about the questionnaire was quickly cleared up. Another factor contributing to the objectivity of the study is that in over 50% of cases, the contact person consulted other employees in the company. Where the effects determined have been compared with business cases compiled by third parties, the results are consistent. In some cases, this study identifies effects that were not identified in the business cases.

- A study is *reliable* when the same results are achieved under the same conditions. As this study is exploratory in nature, the condition can only been proven by carrying out an identical research in the future. However, even now, a few characteristics suggest reliability already. First of all, interviewees gave reasons for their answers, allowing the relationship between operational causes and effects to be assessed. In cases where several factors have changed, the study identifies the CRM effect. In addition, the author gathered and evaluated all the information personally; this eliminates the possibility of variation between different interviewers.

- The *validity* of the study is assessed in terms of internal and external validity. Internal validity (the extent to which the effects identified are due to the use of mySAP CRM rather than other variable factors) is ensured by the research design. External validity (universality of the results) cannot be ensured because the results have the double focus on mySAP CRM and on D-A-CH. A range of industries and dimensions was surveyed, however, which does contribute to the external validity.

5.2 Limitations of the Study: Small Sample, and Limited Geographic Scope

Some limitations need to be borne in mind in order to draw adequate conclusions:

- The first and maybe most severe limitation of the study is that the sample size of only 35 participants is relatively small given the size of the base population of mySAP CRM users and the high level of variation among the individual companies for almost all key indicators of success. So the *range of probable outcomes[162] for a future CRM user remains large*. Also the sample process itself is unclear, and to consider the results to be indicative, one has to believe in the promise of SAP that at least no conscious bias for

---

[162] In statistical terms the "confidence intervals" at 95% or 99% likelihood

the positive cases has taken place. So the results need to be seen as what they were announced: empirical evidence in an exploratory type of research. The participants in the sample did indeed experience the improvements on all levels as described – but that is no guarantee that the same will happen for any other user. For many in the situation of deciding on CRM it may nonetheless be useful to have some systematically gathered factual and quantitative evidence now for an initial feasibility check.

- Only *few of the plausible hypothesized factors of CRM success were found to be statistically significant*. Therefore the hypotheses still need to be tested rigorously on the basis of a larger sample.
- The study represents the most comprehensive comparable analysis of the potential of mySAP CRM to create value in Germany, Austria, and Switzerland. But *that double focus also limits applicability of results* to Europe outside the German speaking countries as well as to the US or Japan. Furthermore, the results do not claim any superiority of mySAP CRM over other comparable applications: The study does not compare software products. This question, which is also important for a decision maker, remains unanswered. The same methodology can of course be applied to other countries as well as to other software vendors – so there is ample space for future research in the area.

5.3 Best Use of the Results: Guidance for the Company Specific Business Case

Given the strengths and limitations of the study, its results should neither be read as a recommendation to invest in a CRM-system – nor as a vote not to invest. It has been empirically shown that users of CRM have achieved significant financial benefits. With a 99.9% chance, the investment in mySAP CRM for users in D-A-CH has on average returned a positive CFROI and increased the company's value. This clear and strong evidence should lead decision makers to take a closer look at the CRM business opportunity. However, there were several cases in the study that did not achieve their financial or operational targets. Therefore the best use of the results is to take them as guidance in crafting a company- and situation-specific business case on CRM.

Chapter 4 pinpoints some situations which are especially prone to yield a positive return: post-merger organizations with a high degree of inefficiency, the need for international coordination of CRM functions, high competitive pressure, numerous diverse products or services with a high degree of customization, or a narrow market with few and therefore especially valuable customers. If one or several of these situational parameters apply, an assessment of the value of CRM should be high on the management agenda.

The first step towards a CRM value assessment is to form a cross-functional team. As the study's findings highlight: CRM should not be an "IT project", rather a business project with a strong enabling IT component. So specialists from the CRM-functions, that is, from marketing, sales, services, E-sales, and the Interaction Center, as well as specialists from the IT department should form the team's nucleus. A controller ought to be involved for the financial modeling. Furthermore, there should be at least one generalist member with sufficient knowledge of CRM systems and CRM business processes, experience in business process redesign, and finance to bridge the differing perspectives. According to the study's results, management support is paramount and should be present from the start. The CRM Value Metric from Chapter 2 may provide logic and rigor in the assessment of operational and business benefits. In addition, it helps to integrate the differing points of view as it builds systematically from the diverse operational process improvements to the financial impact indicators. Finally, the deployment of the CRM Value Metric may increase the willingness of team members to make a commitment through an enhancement of understanding. So while it is difficult to commit to whatever percentage of cost reduction – it is easier to promise a certain reduction in time needed for a marketing campaign, for example, given that these and these features of the CRM application will be implemented. So every team member only has to assess and approve what is in his or her scope of experience; the financial impact of CRM will result almost automatically from these individual assessments.

Chapter 3 can be supportive in making informed assumptions when otherwise relevant data is missing. Furthermore it helps to focus on the key value drivers of an investment in CRM which shortens the planning cycle, saves resources, and yields better results, all at the same time. When the business case has been approved by those who will be impacted, management needs to decide. This decision will now be founded on a clear understanding of the financial consequences as well as on committed figures and assumptions.

If it is decided to implement a CRM system, Chapter 4 identifies empirically some of the key factors of project success – continued management support, employee buy-in, and proficient project management. Throughout the implementation project, the business case provides for guidance. That is not a claim that the business case correctly anticipates the future; no one can do so. However, all available information is systematically assessed and evaluated. And especially in uncertain situations with the high likelihood of changes in the assessments, new information about the customers' preferences, and so on, a business case that is designed according to the principles of the CRM Value Metric proves to be a valuable steering device: Every new information can quickly and thoroughly be checked about its financial impact. Thus management can focus on the most serious issues. Investments will only be made, if they still promise to be profitable – and they are stopped immediately when the situation or the understanding of the situation changed so much as to render the business case negative. To ensure this level of flexibility, however, requires that operational and financial indicators be systematically linked.

So the study's results support all four steps on the way to a value-adding CRM investment: the identification of CRM as a potential business opportunity, the assessment of and commitment to operational improvements by a cross-functional team, the decision, and the CRM project steering. Nonetheless, as users and uses of CRM widely differ, the results will not answer all questions. So the author of the study gladly engages in a discussion on how to tailor-make these steps to the specific needs of the company to ensure that the decision maker will achieve the utmost value of this research.

6 Appendix

6.1 References

Adolf, Ruediger, Stacey Grant-Thompson, Wendy Harrington, and Marc Singer (1997) What Leading Banks are Learning About Big Databases and Marketing, in: McKinsey Quarterly, No. 3, p. 187-192

AMR Research (2003) quoted from: CRM and Business Intelligence Insights, Market Size Insights, in: intellibusiness.com, http://www.intellibusiness.com/c2c/fc/market-stats-c2c-01.htm, June 17, 2003

Avlonitis, George J. and Despina A. Karayanni (2000) The impact of the Internet Use on Business-to-Business Marketing, in: Industrial Marketing Management, Vol. 29, p.452-460

Bauer, Hans H., Mark Grether and Mark Leach (2002) Building Customer Relationships over the Internet, in: Industrial Marketing Management, Vol. 31, p.155-163

Blattberg, Robert C., Gary Getz and Jacquelyn S. Thomas (2001) Customer Equity, Boston

Campbell, Alexandra J. (2003) Creating Customer Knowledge Competence: Managing Customer Relationship Programs Strategically, in: Industrial Marketing Management, Vol. 32, No. 5, p. 375-383

Caulfield, Simon (2001) Does CRM Really Pay? A General Management Perspective, in: SCN Education B.V. (eds.) Customer Relationship Management – The Ultimate Guide to the Efficient Use of CRM, Braunschweig, p.17-21

Copeland, Tom and Vladimir Antikarov (2001) Real Options, New York

Copeland, Tom, Tim Koller, and Jack Murrin (1995) Valuation: Measuring and Managing the Value of Companies, 2nd ed., New York

Dangelmaier, Wilhelm, Matthias F. Uebel and Stefan Helmke (2002) Grundrahmen des Customer Relationship Management – Ansatzes, in: dieselben (eds.) Praxis des Customer Relationship Management. Branchenlösungen und Erfolgsberichte, Wiesbaden, p.3-16.

Dombrowski, Ines and Alexander Messinger (2003) Einführung einer ganzheitlichen CRM-Strategie bei Schott-Glas: Konzeption und Vorgehensweise, in: Teichmann, René (ed.): Customer und shareholder relationship management: erfolgreiche Kunden- und Aktionärsbindung in der Praxis, Berlin, p.242-246.

Dull, Stephen F., Timothy Stephens, and Mark. T. Wolfe (2000) How much are Customer Relationship Management capabilities really worth? What every CEO should know – Executive Summary, Accenture, www.accenture.com/xdoc/en/services/crm/whatceos.pdf, Sept. 5th, 2003

Dyché, Jill (2002) The CRM Handbook – A Business Guide to Customer Relationship Management, Boston

Fielding, Rachel (2003) CRM Boom Will Boost Project Success, in: crmdaily.com, May 29, 2003, www.crmdaily.com/perl/story/21630.html from June 17th, 2003

Fischer, Marc, Andreas Herrmann and Frank Huber (2001) Return on Customer Satisfaction, in: Zeitschrift für Betriebswirtschaft, Vol. 71, No. 10, p. 1161-1190

Frielitz, C, Hajo Hippner, S. Martin, and Klaus D. Wilde (2000) CRM 2000 – Erfahrungen, Einschätzungen und Bedürfnisse aus Anwendersicht, in: Wilde, Klaus D. and Hajo Hippner (eds.) CRM 2000, Düsseldorf

Gardner, Christopher (2000) The Valuation of Information Technology – A Guide For Strategy Development, Valuation, and Financial Planning, New York.

Gartner (2002) CRM Sales Suite General Reference Check Questions at: www.gartner.com, http://eventsurvey.gartner.com/Infopoll/surveys/s300.htm, Nov. 11th, 2002

Gartner (2003) quoted from: CRM and Business Intelligence Insights, Market Size Insights, in: intellibusiness.com, http://www.intellibusiness.com/c2c/fc/market-stats-c2c-01.htm, June 17, 2003

Giering, Annette (2000) Der Zusammenhang zwischen Kundenzufriedenheit und Kundenloyalität : eine Untersuchung moderierender Effekte, Wiesbaden

Grant, Alan W. H. and Leonhard A. Schlesinger (1995) Realize your customer's full profit potential, in: Harvard Business Review, Vol. 73, No. 5, p.59-72

Hauke, Ulrich and Andreas Schuh (eds.) (2002) Business Scenarios for mySAP Customer Relationship Management – Using SAP CRM 3.0, Walldorf

Henn, Harald (2001) Wie rentabel sind CRM-Projekte, in: Call Center Profi 2001, Nr. 7-8, p.40-45

Helmke, Stefan, Dörte Brinker, and Helge Wessoly (2001) Change Management für den erfolgreichen Roll Out von CRM-Systemen, in: Helmke, Stefan and Wilhelm Dangelmaier (eds.) Effektives Customer Relationship Management, Wiesbaden, S. 291-302

Hippner, Hajo and Klaus D. Wilde (2003) Customer Relationship Management – Strategie und Realisierung, in: Teichmann, René (ed.) Customer und Shareholder Relationship Management – Erfolgreiche Kunden und Aktionärsbindung in der Praxis, Berlin, 2003, p.3-52

Homburg, Christian and Frank Sieben (2000) Customer relationship management: strategische Ausrichtung statt IT getriebenem Aktivismus, Mannheim

Horváth, Péter (1988) Grundprobleme der Wirtschaftlichkeitsanalyse beim Einsatz neuer Informations- und Produktionstechnologien, in: Horváth, Péter (ed.) Wirtschaftlichkeit neuer Produktions- und Informationstechnologien, Stuttgart, p. 1-14

Huber, Harald (1999) Die Bewertung des Nutzens von IV-Anwendungen, in: von Dobschütz, Leonhard, Ulrike Baumöl and Reinhard Jung (eds.): IV-Controlling aktuell, Wiesbaden, p.107-122.

Johnson, Rod (2003) How You Define CRM Success Depends on Who You Are, in: AMR Research Alert, Jan. 24th, 2003, http://www.amrresearch.com Research/Alerts/Pdf/030124alert15613.pdf, Sept. 3rd, 2003

Kaplan, Robert S. (1986) CIM-Investitionen sind keine Glaubensfrage, in: Harvard-Manager, Vol. 3, p. 78-85.

Kehl, Roger E. and Bernd J. Rudolph (2001) Warum CRM-Projekte scheitern, in: Link, Jörg (ed.) Customer Relationship Management, Berlin, p.253-273

Keltz, Heather and Laura Preslan (2003) ROI Still Elusive in Customer Management, in: AMR Research Alert, Sept. 4th, 2003, http://www.amr research.com/Alerts/Pdf/030904alert16556.pdf, Sept. 5th, 2003

Kieser, Alfred and Herbert Kubicek (1992) Organisation, 3rd ed., Berlin

Kotler, Philip (2000) Marketing Management, 10th ed., New Jersey

Leek, Sheena, Peter W. Turnbull, and Peter Naudé (2003) How is information technology affecting business relationships? Results from a UK survey, in: Industrial Marketing Management, Vol. 32, No.2, p.119-126

Li, Tiger and Roger J. Calantone (1998) The impact of market knowledge competence on new product advantage: Conceptualization and empirical examination, in: Journal of Marketing, Vol. 62, Oct., p.13-29

Meltzer, Michael (2001) Building the Business Case Blues or Business Case Blues, in: SCN Education B.V. (eds.) Customer Relationship Management – The Ultimate Guide to the Efficient Use of CRM, Braunschweig,, p.311-321

MicroStrategy (2002) Retail Success Stories, at: http://www.microstrategy.com/download/files/customers/success/retail.pdf, Sept. 5th, 2003

Morphy, Erika (2003) Surge in CRM spending, Satisfaction Forecast, in: CRMDaily.com, http://www.crmdaily.com/perl/story/21066.html, March 31, 2003

Muther, Andreas (2002) Customer Relationship Management – Electronic Care in the New Economy, Berlin

Naudé, Peter and Francis Buttle (2000) Assessing Relationship Quality, in: Industrial Marketing Management, Vol. 29, p. 351-361

Newell, Frederick (2001) Customer Relationship Management im E-Business: neue Zielgruppen optimal erschließen, individuell ansprechen, mit E-Strategien langfristig binden, Landsberg/Lech

Nucleus Research (2003a) Assessing the Real ROI from SAP, Research Note D23, http://www.nucleusresearch.com/research.html, August 29th, 2003

Nucleus Research (2003b) Assessing the Real ROI from Siebel, Research Note C47, http://www.nucleusresearch.com/research.html, August 29th, 2003

Ozer, Muammar (2000) Information Technology and New Product Development: Opportunities and Pitfalls, in: Industrial Marketing Management, Vol. 29, p. 387-396

Peters, Tom and Robert Waterman (1982) In Search of Excellence, New York

Pirnar, Ali, Linda Plazonja, and Robert Scalea (2002) The Tyrolit Group Case Study, in: The ROI Report, Vol.6, No. 2., p. 4-22

Porter, Michael E. (1989) Wettbewerbsvorteile (Competitive Advantage): Spitzenleistungen erreichen und behaupten, 4th ed., Frankfurt/M./New York

Primus (2002) Return on Investment (ROI) with Primus Software: Actual Customer Results, June 2nd, 2002, http://www.primus.com/products/whitepapersResearch/#579, Sept. 5th, 2003

Rajola, Federico (2003) Customer Relationship Management – Organizational and Technological Perspectives, Berlin

Rapp, Reinhold (2001) Customer Relationship Management, 2nd ed., Wiesbaden

Reichheld, Frederik F. and William Earl Sasser (1990) Zero Defections: Quality Comes to Service, in: Harvard Business Review, Vol. 68, Sept/Oct, p. 105-111

Reichheld, Frederick F. and Phil Schefter (2000) E-Loyalty: Your Secret Weapon on the Web, in: Harvard Business Review, Vol. 78, July/August, p.105-113

Rigby, Darrell K., Frederick F. Reichheld, and Phil Schefter (2002) Avoid the Four Perils of CRM, in: Harvard Business Review, February, p.101-109

Rohde, Laura (2002) Gartner: CRM revenues to rise 15 percent this year, in: ITworld.com, http://www.itworld.com/App/651/020409crmrevenue/pfindex. html, April 9th, 2002

Rust, Roland T., Christine Moorman and Peter R. Dickson (2002) Getting Return on Quality: Revenue Expansion, Cost Reduction, or Both?, in: Journal of Marketing, Vol. 66, p.7-23

Schmidt, Sebastian (2001) Möglichkeiten der Erfolgskontrolle im eCRM, in: Link, Jörg (ed.) (2001): Customer Relationship Management, Berlin, p.235-251

Schneider, Martin (2003) CRM License Sales Down 25 Percent in 2002, in: destinationCRM.com, http://www.destinationcrm.com/articles/default.asp?articleid=3257, June 12th, 2003

Schwetz, Wolfgang (2001) Customer Relationship Management: mit dem richtigen CRM-System Kundenbeziehungen erfolgreich gestalten, 2. ed., Wiesbaden

Selchert, Friedrich-Wilhelm (1999) Einführung in die Betriebswirtschaftslehre, 7th ed., Wiesbaden.

Selchert, Martin (1997) Organisationsstrukturen und Professionalität – Formen und Funktionen professioneller In-house Dienstleistungen, Hamburg

Shaw, Robert (2001) CRM Definitions – Defining customer relationship marketing and management, in: SCN Education B.V. (eds.) Customer Relationship Management – The Ultimate Guide to the Efficient Use of CRM, Braunschweig, p.23-27

Sims, David (2001) CRM Vendors Don't Walk the Talk, in: CRMguru.com, http://www.crmguru.com/features/sims/2001_10_11.html, June 9th, 2002

Speier, Cheri and Viswanath Venkatesh (2002) The Hidden Minefields in the Adoption of Sales Force Automation Technologies, in: Journal of Marketing, Vol. 66, p.98-111

Stengl, Britta, Renate Sommer and Reinhard Ematinger (2001) CRM mit Methode. Intelligente Kundenbindung in Projekt und Praxis mit iCRM, Bonn

Stojek, Michael (2000) Customer Relationship Management – Software, Strategie, Prozess oder Konzept?, in: Information Management & Consulting, Vol. 15, No. 1, p. 37-42

Stojek, Michael and Thomas Ulbrich (2001) e-Loyalty. Kundengewinnung und –bindung im Internet, Landsberg/Lech

Stokburger, Gregor and Mario Pufahl (2002) Kosten senken mit CRM. Strategien, Methoden und Kennzahlen, Wiesbaden

Temkin, Bruce D., Eric Schmitt, and Liz Herbert (2003) CRM Status: Satisfaction Rate Approaches 75%, Feb. 12th, 2003, http://www.forrester.com/ER/Research/Brief/01317,16392,00.html, June 17th, 2003

Thompson, Bob (2002) What is CRM?, in: CRMguru.com, The Customer Relationship Management Primer, April 2002, http://www.crmguru.com/members/primer/01.html, Sept. 5th, 2003, p.1-3

Thompson, Bob (2003) CRM Vendor Satisfaction: Reloaded, in: customerthink newsletter, Vol.6.11, June 3rd, 2003, http://www.crmguru.com.custhelp.com/cgi-bin/crmguru.cfg/php/enduser/std_adp.php?p_sid=8x7, p.1

Walz, Hartmut and Dieter Gramlich (1997) Investitions- und Finanzplanung, 5th ed., Heidelberg

Wehrmeister, Dierk (2001) Customer Relationship Management – Kunden gewinnen und an das Unternehmen binden, Köln

Wessling, Harry (2001) Aktive Kundenbeziehungen mit CRM, Wiesbaden

Wiedmann, Klaus-Peter and Jürgen Greilich (2002) Customer Relationship Management (CRM) in der chemischen Industrie in Deutschland – Forschungsergebnisse und Tendenzen, in: Uebel, Matthias F., Stefan Helmke, and Wilhelm Dangelmaier (eds.) Praxis des Customer Relationship Management, Wiesbaden, p.281-300

Wilde, Klaus D. (2002) Customer Relationship Management – Charts & Checklists, in: Absatzwirtschaft, Nr. 2, p.43

Zingale, Alfredo and Matthias Arndt (2002) Das E-CRM Praxisbuch, Weinheim

6.2 Table of Figures

Figure 1: Fundamental choices about the CRM value measurement concept

Figure 2: Overview: CRM Value Metric

Figure 3: Phases of research on CFROI of Customer Relationship Management

Figure 4: Range of participants' mySAP CRM experience

Figure 5: Structure of participants by industry sector groups

Figure 6: Structure of participants by size

Figure 7: Degree of reaching mySAP CRM project goals

Figure 8: Conceptual framework for NPV of CRM

Figure 9: Increase in company value from mySAP CRM as NPV without terminal value in EUR millions

Figure 10: Increase in company value from mySAP CRM as NPV with terminal value in EUR millions

Figure 11: Cash flow return on investment (3 years) from mySAP CRM in percent

Figure 12: Break-even period interpolation for typical cash-flow structure

Figure 13: Break-even period for investment in mySAP CRM

Figure 14: Time-to-steady state for mySAP CRM functional modules

Figure 15: Positive feedback loop of customer information improvement through CRM deployment

Figure 16: Overview: Customer information improvement through CRM

Figure 17: Improvements of customer information through mySAP CRM

Figure 18: Distribution of improvements of customer information through mySAP CRM

Figure 19: Average productivity growth in marketing through mySAP CRM

Figure 20: Distribution of present productivity growth in marketing through mySAP CRM

Figure 21: Average productivity gains in sales processes

Figure 22: Distribution of present productivity gains in reporting

Figure 23: Distribution of time-weighted average productivity gains through mySAP CRM

Appendix – Table of Figures

Figure 24: Contribution of sales processes to overall productivity improvement in sales through mySAP CRM

Figure 25: Productivity gains in the Interaction Center

Figure 26: Overview: Sources for productivity improvement in Internet sales through CRM

Figure 27: Distribution of productivity improvement in order management through mySAP CRM Internet sales

Figure 28: Comparison of producitivity gains in order management for users of Internet Sales versus other participants

Figure 29: Overview: Drivers of additional revenue through CRM

Figure 30: Distribution of increase in revenue

Figure 31: Distribution of the share of revenue increase through additional customers

Figure 32: Distribution of sources of additional revenue through CRM

Figure 33: Causal chain: New customers (via lead process) through CRM

Figure 34: Mean average increase in the number of leads generated and the lead conversion rate in sales, marketing, and the Interaction Center

Figure 35: Improvements of influencing factors driving new customer acquisition

Figure 36: Improvements in channel coordination

Figure 37: Causal chain: Reduced customer churn through CRM

Figure 38: Mean average improvement of customer satisfaction and retention

Figure 39: Distribution of increases in customer satisfaction and customer retention among participants

Figure 40: Causal chain: Increased quantity of goods sold per customer

Figure 41: Causal chain: Extra revenue from the Interaction Center

Figure 42: Change of revenue drivers in the IC through CRM

Figure 43: Speed target concepts and indicators

Figure 44: Acceleration of CRM processes as a result of mySAP CRM

Figure 45: Distribution of reduction of the time-to-volume

Figure 46: Distribution of median CFROI (3 year and 5 year) across sectors

Figure 47: Distribution of coefficients of variation across sectors

Figure 48: Distribution of median NPV's across sectors

Figure 49: Distribution of median Break Even across sectors

Figure 50: Overview of factors for CRM success

Figure 51: CFROI according to sector complexity

Figure 52: Mean average CFROI from participant sub-groups distinguished by the number of customers

Figure 53: Mean average and median CFROI from participant sub-groups distinguished by the situation before the implementation of mySAP CRM

Figure 54: Overview: Parameters influencing CRM usage as a target of change management

Figure 55: Mean average 3-y-CFROI for sub-groups according to leadership in the CRM project

Figure 56: Distribution of the number of months of software implementation

Figure 57: Distribution of the percentage change of processes upon CRM implementation

Figure 58: Overview: CRM value drivers by sector

6.3 Glossary of Terms and Abbreviations

Break-even period is the time needed until the present value of all payments from an investment is equal to zero. As for most investments cash-outs in the beginning are followed by cash-in later, the break-even period is typically expressed as a positive amount of months or years

B2B and B2C stand for "business-to-business" and "business-to-consumer" and denote the direction of commercial activities

Business dynamics capture developments that evolve from mutual interdependencies between different parameters. It is an own scientific branch with a set of modeling tools, like for example, causal feedback loops

Business cases consist of an explicit and detailed, fact-based reasoning of the value that is to be created by an investment and a financial model that results in financial indicators that enable an informed decision

Cash-flow is the difference of all payments for a period of time

CFROI stands for cash flow return on investment. It is computed as the internal rate of return of the operative gross cash flow from an investment. Depending on the range of values taken into consideration, the CFROI varies. Therefore, the range of years and the interest rate factored in should be explicitly noted

Coefficient of variation is a ratio of the standard deviation to the mean average, expressed as a percentage. It is a measurement of the relative dispersion of a data series and requires all values in the series to be positive

Confidence interval indicates a range of values in which the "true" mean average of the base population will be located with a 95% or 99% (sometimes also a 99.9%) probability

Conversion rate indicates the number of successes over the number of trials. For example, a lead conversion rate divides the number of customers won by the number of initial leads

Correlation coefficient according to Bravais-Pearson is a standardized measurement of the strength of the linear relationship between two variables. Commonly designated as r, its values range from -1 to $+1$, indicating a strong negative relationship, through zero, to strong positive association. Values of $r = 0$ to 0.2 are considered to be a very low relationship, up to 0.4, the relationship is seen as low, up to 0.6 as medium, up to 0.8 as strong, and beyond that it is a very strong relationship.

D-A-CH stands for the German-speaking countries: Germany (D), Austria (A), and Switzerland (CH)

Delivery-to-promise is understood as the portion of orders delivered as it was promised, that is, the right goods or services at the right place, at the right time, with the right quality

Effectiveness expresses the ratio of the level achievement over the target. It is commonly expressed as "doing the right thing"

Efficiency stands for the relation of output to input. It is also commonly referred to as "doing things right"

E-shops differ from websites in that they enable commerce, either by simply offering a static product catalogue with an address for ordering, or by providing rich functionality in product search, configuration, and online payment

Feedback loops – also referred to as causal loops – stand for self-reinforcing or counterbalancing closed chains of cause-and-effect that feed back on each other

FTE stands for full time equivalents. An FTE signifies the amount of work hours that an average full time employee is available for the company. This measure enables comparisons of workforces without regard to the part-/full-time contracts as two half-time employees add up to one FTE

Histogram is a graphical depiction of a data series whereby the values are grouped and the frequency per group is represented by the area of a rectangle covering the space above the group's range.

Leads is a term with widely differing meanings. Here it is used to describe any potential customer that is known to the company by name and that has a particularly high likelihood to buy from the company

Logic trees structure possibilities so that the results are mutually exclusive and collectively exhaustive

Mean average also arithmetic mean or simply mean for a group of items is defined by the sum of the values of these items divided by the number of items.

Median is often used as a measurement of location for a frequency distribution. The median of a group is the value of the middle item when all the items are arranged in either ascending or descending order of magnitude. In case of an even number of items, the median is calculated as the mean average of the two middle items.

Mode denotes the class in a frequency distribution that includes the highest portion of items.

Net present value (NPV) stands for the accrued current value of operative gross cash flows from an investment minus the initial investment itself. It signifies the value added from an investment.

Normal distribution is a probability distribution which is widely used for naturally occurring variables. It is represented by a bell-shaped curve. Sometimes it is also referred to as the Gauss-distribution.

Outsourcing is a process by which assets and/or employees are transferred out to a service provider from which in turn services are sourced on a continuous basis according to the specified service level agreement.

Percentage-point and percentage differ significantly. If through using CRM, the number of successful leads rises from 10% to 15%, it has risen by 50% but the difference between the two figures is only 5 percentage-points.

Productivity is a ratio of output over input, whereby only one kind of input can be calculated at a time as different kinds of inputs don't add up.

Profitability is the ratio of the profit from an investment over the invested amount itself. CFROI is one possible measure of profitability.

Statistical significance of a correlation coefficient is given when the base hypothesis that there is no linear relationship between two variables can be rejected as being less than a 5% or 1% probability of making a mistake.

Student's t-distribution signifies a whole family of distributions which resemble the bell-shaped standard normal distribution and are, in fact, approximated by it for a sample size of $n \geq 30$. Nonetheless, as the t-distribution is more flat than the normal distribution, it's values are more conservative so it has been chosen as the base for confidence intervals and testing for statistical significance of, for example, correlation coefficients. The distribution's probability density function differs according to "degrees of freedom", that is, the number of observations.

Terminal value stands for an investment's value that materializes after the explictly planned and modeled period of time. It is typically calculated as the perpetuity of a normalized cash flow.

Time-to-delivery spans between the customer's request and its fulfillment

Time-to-market measures the span of time from an idea to the marketable product

Time-to-volume measures the time from the tested product to reaching the anticipated roll-out of the product into the market

Two-tailed t-tests apply when the significance of a mean average of normally distributed variables is to be tested for statistical significance and when the unknown variance of the base population has been estimated by the sample's variance. The t-statistic is $t = r * ((n-2)/(1-r^2))^{0.5}$ with r = Bravais-Pearson correlation coefficient, n = sample size. The t-statistic follows a Student's t-distribution with n-2 degrees of freedom.

WACC stands for the weighted average cost of capital which is calculated as the weighted average of the cost of equity and the cost of liabilities

Appendix – Questionnaire

6.4 Questionnaire "Value Creation by mySAP CRM"

Information on the Participant and the Use of mySAP CRM

- General information on the participant

Company	
Sector(s)	
Contact (Name, Phone, E-Mail)	
Position	

- Information on the use of mySAP CRM

Situation before using mySAP CRM	
Specific goals for the use of mySAP CRM (top 5 KPIs[163])	
Reasons for choosing mySAP CRM[164]	
Department driving the project	
mySAP CRM release in use	
Productive since x months	

---

[163] KPI = Key Performance Indicators
[164] Versus other software providers

Appendix – Questionnaire

Value-Effects of mySAP CRM across Different CRM functions

- Did you capture any value from the mySAP CRM so far?

Possible value	Type and scope of value captured (+ examples)
To which extent have the CRM goals (KPI) been reached (%)	
To which extent have cost savings been enabled by CRM	
To which extent have revenue increases been enabled by CRM	

- Possible quality effects through the use of mySAP CRM across CRM functions (that is, marketing, sales, service, and so on):

Possible effects	Type and scope of possible value (+ examples)				
Increase in customer satisfaction	0%	1-10%	11-20%	21-30%	>30%
Increase in price of existing products and services[165]	0%	1-10%	11-20%	21-30%	>30%
Increase in number of goods sold per customer[166]	0%	1-10%	11-20%	21-30%	>30%
Increase in revenue through cross-sales and up-sales	0%	1-10%	11-20%	21-30%	>30%
Increase in the average duration of contract[167]	0%	1-10%	11-20%	21-30%	>30%

---

[165] Only in so far as it is related to the mySAP CRM use; separate initiatives are not to be included
[166] Within the range of products or services that the customer used to buy before the CRM use
[167] Average across all contracts; only if duration of contract is proportional to an increase in revenue

Appendix – Questionnaire

Increase in average customer profitability	0%	1-10%	11-20%	21-30%	>30%
Increase in delivery-to-promise[168]	0%	1-10%	11-20%	21-30%	>30%
Increase in customer loyalty (decrease in percentage of customers lost p.a.)	0%	1-10%	11-20%	21-30%	>30%
Reduction of inventory[169]	0%	1-20%	21-40%	41-60%	>60%
Reduction of coordination problems among channels[170]	0%	1-10%	11-20%	21-30%	>30%
Other quality effects across the CRM functions by the use of mySAP CRM					

- Speed-effects through the use of mySAP CRM across different CRM functions:

Possible effects	Type and scope of possible value (+ examples)				
Reduction of time-to-market	0%	1-10%	11-20%	21-30%	>30%
Reduction of time-to-volume	0%	1-10%	11-20%	21-30%	>30%
Reduction of time-to-delivery	0%	1-10%	11-20%	21-30%	>30%

---

[168] For example, by easier and more reliable delivery date check in the order process, improved prioritization of orders, seamless order management, improved integration of business partners ("collaborative CRM")
[169] For example, by a streamlined product scope, faster replenishment, more accurate forecasts
[170] For example, uniform pricing information on the Internet, Call Center, and sales

Appendix – Questionnaire

Other additional speed-effects across the CRM functions	

- Cost advantages through the use of mySAP CRM across different CRM functions:

Possible effects	Type and scope of possible value (+ examples)
Increase in productivity by in-/ outsourcing of CRM functions	
Increase in productivity by improved coordination among business partners	
Other cost advantages across the CRM functions through mySAP CRM	

Value-effects of mySAP CRM in Marketing

- Did you observe any increase in value due to the use of mySAP CRM in marketing? In which areas? To what extend?

- Possible productivity gains in marketing by main clusters of activities:

Possible effects	Type and scope of possible value (+ examples)				
Marketing-analyses (customer lifetime value, customer profitability, market segmentation)	0%	1-10%	11-20%	21-30%	>30%

199

Appendix – Questionnaire

Marketing planning and campaign management	0%	1-10%	11-20%	21-30%	>30%
Lead[171] management (generation, qualification, tracking, and reporting)	0%	1-10%	11-20%	21-30%	>30%
Other marketing processes impacted by mySAP CRM					

- Other possible value-effects by the use of mySAP CRM in Marketing:

Possible effects	Type and scope of possible value (+ examples)				
Reduction of double work, redundant documents	0%	1-10%	11-20%	21-30%	>30%
Increase in the number of leads generated in marketing	0%	1-20%	21-40%	41-60%	>60%
Increase in the quality of leads generated, for example by better marketing analytics	0%	1-20%	21-40%	41-60%	>60%
Increased amount and quality of market information	0%	1-10%	11-20%	21-30%	>30%
Reduction in time to assemble the same amount of customer information now	0%	1-10%	11-20%	21-30%	>30%

---

[171] No differentiation between lead (of different quality) and opportunity

Appendix – Questionnaire

Increase in completeness and context of customer information	0%	1-10%	11-20%	21-30%	>30%
Increased use of customer information by CRM staff (e.g. Sales)	0%	1-10%	11-20%	21-30%	>30%
Increased frequency of event-triggered customer interaction	0%	1-10%	11-20%	21-30%	>30%
Identification of potential for price optimization	0%	1-10%	11-20%	21-30%	>30%
Increase in marketing budget spent on A-/B- customers	0%	1-10%	11-20%	21-30%	>30%
Increased return-on-marketing (revenue over marketing budget)	0%	1-10%	11-20%	21-30%	>30%
Increased effectiveness of communication (e.g. recall)	0%	1-10%	11-20%	21-30%	>30%
Other effects of the use of mySAP CRM in marketing					

- Expected development of value-creation through mySAP CRM in marketing:

Current level of use (due to possibly inadequate skills, poor data quality, licenses available) as percentage of max	%	
Estimated time until the maximum level will be reached (in month after going live)	Months	

Appendix – Questionnaire

Value-effects of mySAP CRM in Sales

- Did you observe any increase in value due to the use of mySAP CRM in sales? In which areas? To what extend?

- Possible productivity gains in sales by main clusters of activities:

Possible effects	Type and scope of possible value (+ examples)				
Sales planning[172]	0%	1-10%	11-20%	21-30%	>30%
Lead (and opportunity)- management	0%	1-20%	21-40%	41-60%	>60%
Customer interaction[173]	0%	1-10%	11-20%	21-30%	>30%
Reporting	0%	1-10%	11-20%	21-30%	>30%
Order mgmt.[174]	0%	1-20%	21-40%	41-60%	>60%
Contract mgmt.[175]	0%	1-10%	11-20%	21-30%	>30%
Sales cycle time	0%	1-20%	21-40%	41-60%	>60%
Reduction of time for internal coordination	0%	1-10%	11-20%	21-30%	>30%

---

[172] Goals, campaigns, measures, sales areas, and so on
[173] Gathering of information on the customer, product configuration, pricing, travel, discussion
[174] Proposal writing, order check and completion, check of invoice, status tracking
[175] Contract review, adaptation, renewal, price renegotiations

Appendix – Questionnaire

Other productivity gains by the use of Mobile Sales	
Other processes impacted by mySAP CRM	

- Other possible value-effects by the use of mySAP CRM in sales:

Possible effects	Type and scope of possible value (+ examples)				
Increase in time spent on key customers (A, B)	0%	1-10%	11-20%	21-30%	>30%
Increase in the number of leads generated by sales	0%	1-20%	21-40%	41-60%	>60%
Increase in the sales-to-lead ratio in sales	0%	1-10%	11-20%	21-30%	>30%
Increase in the number of customer visits	0%	1-10%	11-20%	21-30%	>30%
Increase in sales-to-visits ratio	0%	1-10%	11-20%	21-30%	>30%
Reduction of early cancellation of contracts	0%	1-10%	11-20%	21-30%	>30%
Reduction of write-downs on accounts receivable	0%	1-10%	11-20%	21-30%	>30%
Other effects of the use of Mobile Sales					
Other effects of the use of mySAP CRM in sSales					

Appendix – Questionnaire

- Expected development of value-creation through mySAP CRM in sales:

Current level of use (due to possibly inadequate skills, poor data quality, licenses available) as percentage of max	%	
Estimated time until the maximum level will be reached (in month after going live)	Months	

Value-effects of mySAP CRM in Internet Sales

- Did you observe any increase in value due to the use of mySAP CRM in Internet Sales? In which areas? To what extend?

- Possible productivity gains in Internet Sales:

Possible effects	Type and scope of possible value (+ examples)				
Increase in the number of e-Sales orders (B2B/B2C)	0%	1-10%	11-20%	21-30%	>30%
Increase in average revenue/e-Sales order (B2B/B2C)	0%	1-10%	11-20%	21-30%	>30%
Thereof additional revenue (not just rechanneled)	0%	1-20%	21-40%	41-60%	>60%
Difference of time spent for an online vs. offline order	0%-20%	21-40%	41-60%	61-80%	>80%
Difference of time spent for an online order with and without mySAP CRM	0%-20%	21-40%	41-60%	61-80%	>80%

Increase in conversion rate (sales-to-hits ratio)	0%-20%	21-40%	41-60%	61-80%	>80%
Other effects of the use of e-Sales					

- Other possible value-effects by the use of mySAP CRM in other scenarios :

Possible effects	Type and scope of possible value (+ examples)
Web Auction	
One-Step Buying	
Web Analytics	
Live Web Collaboration	

- Expected development of value-creation by mySAP CRM in Internet Sales:

Current level of use (due to possibly inadequate skills, poor data quality, licenses available) as percentage of max	%	
Estimated time until the maximum level will be reached (in month after going live)	Months	

Value-effects of mySAP CRM in Service

- Did you observe any increase in value due to the use of mySAP CRM in service? In which areas? To what extend?

- Possible productivity gains in service by main clusters of activities:

Possible effects	Type and scope of possible value (+ examples)				
Help Desk services[176]	0%	1-10%	11-20%	21-30%	>30%
Administrative handling of service-orders[177]	0%	1-10%	11-20%	21-30%	>30%
Fulfillment of service-orders[178]	0%	1-10%	11-20%	21-30%	>30%
SLA-management (drafting, changing)	0%	1-10%	11-20%	21-30%	>30%
Reduction of over-capacity by more accurate forecasts	0%	1-10%	11-20%	21-30%	>30%
Other effects of the use of Mobile Service/e-Service					
Other processes impacted by mySAP CRM					

---

[176] Answering questions, distant problem solving, complaints and trouble ticket tracking; refers to net-effect, that is, reduction in time spent for help desk services less additional time spent for content-management/scripting
[177] Writing, tracking, billing, documenting
[178] Spare parts management, scheduling, diagnostic, coordination, solution

Appendix – Questionnaire

- Other possible value-effects by the use of mySAP CRM in service:

Possible effects	Type and scope of possible value (+ examples)				
Increase in service first-time-right	0%	1-10%	11-20%	21-30%	>30%
Increase in customer self-service	0%	1-20%	21-40%	41-60%	>60%
Increase in availability of service	0%	1-10%	11-20%	21-30%	>30%
Increase in lead generation by service	0%	1-10%	11-20%	21-30%	>30%
Reduction of time between customer interest/complaint and solution	0%	1-10%	11-20%	21-30%	>30%
Increased customer satisfaction with complaint mgmt.	0%	1-10%	11-20%	21-30%	>30%
Reduced time between service and billing	0%	1-10%	11-20%	21-30%	>30%
Other effects of the use of mySAP CRM in service					

- Expected development of value-creation through mySAP CRM in service:

Current level of use (due to possibly inadequate skills, poor data quality, licenses available) as percentage of max	%	
Estimated time until the maximum level will be reached (in month after going live)	Months	

Appendix – Questionnaire

Value-effects of mySAP CRM in the Interaction Center (IC)

- Did you observe any increase in value due to the use of mySAP CRM in the IC? In which areas? To what extend?

- Possible productivity gains in service by main clusters of activities:

Possible effects	Type and scope of possible value (+ examples)				
Help Desk services[179]	0%	1-10%	11-20%	21-30%	>30%
Reduction of time for inbound telesales	0%	1-10%	11-20%	21-30%	>30%
Reduction of time for outbound telesales[180]	0%	1-10%	11-20%	21-30%	>30%
Documentation of customer interaction, reporting, general admin	0%	1-10%	11-20%	21-30%	>30%
Reduction of temporary IC overcapacity by more accurate forecasts	0%	1-10%	11-20%	21-30%	>30%
Reduction of initial training per average new call center operator[181]	0%	1-10%	11-20%	21-30%	>30%

---

[179] Answering questions, distant problem solving, complaints and trouble ticket tracking; refers to net-effect, that is, reduction in time spent for help desk services less additional time spent for content-management/scripting
[180] Preparation, average time per call
[181] For example by better scripting, easier processes, better support

Appendix – Questionnaire

Other processes impacted by mySAP CRM	

- Other possible value-effects by the use of mySAP CRM in the IC:

Possible effects	Type and scope of possible value (+ examples)				
Increase in the number of in- and outbound telesales	0%	1-10%	11-20%	21-30%	>30%
Increase in sales-to-calls ratio (in- and outbound)	0%	1-10%	11-20%	21-30%	>30%
Reduction of average time waiting per call	0%	1-10%	11-20%	21-30%	>30%
Reduction of referrals (first to second level) by for example better scripting	0%	1-10%	11-20%	21-30%	>30%
Increase in revenue per order in the IC	0%	1-10%	11-20%	21-30%	>30%
Thereof additional revenue (not just rechanneled)	0%	1-10%	11-20%	21-30%	>30%
Other effects of the use of mySAP CRM in the IC					

Appendix – Questionnaire

- Expected development of value-creation through mySAP CRM in the IC:

Current level of use (due to possibly inadequate skills, poor data quality, licenses available) as percentage of max	%
Estimated time until the maximum level will be reached (in month after going live)	Months

Data needed for the ROI calculation

- Financial data

Total revenue	MEuro	0-50	51-250	250-500	501-2500	>2500
Average revenue per e-Sales B2B and B2C	TEuro					
Average revenue per sales order	TEuro					
Average revenue per IC order	TEuro					
Ebitda[182]-margin	%					
WACC[183]	%					

- Information on employees

	Marketing	Sales	IC	e-Sales	Service
FTE					
Total av. cost per employee p.a.					

---

[182] Earnings before interest, tax, depreciation, and amortization = operative gross cash flow
[183] WACC = minimum return required for investments

Appendix – Questionnaire

- Overview of activities

	Activities	Time %	Activities	Time %
Marketing	• Analyses • Planning and campaigns		• Lead-mgmt. •	
Sales	• Planning • Lead- and opport. mgmt. • Customer visits • Reporting		• Order mgmt. • Contract mgmt. • Sales cycle time • Internal coordination	
Service	• Help desk • Serv. order admin		• Serv. order fulfillmt. • SLA mgmt	
IC	• Help desk • Inbound • Outbound		• Reporting • Initial training •	

- Value drivers in CRM

Value drivers	Units	Amount
Leads generated (Marketing, Sales, Service)	# p.a.	
Visits/sales employee (average for entire sales staff)	# p.a.	
Conversion rates (Sales, IC)	%	
Orders in e-sales (B2B and B2C)	# p.a.	
Telesales in the IC	# p.a.	
Total number of orders	# p.a.	
% of cancelled orders	%	
Total number of contracts	# p.a.	
Cancelled contracts and/or write downs on accounts receivable	%	
Total number of customers	#	
Average yearly inventory	MEuro	

Appendix – Questionnaire

Investment and cost

- Pilot-project

Position	Units	Amount and comments
Investment	TEuro	
Time spent	MM	

- Hard/Software

Position	Units	Amount and comments
Price per mySAP CRM license	TEuro	
Number of licenses	#	
Investment in additional needed hardware (server, network)	TEuro	
Expected additional investment (5 year horizon)[184]	%	

- Implementation (external and internal)

Position	Units	Amount and comments
Time spent on implementation	MM	
Price per MM implementation	TEuro	

- Training/time investment

Position	Units	Amount and comments
Days/employee training	Days	
Number of employees trained	#	
Fee for training/day	TEuro	
Reduction in productive time due to learning in %	%	

---

[184] Relative to initial investment; only hard- and software

- Recurrent cost

Position	Units	Amount and comments
External system administration	MM pa	
Internal system administration	MM pa	
Additional effort for content mgmt (e-sales, e-service)	MM pa	
Expected increase (5 years)	% p.a.	

- Reduction of cost and investment by mySAP CRM

Position	Units	Amount and comments
Reduction of system admin by reduction of legacy systems	TEuro	
Avoidance of otherwise necessary investment	TEuro	

KPI for the implementation project

Position	Units	Amount and comments
Time of implementation project	months	
product decision	months	
feasibilitiy	months	
blueprint and process reengineering	months	
implementation	months	
test/adaption	months	
initial data load	months	
Clarity and quality of concept	1-5[185]	
% of standard interfaces	%	

---

[185] German grades from 1 = very good, 5 = insufficient

Appendix – Questionnaire

Number of new interfaces	#	
% of software modified	%	
Scope of change in processes[186]	%	
Functionality available when going live	%	
No. of employees initially live	%	
Change in the number of employees using mySAP CRM	%	
Use of mySAP CRM by employees relative to expectations	%	
% of company data available in the system (when going live, change over time)	%	
Support by top-management	1-5	
Involvement of top management in the project	1-5	
Number of employees involved in mySAP CRM project	#	
Existence and size of change management teams	FTE	
Quality of implementation partner	1-5	
Acceptance by users	1-5	

---

[186] Eliminination of steps from the process, reduction of interfaces, optimization per step, and so on

Herausgeber

Prof. Dr. Beate Kremin-Buch
Prof. Dr. Beate Kremin-Buch vertritt die Fächer Rechnungswesen und Controlling im Fachbereich Management und Controlling. Forschungsschwerpunkte sind die Internationale Rechnungslegung und das Strategische Kostenmanagement. Diverse Veröffentlichungen widmen sich diesen beiden Gebieten, z. B. Internationale Rechnungslegung, 3. Aufl., 2002, Fachbegriffe der Internationalen Rechnungslegung (zusammen mit Götz Hohenstein), 2. Aufl., 2002 und Strategisches Kostenmanagement, 3. Aufl., 2004.

Prof. Dr. Fritz Unger
lehrt Betriebswirtschaftslehre und Marketing im Berufsintegrierenden Studium (BIS), ist Autor, Mitautor und Herausgeber zahlreicher Bücher (u.a. Management der Marktkommunikation, 2. Aufl., 1999, Integriertes Marketing, 3. Aufl., 2001, Marktpsychologie, 2001, Mediaplanung, 2. Aufl., 2002 und Verkaufsförderung, 2. Aufl., 2003).

Prof. Dr. Hartmut Walz
ist verantwortlich für Bankbetriebslehre und Finanzdienstleistungen im Fachbereich Internationale Dienstleistungen. Durch betriebswirtschaftliche Praxisprojekte und Publikationstätigkeiten (u. a. Investitions- und Finanzplanung, 6. Aufl., 2004) unterstützt er den Know-how-Austausch zwischen Hochschule und Wirtschaftspraxis.

Printed by Libri Plureos GmbH
in Hamburg, Germany